THE FACES OF HOMELESSNESS IN LONDON

The Faces of Homelessness in London

JEANNE MOORE
DAVID CANTER
DES STOCKLEY
MADELINE DRAKE

Dartmouth
Aldershot • Brookfield USA • Singapore • Sydney

Published by
Dartmouth Publishing Company Limited
Gower House
Croft Road
Aldershot
Hants GU11 3HR
England

Dartmouth Publishing Company
Old Post Road
Brookfield
Vermont 05036
USA

British Library Cataloguing in Publication Data
Moore, Jeanne
Faces of Homelessness in London
I. Title
362.509421

Library of Congress Cataloging-in-Publication Data
The faces of homelessness in London / by Jeanne Moore ... [et al.].
p. cm.
Includes index.
ISBN 1-85521-252-8
1. Homelessness–England–London. 2. Homeless people–England–London. 3. London (England)–Social conditions. I. Moore, Jeanne.
HV4546.L66F33 1995
362.5'09421–dc20 94-42385
CIP

ISBN 1 85521 252 8

Printed in Great Britain by Antony Rowe Ltd,
Chippenham, Wiltshire

Contents

List of Tables

Chapter 5: The Street

Chapter 6: The Experience of Hostels

Chapter 8: Squatting in London

Chapter 9: Living in Hotels in London

Chapter 10: Begging

Chapter 11: A Comparison Across Settings

List of Figures

Foreword

Despite all the debates about Homelessness over the last few years there is still a great deal of misunderstanding of the nature of the people who find themselves homeless. The policies of many agencies that are concerned about Homelessness, from national governments to local voluntary groups, therefore have much to gain from a careful consideration of how and why people become homeless, the consequences that experience itself has for them as well as the consequences of how the agencies respond to people who become homeless.

The present volume provides fresh insights into the experiences of being homeless by exploring a wide range of manifestations of that experience, the many 'faces' of homelessness. This includes somewhat novel studies comparing the perceptions of hostel residents and staff, as well as studies of squatting and begging.

The finding, from careful observation, that the number of people sleeping rough on the streets of London ran into hundreds rather than thousands, did help to convince the British government that they could have an impact on this problem with less resources than previously thought necessary and therefore well within the resources that could readily be made available. The detailed methodology of that crucial study, since used as a model for 'street counts' in other major cities around the world, is published here for the first time.

The Salvation Army, who commissioned the original research, have developed a strategy for their London services to homeless people that draws heavily on the findings reported in the following chapters. Recognising that there are many faces to homelessness, not just people sleeping rough on the streets, the Salvation Army now see it is vital to have a focused strategy covering all aspects from initial contact to final resettlement into permanent accommodation.

The more subtle findings presented on the following pages, derived from the many surveys of homeless people, will probably take more time to find their way into the consciousness of government ministers. The findings make it clear that people very rarely choose to be homeless or wantonly turn down appropriate accommodation.

The studies reported here show that people become homeless from many different types of crisis and therefore require various forms and degrees of help. Some will find homes by themselves, others will use the advice and information available from agencies in order to move on, while yet other homeless people will require help and support over time. These studies serve to emphasise that it is not just inadequate or mentally disturbed people who become homeless. People with jobs and other personal resources can find themselves in domestic crisis even within a stable life style.

Different forms of support and accommodation will be required to meet the needs of different homeless people. Furthermore, housing management is just as important as various forms of therapeutic help, the one supporting the other. Perhaps paradoxically, the caring objectives uppermost in the minds of many agencies may lead them to emphasise therapy at the expense of the more prosaic goals of helping to find permanent residence.

There may be signs that Homelessness is not on the increase, but Homelessness will certainly continue to be a challenge to any civilised society that does not have an adequate supply of housing for people on low incomes. So, although the studies reported were completed before Margaret Thatcher was dismissed by her party, their message of how we are all vulnerable in an uncaring society is still a fresh one that needs to be widely broadcast.

The current British Government is in the process if passing legislation for which the studies reported in the present volume have a special relevance. The first is the new homeless legislation that no longer requires local authorities to provide permanent accommodation for those people accepted as homeless. They will receive temporary accommodation and take their turn on the housing register. If this legislation is acted on constructively so that after a period of time in decent temporary accommodation they will find their way into permanent housing, then it could be an improvement on current conditions. But, if it means that more people in various states of crisis will spend long periods of their lives being shunted between various kinds of temporary accommodation then their standard of life will deteriorate and we will all be the worse off.

The present British Government has increasingly emphasised the importance of the private rented sector in playing a part in meeting housing needs. Exactly what role it should play is hotly debated, but there can be no doubt that reasonable private rented housing provides far better temporary accommodation than 'Bed and Breakfast' Hotels. Any move away from reliance on this form of hotel option can only be good.

The new Criminal Justice Act also has important implications for Homelessness. It proposes to make squatting a criminal offence. As studies reported in the following pages show, for many years there has been an acceptable role for squatting as a way into the housing market for some, especially younger, people. Indeed, housing co-operatives and their later evolution as housing associations can trace their roots in part to the squatting movement of the 1950's and 1960's. Certainly local authorities have seen the value of offering tenancies to squatters who have proven themselves to be good tenants, which our research shows is not an inconsiderable proportion of squatters. Squatting is a complex social and legal issue, but it would be counter productive if the new legislation reduced the possibility of effective use of empty housing, and the development of new forms of short-term tenure, by making all squatters criminals and thereby making them a burden on the agencies for the homeless.

Any understanding of all these complex issues, though, requires direct contact with the people who are homeless, as people not as statistics. Otherwise there is a danger that 'Homelessness' becomes too all-embracing a term vaguely perceived as the cause of many evils in society. This problem is exacerbated by the rarity of homelessness studies that focus on the experiences of individuals, psychological studies. Sociological studies that deal with statistical trends at the aggregate level are far more common. This is partly because it is easier to see the policy implications of aggregate trends. The present volume therefore does incorporate some of those considerations. However, if the work is carried out in an appropriate way the psychological perspective is also essential, since policy cannot be effective unless it takes account of the experience of individuals . The present volume therefore also acts as an example of some ways in which action research can be carried out that takes account of the experiences of the homeless individuals who go to make up the general statistics.

Some of the consequences of the research reported has already been acted on. The readiness with which some policy makers have followed up our results may be taken as one indication of their utility and validity. However, if the ideas and results are not to be swallowed up in policy priorities or distorted by trends in the fashions of caring then it is essential that a thorough record of the studies is openly available for challenge and debate. We hope that such a record will also have value beyond the confines of the original practical objectives. If it helps us to understand more about how people find their way into crisis and the processes they have for coping, and if it shows how the various institutional attempts at help interact with the capabilities the people at risk bring with them, then it is possible that the principles and approaches taken to studying Homelessness in the present volume will have relevance to the many other areas where academic research can help reduce human suffering.

1 A Portrait of Homelessness

Introduction

Homelessness is often discussed as a single phenomenon, both within a country and internationally. The media is often drawn towards the more extreme types within the third world, such as flood or earthquake victims. In Britain and the United States, the emphasis falls on those on the street who are observable and therefore in the public eye. The plight of these people has become synonymous with homelessness. Even people living in temporary hostels and shelters do not consider themselves as homeless (cf. Watson and Austerberry 1986; Moore and Canter 1992), despite wanting a place of their own. However, people living in hostels and temporary accommodation are without permanent accommodation and do want their own housing and by our definition they are homeless. As this book will make clear there are roughly 35 times more single people in homeless settings such as hostels, hotels and squats than are on the streets. This book seeks to explore below the tip of the iceberg to document the characteristics, and defining features of the faces of homelessness.

Each of the faces of homelessness presented here has distinct features and characteristics. The physical setting differs for each, from the niches, corners, parks and alleys of the street, to the often cramped quarters of a bed and breakfast hotel, the bare and twilight atmosphere of the squat to the supervised and orderly hostel. None of these methods of survival in the state of homelessness are satisfactory in any permanent sense. However some are more tolerable than others.

London, like many cities, has always contained some people for whom there does not seem to be any suitable housing option. Today, the range and extent of homelessness in London is such that present coping mechanisms are faltering. Two aspects need to be considered. Firstly, the management of existing resources and the lack of a comprehensive strategy for coping with homelessness in London. Secondly, homeless people themselves have goals, expectations and requirements which have to be better understood. Both these areas have to be explored if the accommodation provided is to be effective in helping people to find their way back into traditional forms of housing and in some cases, lifestyle.

The difficulty in the first area, would seem to lie not in the amount of temporary accommodation being offered, but in the combination of a lack of permanent affordable housing, coupled with no comprehensive strategy for providing the wide range of temporary accommodation required. The research reviewed in this book indicates that the homelessness problem in London, is a manageable one, but it needs a new strategy. Charting the variety and distribution of homeless people is a necessary pre-requisite for the development of this strategy.

With regard to the second area, the focus on the experience of homeless people in a variety of homeless settings is vital. No comprehensive range of accommodation can be effective without some understanding of both the differences between sub-groups of homeless people and their shared perspective.

These are the main driving forces behind the present book. The attempt to combine an investigation into the scale of the problem, with an exploration of the experience of being part of that problem: being homeless in London. The book provides an account of a project which was commissioned by the Salvation Army to help them better cope as providers of accommodation in London. The research carried out by the University of Surrey lasted two years and has over this time assisted the Salvation Army in their development plans. The account provided here takes the general themes and findings of the research and attempts to make them of use to those concerned with homelessness in general.

Background to Research

The study of homelessness has generally emerged from a social or economic perspective. Social or demographic trends have been the subject of many discussions, and the economic forces which may lead to homelessness as a large phenomenon. However, the psychological approach has an important contribution to make in that it focuses on the individual and in this instance, the individual within a particular social context. This section presents an overview of recent literature on homelessness and sets out a new perspective originating in social psychology. It presents definitions of homelessness and sets out the aims of the research.

A number of investigators, over the past few years, have emphasised the heterogeneity of people who are homeless. Less attention has been paid to the variety of settings in which homeless people exist or the ways in which they may move between these settings. The current research deliberately chose to consider as many settings as possible in which homeless people may be found and to get at least a preliminary picture of those settings and the people who may be found in them.

This research has made it quite clear that in present day London the majority of homeless people do not live on the streets with no roof at all over their heads. The number who do, may well have increased at least three fold, and possibly ten fold, over the last 20 years. There are still many opportunities, both legal and illegal, for people to find shelter from what the sky may inflict. However, whereas sleeping on the streets presents many obvious threats to health and wellbeing, as well as severely limiting the opportunities for personal development, the threats and advantages posed by living in an illegal squat, being crowded with a number of strangers into an old hostel, or trying to bring up children in a bed and breakfast hotel are not so immediately obvious. The possibilities and problems of all these ways of being homeless need further examination.

London has a shanty town as large as might be expected in a Latin American city, but it is hidden. People live illegally in squats or in cramped, badly equipped hotels and crowded hostels. If they do not fall into a group that the government recognises as having a special need, or they cannot find a place in one of the spaces indoors, they find they have no choice but to survive on the streets. Homeless people form a floating, changing group of people trying to cope as best they can with a legislative provision that is not aimed at caring for people but providing for particular needs.

This examination was directed at the particular experiences people have of the different facets of homelessness and how they move between them. The objectives and criteria that homeless people have for the temporary places in which they stay and how these evolve during their experiences of being without a home were also examined. Such considerations move us beyond dealing with the physical conditions and include a focus on the types of assistance or support that is considered appropriate to different groups.

The present studies indicate that each of the faces of homelessness has its own qualities, covering the range from being roofless to lack of legal tenure. Within this range, attention is given here to the significance of 'hearthlessness', having a roof but no homelike qualities to that residence.

Social/Environmental Perspective

The University of Surrey's Department of Psychology has a strong research interest in Environmental Psychology. The focus of this particular aspect of psychology is on the relationship between the physical, the social and the individual, that is the interaction between the built environment and the people that use it. Research has tended to focus on offices, schools, hospitals, and houses, exploring not only the physical attributes of a place, but also the concepts that people hold of a place, and the activities which occur therein. A knowledge of how these interact with each other can help to improve these facilities. The experiential approach underlies this perspective. It argues that any exploration of a place must take as its basis the users' experience of that place. There is a focus on the conceptions of the individual within a particular role or organisational system, aspects of how the individual 'views' the world. Implicit in this approach is the view of people as purposive and goal-oriented, which suggests that people have reasons for their actions. Thus the experience of the individual and the understanding of their motivation and goals is of prime importance to the environmental psychology approach, to be drawn on in any evaluation or design of a building in which that person works or lives.

What this implies about facilities for homeless people, is that before any design or plan can be considered, some understanding of their experience is essential. It is from this basis that this research identifies the different subgroups of homeless people, and explores the experience of each of these groups in some detail.

The University of Surrey's Psychology Department has over a ten year involvement in the study of therapeutic environments. For the purposes of this research, the term therapeutic refers to any type of help or support offered in a range of settings from hospitals at one extreme to sheltered housing at the other.

In 1979 Canter and Canter edited a book on therapeutic environments which provided the framework for a number of research projects. They argued that the failure to create therapeutic environments may be as a result of inadequate (fuzzy) definitions of therapeutic goals (Canter and Canter 1979 p.9). Six therapeutic models were suggested which embraced all therapeutic environments: individual growth, self enhancement, medical, custodial, prosthetic and normalisation. Each of these models had implications for the physical and social environment in terms of its design and organisation.

Some of the studies that then emerged set out to validate empirically the existence of these models. The studies that followed Canter and Canter (1979) focused on the experience of users of various facilities in order to evaluate the existing environment and to put forward suggestions for the design of new facilities.

Moran (1979) examined the concepts that users of a women's day centre in Cork had about their ideal day centre. Using a questionnaire based on activities that went on at the day centre, users rated the suitability of aspects (e.g. size of room) of the various locations within the building for specified activities (e.g. eating). Taking the results of this and other design briefing exercises, she put forward design suggestions, some of which were later included in a new day centre. This day centre was evaluated in turn by Cody (1982) who found high satisfaction rates with the new building.

King (1987) explored a psychogeriatric hospital and focused the differences between staff and patients in their perception of other patients. Results reflected the existence of a fundamental variation in viewpoint between staff and patients due to their different environmental roles. In other words they did not share the same objectives with regard to that environment. In the case of a hospital this would probably be due to different organisational roles within the hospital. Further design briefing exercises with the staff revealed a perceived distinction in activities within the hospital in terms of their social and non-social aspects. Thus proposed changes in the hospital were proposed which reflected this distinction (Canter and King 1990).

Shattock (1988) similarly explored the staff's conceptions of hospital wards. Using a questionnaire designed to assess the models in use, a ward satisfaction questionnaire and a design briefing exercise, she sought empirical validation for Canter's therapeutic models (1979). Results suggested two therapeutic models were in use, the medical and the social, representing broader groups of Canter and Canter's (1979) proposed six models. The study has implications for any therapeutic facility, attempting to expose the models in use and linking them to aspects of the physical environment and preferred designs.

Oakley (1980) sought to establish criteria which would enable hostels for single homeless people to be assessed as to their suitability. He focused on the profiles and perspectives of hostel residents and suggests Canter and Canter's individual growth model (1979) as the model around which designs should focus. As the staff architect for the Salvation Army, he then designed a series of hostels around the country based on this design theory, taking the physical attributes of domesticity/homeliness and individual rooms as the basic form. Moore (1989) tested this theory by studying four of the hostels influenced by his design. She found in part, very high rates of satisfaction among both staff and residents, which ranged from the highest rates at the newest and most theory-driven designed hostel and lowest at the oldest largest and least influenced by Oakley's theory. This would seem to suggest at the least, that Oakley's hostel design has succeeded in eliciting strong approval from its users.

In summary, the University of Surrey has conducted a series of research projects into the use of therapeutic environments. By exploring and evaluating the therapeutic models in use therein, as well as the conceptions of residents, design criteria can emerge which help to shape a wide range of different types of environments. It is important to stress again that the term therapeutic is not used here in a limited sense but includes a range of support and help. Furthermore, all types of facility and housing will be explored and not just a range of therapeutic environments. Thus this research has important implications for the future design and organisation of facilities for homeless people.

Existing Perspectives

In the context of numerous socio-economic accounts of homelessness, the psycho-social approach is developing in the US and in Britain. Recent American reports have started to take the individual within a social context as their framework but tend to list features of the homeless person's experience (Rossi (1989), Caton (1990)). They have not developed any interpretative framework or model to guide research, nor have they included views of homeless people themselves. Indeed these accounts are only general frameworks, and do not contain any research findings. This book explores homeless people in London within a psycho-social framework which takes the many different types of experience of homelessness as its starting point.

Perspectives

Studies on homelessness from the United States rarely get included in British reviews and vice versa. Although the problem of homelessness is chronic in the United States and some of the ways of coping with it are quite different, there are great gains to be made from a common explanation. The two fields of research have tended to adopt similar approaches: the socio-economic and psychopathological. As Caton (1990) suggests:

> Those who view homelessness solely in terms of faulty economics or a lack of a home, will see the problem and its solution differently from those who see homelessness as the profound deterioration of social and psychological functioning.

Social or demographic trends have been the subject of many discussions, as have the economic forces which may lead to homelessness as a large phenomenon. However, the psychological approach has an important contribution to make in that it focuses on the individual and in this instance, the individual within a particular social context.

The field of homelessness research has tended to polarise between the socio-economic and the psychiatric approaches. Caton (1990) argues that the recent literature on homelessness had attributed the condition to economic and social policy failure. The former has tended to be the most common approach discussing broad economic and social changes that have contributed to the growth of homelessness in Britain (see for e.g. Drake 1981; Greve 1971; Greve and Currie 1990).

Within this general distinction there have been a wide range of studies, some of which review current literature and others which have provided a large amount of background information on homeless people. While these studies have been influential and have provided a useful framework for more detailed study, they do not on their own provide a comprehensive focus on homelessness. Their approach is to focus on broad societal changes and trends and to focus on samples of homeless people to illustrate those trends. Drake et al (1981) in their national study of single homeless people stated their objective as 'to provide a broadly based understanding of the characteristics, needs and housing preferences of single homeless people'. This 'broadly based understanding' is valuable, but it has not been followed by studies which attempt to go beyond a broad societal analysis and focus on the individual.

Greve and Currie (1990) in their overview of homelessness in Britain provides a full account of the socio-economic forces and policy decisions which have increased homelessness over the last ten to 30 years. They argue that the primary cause is the critical shortage of affordable rented housing. The report discusses further structural factors and immediate reasons for homelessness. The structural factors were given as:

1. Personal and Household Characteristics
2. Precipitating Event
3. Income
4. Housing Market
5. Employment and Incomes
6. Policies

The immediate reasons provided for households accepted by Local Authorities in 1988 were:

1. Breakdown of Sharing Arrangements
2. Dissolution of Marriage or Other Partnership
3. Loss of Privately Rented or Service Tenancy
4. Other Reasons
5. Mortgage Default
6. Rent Arrears

This account does refer to 'personal characteristics' and 'breakdown of marriage' as part of the reasons, but these could hardly be considered to be a reasonable reference to the experience of homelessness from a personal level. Indeed the problems with this account arise when it is used to explain homelessness in full. There is no doubt that a lack of affordable housing, poverty and the policies discussed by Greve have led to an increase in homelessness, but without an account of the differences within this huge, disparate group of people and their experiences and views, it is hard to see how this information can be fed into the development of a strategy to help them.

Rossi (1989) goes beyond a simple economic and social causal model. He argues 'No matter what the availability of inexpensive house, personal characteristics are likely to explain who becomes homeless'. Rossi does present useful comparisons between his sample of Chicago homeless and other studies of impoverished but housed groups. This is one of the ways forward in understanding some of the characteristics of homelessness as he demonstrated that among the extremely poor, those with disabilities are the most vulnerable to homelessness (Rossi 1989, p.179). However his approach consists of providing a list of symptoms of homeless people without linking them in a holistic model. He lists, mental illness, demoralization, alcoholism, criminal convictions, social networks etc. and in this way addresses only the problems associated with homelessness. He does not bring us any nearer to understanding the homeless person's view or perspective on the world, his rationale for making certain decisions, and following certain paths of action. By regarding homeless people as one large group with higher incidence of all of these problems, he falls short of providing a holistic psychological model of types of homeless people.

The other general approach to the study of homelessness has tended to be the psychopathological in which the individual's behaviour or character has been used to explain why they are homeless and implies that through their deviancy or pathology they have become homeless. It denies any socio-economic influences and implicitly blames the individual. While the former may also be seen to be a part of the overall housing system approach (Watson and Austerberry (1986), it is not reasonable to argue that studies such as those by Lodge Patch (1978), or Tidmarsh (1978) which focus on the incidence of mental illness in the homeless population, are psychological in focus (Watson and Austerberry ibid.), but are rather, in part psychiatric and psychopathological. The psychopathological approach tends to 'blame homelessness within the individual' (Watson and Austerberry 1986 p.17), for example Whiteley (1955) who states 'To his environment the down and out contributes nothing. To exist in it he must be as psychopathic as his neighbour'. The psychiatric approach offers much the same as for example, when Lodge Patch (1971) argues 'the homeless man.... is not simply one who happens not to have a home, he is also a man incapable of sustaining one, and may be incapable of any other kind of life than the one he has adopted'.

Examples of such an approach are particularly scattered in the area of psychiatric illness and homelessness (c.f. Priest 1971,1976; Patch 1971). Much of the early work in the 1970's was also fraught with methodological problems. Kroll (1986) suggests that:

> Before Bassuk in 1984 there were no published American studies that surveyed either representative, randomly selected homeless persons or the entire population of a single shelter.

The politically sensitive nature of homelessness has led to criticism and possible acceptance of particular approaches. For example, the socio-economic approach attributes causation and societal forces and policy decisions, which can be changed or tackled politically. The psychopathological perspective has tended to focus on the individual as social pathological deviant. This renders the homeless person as master of his own fate and thereby excuses society for not managing to cope. This has been the approach generally adopted by governments, for example Reagan who reportedly said :

> People who are sleeping on the streets, the homeless who are homeless you might say, by choice.

This could be interpreted as a way of absolving responsibility. However in the flurry to find an approach which will generate a public response, the exploration of homelessness has been superficial and insufficient. Other writers in the United States are commenting on this and are trying to put together a more comprehensive account.

Social Psychological Approach

While Rossi (1989) has gone some way to placing personal characteristics on the research agenda for homelessness, as yet no working model or approach has emerged from the social sciences to explore this growing problem. However, some recent approaches by psychologists have been encouraging. Toro et al (1991) have suggested that there are promising signs that psychology may be gaining momentum in its concern with homelessness. They have put forward an ecological perspective which sees:

> behaviour as transactional which cannot be understood without reference to context.

The goal as they see it is to clarify the person-environment transactions between individuals and multiple levels of the social context, and not conceptualise homelessness as a person based problem (Toro et al 1991). This approach may be only one of several approaches to the relationship between homeless people and their social and physical context.

The focus of this research is psychological in the sense that the individual's own perspective on the world is seen as relevant and central. Rather than blaming the individual, this approach seeks to take account of him or her. As Caton (1990) argues:

> At present there is very little understanding of how homelessness evolves out of an individual's life experience or how it is related to personal characteristics and larger social and economic issues.

This book offers a Place Theory approach (Canter 1977) in which the individual's experience is considered within a particular physical and social context and is not solely a product of the society or determined by his or her own action.

Part of any definition of homelessness therefore must take into account the heterogeneity of the homeless population. While for the purposes of this research, a homeless person is defined as anyone who has no 'fixed residence' and wishes to obtain one, people can be defined according to a number of different criteria.

They can fall along a continuum, from those that have legal tenure to those who sleep rough on the streets (Watson and Austerberry 1986 p. 21). Along this continuum falls those in hostels, in hotels, in squats and those on other people's floors. However there are other factors to be considered. One could argue that this continuum may be further refined to take into account the lack of any focus or home-like identity within a place of abode. Traditionally the family has been thought of as having its centre of gravity around a 'hearth'. This may therefore act as a useful symbolic reference for considering another important dimension: 'hearthlessness'. Those in hotels for example are more hearthless than those in squats, but may be less hearthless than those in hostels, depending on the type of facility. The symbolic nature of this concept does not necessarily include the family as the only image for home but adds symbolic qualities to the usually cited physical qualities of home. Home is a multivariate concept with meanings varying across individuals, culture and time (cf. Chapters 4 and 5; Moore and Canter 1991a; Moore and Canter 1991b). There are homeless people for whom the traditional notion of a home, with a family at its core is something of a nightmare and not to be repeated. Their idea of home may be very different to other people's conceptions. The simple way of expressing this idea is that there has to be more to describing a whole variety of people with degrees of problems, ranges of experience and different goals, and circumstances than just as needing roofs or collectively having a series of pathological characteristics.

Banishing Stereotypes

While research has indicated the existence of different demographic descriptions of those sleeping on the street and in hostels, there has been no overall account of this. One of the aims of the first stage of the research was to try to untangle the various strands within the homeless population. At first glance there emerged fairly distinct types of homeless settings. Primarily there was a distinction between family homelessness and single homelessness as defined by English legislation in terms of who the authorities have a statutory responsibility for and for who they do not. The Salvation Army have traditionally helped the single homeless and it was this group that was targeted. Focusing on this heterogeneous group many other differences became apparent, most specifically between people who may sleep rough, stay in hostels, bed and breakfast hotels and squats.

Different Ways of Being Homeless

By concentrating attention on these discrete groups for methodological reasons, there was not the intention to suggest that they are distinct or independent of each other. It appears that a proportion of each group forms part of a moving fluid pool which goes from one type of place to another, and that a further proportion has a permanent residence in one type. For hostels, the fixed group could be those who consider the hostel as their home and have lived there for some years, while the floating population could move from one hostel to the next, from one hostel to the street and back again etc. This does not imply that there is a completely free choice being made between types of homelessness. However why one person decides that the street is a better alternative than a hostel bed and another decides the opposite is worthy of study,or why one person will go to a squat where another will stay on the streets. Clearly there is a complex interaction between opportunity and the person, which involves some element of choice and decision, which needs to be understood.

It is important to try to understand for example, what aspects of street living are lost when in a hostel, where do people think the best places to sleep rough are, who sleeps in groups and on their own, and for what reasons? The social and psychological processes involved not only in becoming homeless but also being homeless have to be understood in the consideration of the provision for different types of facilities.

This is an holistic approach to the homeless individual who may be hearthless or may be close to being homeful. The homeless experience and its amelioration requires a perspective which takes account of social context, personal and physical situation. To be homeful, an individual has to be happy with all three aspects, and any individual may or may not need help with all or one of them. This perspective can live alongside other perspectives as it acknowledges the need for affordable housing, for a better understanding of health status, and other problems some homeless people face, and of a common understanding of the complexity of being without shelter and being without a home.

The psychological approach is one which seeks to account for differences between people and examines these in terms of a person's experience within a specific context. It is therefore important to examine both each individual setting and its characteristics and the variety of experiences the people who stay in them have, and to compare across settings to examine the similarities and differences. This perspective is one of compromise, it neither places the individual as a victim of social or economic forces nor as creator of his/her own destiny. The approach outlined here is exploratory and is not presented as a model or theory but rather as a framework for thought on homelessness. It is hoped that other studies will follow which can build on this framework. It is clear however that any theory or even framework must allow for a complex set of relationships with no simple causal relationship between a set of factors or associated problems.

Structure of the Book

The book is organised around the faces of homelessness which were examined as part of two and a half years of research. The next chapter provides an overview of the counts of homeless people in London. The full methodological account is to be found in the Appendix. Chapters 4 to 9 present the results of a questionnaire survey as they apply to the overall sample and the four settings; the street; hostels; hotels and squats. Chapter 10 presents another aspect of homelessness: begging. This was not part of the original study but is exploratory in design, providing some insight into this previously unexplored area. The concluding chapters illustrate the differences between the settings and draw some overall conclusions.

2 Homelessness in England: Changing Responses and the Impact of Europe

Homelessness is attracting attention throughout the European Community. Workers with homeless people have identified what is considered a crisis in homelessness. The reasons for this crisis were examined in a European Commission funded study of homelessness (LABOS 1990). Europe-wide concern about homelessness, led to the creation in 1988 of FEANTSA (the Federation of National Organisations Working with Homeless People).

However, it is only in the UK that it is possible to chart the increase in homeless people, and, even here, the national statistics only cover homeless people accepted by local authorities as being in priority need of housing under the 1985 Housing Act. The UK statistics exclude all those not accepted by local authorities and all those who do not apply. Thus the statistics exclude the majority of single people and those refused help as homeless under the various clauses of the Housing Act 1985. Other EC countries do not have any national statistics for homeless people.

The British statistics chart a steep rise in homelessness as expressed in the numbers who apply to local authorities and are accepted for help. The reasons for the increase must be seen in terms of individual difficulties as well as social, demographic and economic trends. In this chapter a causal model is developed for the increase in homelessness in England over the 1980's. The approach taken in this book is a predominantly environmental psychological one, explaining homelessness in terms of both individual and social factors. This chapter reviews the complementary, aspects of the process by examining the historical macro-societal changes that are relevant.

According to this sociological model, homelessness results from a disjuncture between housing supply and demand brought about by changing demographic, economic and social structures, and mobility. This disjuncture particularly disadvantages different geographical areas, such as inner city areas or areas of rapid economic restructuring, and certain vulnerable social groups, such as the long-term unemployed, single parents, young and old single people, chronically sick and disabled people, women, those from ethnic minorities, those discharged from institutions and the armed forces, those leaving tied employment, and drug and alcohol abusers. For further explorations of this model see Drake et al 1981.

The numbers of homeless people in England

Any attempt to enumerate homeless people can only be partially successful. The national statistics enumerate only homeless people contacting the local authorities. Until the abolition of Board and Lodging payments in 1989 other types of homeless people could be approximately enumerated in the Board and Lodging statistics. Board and Lodging payments were benefits to single people living in hostels, lodgings and hotels. An overall figure for homeless people can be obtained by adding the statistics together. The last year for which we have these statistics was 1986. In 1986 approximately 590,000 individuals applied as homeless to local authorities and there were 166,000 Board and Lodging claimants. The figure for applicants for help as homeless is used rather than that for acceptances since it could be argued that most applicants were in reality homeless even though they were, often for technical reasons, not accepted by local authorities. Also the number for individuals is used rather than that for households to make it comparable to the statistics for Board and Lodging applicants. Thus in 1986 there were approximately 756,000 homeless people in England. This can only be a benchmark figure since it is determined by eligibility to apply for help rather than by social reality.

Other attempts to enumerate homeless people have concentrated on London. In 1985 a team of people was assembled by Professor John Greve to undertake a study of homelessness in London for the Greater London Council which was the local authority operating at London-wide level. (The Council was abolished in 1986 leaving London with no city level government at all). That study found that there were 600,000 homeless people in London. These were people who were literally homeless; those living in hostels and hotels; and those sharing with other people, who might be expected to want their own accommodation (SAUS 1986).

Two years later, in 1986/7 The London Research Centre did a study of housing in London. The study found that 133 potential households, or an estimated 338,000 people, were living with other people but acutely needed their own accommodation (LRC).

Two years later again, in 1989, the study commissioned by the Salvation Army and carried out by the University of Surrey and drawn on in this book found that there were 75,000 people who were visibly homeless in London. These were people living in the most basic conditions. They were living in hostels and hotels, squats (that is, illegally occupying accommodation), or sleeping on the streets, 753 were actually on the streets on a very cold April night, three times more than were found to be on the streets in 1965. Among those sleeping rough, men outnumbered women by 7 to 1. Fifty eight per cent (58%) were between the ages of 21 and 50. On the same night 10,000 people were found in a survey of 60% of London's hostels. Only 6% of beds were empty, suggesting that there were likely to be 18,000 people in all London's hostels. 30,000 were estimated to be squatting, and 25,000 were estimated to be living in London's hotels, a third of these were children (Canter et al, 1989).

The increase in homeless people in England

Homelessness in England has risen dramatically since the early 1970's. The statistics about those accepted as homeless by local authorities shows a five fold increase between 1971 and 1991, from 25,468 households to 145,140 households (Table 2.1). The statistics for those claiming Board and Lodging payments increased over three times from 49 thousand to 166 thousand people, over a shorter time, from 1979 to 1989 when statistics ceased (Table 2.2).

Table 2.1: Homeless households: applications and acceptances: 1971 to 1991

	Accepted	Not Accepted	Applications
1971	25,468	7,918	33,386
1973	33,225	14,488	47,713
1976	33,720	18,890	52,610
1979	56,920		
1982	74,800	82,700	157,500
1985	93,980	109,500	203,480
1988	116,000	122,470	242,470
1991	145,140	not given	not given

Note: The legislation and the recording system changed several times over the period.
Source: DOE Local authorities' action under the Homelessness provisions of the 1985 Housing Act: England. Figures for relevant years.

Table 2.2: Numbers claiming board and lodging payments: 1979 - 1986

			thousands
	boarders	hostel dwellers	all
1979	25	24	49
1980	31	29	60
1981	38	31	69
1982	54	31	85
1983	76	36	112
1984	106	57	163
1985	no figures		
1986	140	26	166

Source: Figures supplied by the Social Security Advisory Committee from Department of Social Security statistics.

The statistics clearly show that homelessness increased particularly among single people. Statistics on the homeless accepted by local authorities show that the proportions of single households accepted as homeless increased since the mid 1970's. The large increase in those claiming Board and Lodgings payments, who were mainly single, confirms this. However, of the single households accepted by local authorities a substantial number would have been pregnant women (Table 2.3). The statistics on priority homeless people show that the patterns of acceptances for different types of households differed between London and the rest of England with the increase in acceptances of single households being greater for London than for the rest of England.

Table 2.3: Homeless households accepted by household composition; 1976 to 1989. Figures for the first half of each year, London and the rest of England

	percentages					
London						
Household type	1976	1979	1982	1985	1988	1991
2 parent families	49	30}	63	54	61	61
1 parent families	33	31}				
single, adult, elderly	18	38	37	46	39	39
Rest of England						
2 parent families	51	34}	65	65	66	64
1 parent families	33	40}				
single, adult, elderly	16	26	35	35	34	36

Source: DOE statistics for each year.

The reasons for the increase in homeless people; a sociological model.

The increase in homelessness can be explained in terms of what are called supply factors and need factors. As the supply of habitable low cost rented housing fails to increase to meet escalating housing need, a 'scissors crisis' occurs, resulting in homelessness. Thus examining this crisis involves looking at the need side and the supply side.

Housing need

The main predeterminant of housing need is the increase in the numbers of households and particularly of single households and lone parents. Households increased in England and Wales from 16.2 thousand in 1961 to 19.1 in 1986 and are projected to rise to 21.2 thousand in 2001. However, the increase was particularly marked for single person households and less so for single parents. Two parent households declined over the period. Among single person households, the elderly are particularly increasing. As they are increasing as a proportion of the population, it is single people and lone parents who are particularly increasing among the homeless (Table 2.3).

However, the increase in households itself would not create housing need. Need is created by an increase in the types of households who cannot gain access to housing. Access to housing is determined partly by income. The distribution of income between those in the bottom and those in the top fifth became more skewed throughout the 1980's, with the top fifth increasing its share of income from 37.9% in 1976 to 41.7% in 1986. Over the same period the bottom quintile reduced its share from 7.4% to 5.9% (Table 2.5). Thus English society has become increasingly unequal in its income distribution and this trend was continued through the 1990's.

Table 2.4: Distribution of final household income, UK

	Quintile groups				Percentages	
	bottom fifth	next fifth	middle fifth	next fifth	top fifth	total
1976	7.4	12.7	18.0	24.0	37.9	100.0
1981	7.1	12.4	17.9	24.0	38.6	100.0
1985	6.7	11.8	17.4	24.0	40.2	100.0
1986	5.9	11.4	17.0	23.9	41.7	100.0

Source: Based on Social Trends 19 5.18, p.97.

The proportion of households in poverty increased over the 1980's. Those living in households earning less than four fifths of the average income increased from 42% to 43% (Table 2.6). The increase was particularly marked for lone parent households. While in 1981 86% of people were living in households headed by a lone parent with less than four fifths of average incomes by 1985 the proportion had increased to 90%. The increase was also particularly marked for unemployed households. Seventy five per cent (75%) of all people living in these types of households had incomes of less than four fifths of average incomes in 1981. The proportion had increased to 84% in 1985.

Table 2.5: Proportions of individuals in households with below 80% of the average income by economic status. Great Britain

	% with incomes below 80% of national average		
	1981	1983	1985
Economic status of head of benefit unit			
pensioner	66	60	66
full-time worker	28	26	26
sick or disabled	74	61	70
single parents	86	86	90
unemployed	75	81	84
others	52	54	57
All economic types	42	41	43
Number of individuals (thousands)	22,220	22,250	23,340

Source: Based on Social Trends 19 Table 5.18, p.97.

Lone parents are consistently shown as being the poorest households and disproportionally likely to become homeless. Divorce increased from 1971 when there were 80 thousand or 6.0 divorces to every thousand married people, to 1986 when there were 165 thousand or 12.6 to every thousand (Social Trends 19 Table 2.6, p.43). It has been estimated that an average of 15,000 newly formed households needing specifically low cost rented housing were created every year by divorce in the early 1980's (Social Trends 1987, p.221). Most of these types of households are likely to consist of mothers and children who turn to local authorities under the homelessness legislation. Contrary to common perceptions divorced men are more likely than divorced women to remain owner occupiers and also to remarry.

People from ethnic minorities are among the most disadvantaged in housing. While they do not figure largely among single homeless people, they do among those accepted as homeless by some local authorities. For example a study carried out in 1984 to 1985 found that of the homeless accepted by Tower Hamlets, 69% were Bangladeshi, yet only 9% of the Tower Hamlets population were Bangladeshi. In addition a study and formal investigations carried out by the Commission for Racial Equality found that people from ethnic minorities live in the worst housing conditions and face serious racial harassment where they live (CRE. Race, immigration and housing: A guide. 1989 p.5).

Certain types of people are more vulnerable in conditions of increasing poverty and scarcity of low rented housing. Those discharged from institutions are such a group. The progressive deinstitutionalisation which has followed the various items of community care legislation introduced from the 1968 Health Services and Public Health Act throughout the eighties has resulted in some homeless mentally ill people becoming homeless on discharge for lack of adequate community care. Agencies working with homeless people, report increasing numbers of severely mentally ill people coming to them for help. Inadequately prepared discharge from care is also contributing to homelessness among the young. A recent review of the literature and statistics of young people in care and homelessness suggested that there is a high correlation between the two (Stockley 1990). The reasons for homelessness given by those accepted for housing as homeless by local authorities reflects the trends identified here in the relationship between housing supply and need. Those made homeless because friends or relatives were unable or unwilling to accommodate them increased from 38% during the first half of 1978 to 44% in the first half of 1988. These people were sharing with friends and relatives being what is known as concealed households. The increased loss of shared accommodation as a reason for homelessness either shows that these types of households have increased among the population or that they have become increasingly at risk of homelessness.

Relationship breakdown increased as a reason for homelessness from 15% in the second half of 1978 to 19% in the second half of 1988. Mortgage default increased from 4% to 7% over the period.

Housing supply

The supply of accessible housing at low rent in the right location and of the right bedroom size needs to approximate to the need for such housing if housing need and homelessness is to be avoided. Over the last 15 to 20 years there has been a growing mismatch between the two sides of this equation. For the National Housing Forum, Pat Niner estimated in 1989 that a further 2 million houses were needed to satisfy demand and an additional 3.2 to 4 million would be needed by 2001 (National Housing Forum 1989, p.vii).

Of particular relevance to homeless people is the supply of rented housing. Rented housing both public and private has declined from over 50% of the stock to just over 30%. Privately rented accommodation amounted to 9% in 1989 and social housing rented from local authorities and housing associations to 22% (Table 2.6). The private sector was once the main supplier of housing to the poor and homeless. It was the most accessible type of housing, being cheaper than owner occupation and with unregulated access, unlike access to social housing which depends on eligibility. The role of last resort housing was increasingly transferred from private rented to social rented housing during the 1980's. Social housing has not increased sufficiently to cope with the increase in need even among eligible people. Waiting lists have almost become irrelevant in particularly hard-pressed areas such as the inner cities. In some areas no households are housed from the waiting list, only homeless households have been housed.

Table 2.6: Households by tenure, 1971 to 1989

	Percentages			
	1971	1981	1986	1989*
owner occupied	49	56	62	69
privately rented	20	13	11	9
publicly rented	31	31	26	22

Source: Social Trends 19 Table 8.20, p.147 and joint Charities Group 1989, p.18. Figures rounded.
* provisional figure for March

Over the 1970's and 1980's the numbers of houses completed annually in all tenures decreased sharply from 261,000 in 1977 to 184,000 in 1989. The decrease was particularly dramatic in the public rented sector which decreased from 140,000 in 1977 to 24,800 in 1988 (Table 2.7).

Table 2.7: House completions 1977 to 1988

England	Thousands		
	Public	Private	All
1977	140.0	121.0	261.0
1980	94.1	110,0	204.1
1983	43.8	127.3	171.2
1986	29.6	141.3	170.9
1988	24.8	159.8	184.6

Source: Based on an unnumbered Table on p.12, Joint Charities 1989.

The owner occupied sector has been increasing as a proportion of the total housing stock. At the same time as the owner occupied sector has been increasing the numbers of repossessions have also been rising (Table 8).

In 1982 there were 6,000 repossessions, in 1987, 22,900. In 1993 there are predicted to be over 200,000 repossessions, per annum.

Table 2.8: Repossessions by Building Societies

	Thousands
1982	6.0
1985	16.8
1987	22.9

Source: Social Trends 19. Table 8.19, p.146.

As rented housing has been declining, so has housing of last resort. Religious and philanthropic organisations, such as the Salvation Army are still the largest providers for single homeless people. Many of these types of hostels were built at the end of the last century or at the beginning of this one. The buildings are old and in need of refurbishing or rebuilding. Such large, old hostels are being closed and replaced by smaller, new hostels which do not provide the same number of bedspaces.

The religious organisations first developed their hostels using charitable funds, and, therefore, without extensive government controls over standards and design. They now refurbish or rebuild using government funds which are subject to controls. The old religious organisations have established housing associations. For example Church Housing, the housing association took over almost all of the Church Army hostels. They are now part of a large housing association, English Churches Housing Association. Working within a housing association framework enables the organisation to take advantage of government funding through the Housing Corporation which funds Housing Association development, through the Hostels Initiative started in 1981 and subsequent special needs programmes. However, the Housing Corporation issued guidelines limiting hostel size to 30 bedspaces. In practise the Corporation likes to fund even smaller hostels. Only a few larger hostels have been funded. Thus it is almost impossible for the old 19 century buildings to be refurbished. The organisations, often have to either carry on with their buildings in an unsatisfactory state, or to demolish and rebuild on a smaller scale.

The emphasis on smaller, well designed hostels is commendable in many ways. An unwelcome consequence, however, is that the number of bedspaces in hostels has declined at a time when homelessness has been increasing and when public investment in other types of housing has been decreasing. Bedspaces in London alone declined from 13,579 in 1981 to 10,078 in 1985. The decline was caused by the decline in beds within large old hostels which were more likely to offer direct access to people from the streets than the newer hostels.

These trends have been noted throughout the Member States of Europe where expenditure on social housing is declining, single people are increasing as a proportion of the population, divorce is rising, young unemployed people are found on the streets, the psychiatrically ill are discharged with inadequate care into the community, and so on. FEANTSA has estimated that there are 2.5 million homeless people in Europe. (FEANSTA 1993.) These are the visible homeless on the streets or in temporary accommodation. Yet it is only in England that there is even a limited right to housing for at least some types of homeless people.

The response to homelessness: the history of policy and provision for homeless people in England

There has been a historical progression in responsibility for policy and provision for homeless people. Until the Beveridge revolution of 1948, religious and charitable groups were the prime providers for homeless people. From 1948 till the early 1980's the state increasingly took on responsibility for housing homeless people or for funding those who did provide for them. At the earlier part of this period the responsibility was primarily seen as resting with service departments. By 1977, with the Housing (Homeless Persons) Act the responsibility was transferred to Housing Departments. This marked a change from the explanation of homelessness as the result of social pathology to the view that it was caused by housing shortage and poverty.

The basis of all homelessness policy and provision was the 1948 National Assistance Act which empowered, but did not oblige, local authorities through their Social Services departments to provide a full range of residential provision for those in need who were normally resident in their area, or who were not normally resident but were made homeless in emergency. Indeed if local authorities had made use of the powers available to them under the Act much subsequent legislation would arguably have been unnecessary.

Succeeding legislation introduced duties rather than powers to house ever more types of homeless people. For example the 1959 Mental Health Act explicitly stated that mentally ill people should be housed under the terms of the 1948 Act. The 1966 Ministry of Social Security Act made it possible for the Ministry to compel a local authority to provide for people in urgent need of accommodation. It also made it a duty of the Ministry to provide a network of reception centres throughout the country for homeless people, a network which is now under threat following the DSS policy of closures and transfer of the function to local authorities and voluntary agencies. The 1968 Health Services and Public Health Act was the precursor of modern Care in the Community legislation and empowered local authorities to provide residential services for the ill outside hospitals, and to fund voluntary agencies to provide such services. Protection for ex-offenders was extended under the 1972 Criminal Justice Act.

While care and accommodation for homeless people was generally seen as a Social Services Department responsibility over this time, the Housing Act 1957 did lay a general duty on local housing authorities to 'consider the housing conditions in their district and the needs of the district with respect to the provision of further housing accommodation', and to provide hostels. The few that did provide hostels did so mainly for homeless families rather than single people. In general, housing departments did very little for single people.

The 1977 Housing Homeless Persons Act marked the climax of the increasing state responsibility for homeless people as well as an acceptance that homelessness was not inevitably the result of social pathological behaviour or illness but rather of poverty and inadequate housing for people in extreme housing need. The Act made it a duty of local housing authorities to house those in priority need, replacing the duties laid down by the 1958 National Assistance Act and its amending legislation.

The Act used a two pronged definition of the types of people to be helped by the Act. On the one hand they had to be homeless, namely without a home which they had the right to occupy or could gain access to at the time of application to the local authority for help; or likely to become homeless within one month of the application. On the other they had to be part of the priority groups to have first claim on resources. The four types of priority groups were people with children; those threatened by some kind of emergency such as fire or flood; those vulnerable because of sickness or disability; and those vulnerable because of other reasons such as domestic violence, or pregnancy.

If however, homeless applicants can be shown to have made themselves homeless 'intentionally' the authority does not have a duty to rehouse them. In effect 'intentionality' is defined following the large body of Case Law which has developed as a result of litigation between homeless applicants and local authorities. 'Intentionality' often has little to do with the actual intentions of homeless people but rather more with how their actions can be interpreted by housing authorities, trying to limit the call on their resources..

In practice many local authorities are said to extend the 'intentionality' clause to avoid their responsibilities. People who have left violent homes, or have been evicted for rent or mortgage arrears, may be declared 'intentionally' homeless. In a 'cause celebre', Bengali families living in Tower Hamlets were declared 'intentionally homeless' because they left their homes to go and fetch their families from Bangladesh. The council was taken to a Judicial Enquiry by the Commission for Racial Equality. The council won the right to declare the families 'intentionally homeless'.

Like 'intentionality','vulnerability' has less to do with peoples' actual vulnerability as with whether or not their vulnerability is of the sort that the legislation recognised. For example many young people are actually vulnerable because of their age and the likelihood that they might be exploited. But they are not generally classified as vulnerable and therefore as priorities, by the local authorities.

The Act was accompanied by a Code of Guidance which explained exactly how it was to be interpreted. A large body of Case Law has built up over the years the Act has been in operation. The Act is operated in the light of both the Code and The Case Law.

The Act was passed following fierce lobbying by its supporters and their opponents. The supporters argued that housing homeless people should be a statutory duty of local housing authorities. Homelessness led to, for example, families being split up, and children being received into care. 'Cathy Come Home', a film which graphically depicted the tragedy of a young woman and her children being forcibly separated because of their homelessness, lent powerful support to the campaign behind the Act.

Opposition came from two directions. On the one hand were those who argued that in offering accommodation only to priority homeless people, the policy did not go far enough. It excluded most single and childless people. It also retained the infamous 'intentionality' clause and a restrictive definition of vulnerability.

On the other hand, fundamental opposition to the very principle of giving homeless people rights came from those who argued strongly that it was a 'queue jumpers Charter'. Many housing authorities felt the Act was forcing them to abandon one of their most sacred shibboleths, the primacy of the waiting list. Depending on their age and family status, any local person can go on the waiting list. A pointing system gestures in the direction of taking account of special needs or vulnerability. The Act would, they feared, open the floodgates to outsiders who would usurp the rights of local people to housing.

Even today the main arguments against the Act remain those which were made when it was passed. Some argue that the main cause of homelessness is the increase in single mothers, that young women get pregnant to jump the waiting list. They point to the increase in births to unmarried mothers from 6% of births in 1961 to 23% in 1988. Yet the great majority of these births are registered in two names, that is to people living in stable cohabiting couples. Some also blame the increasing divorce rate, and here they have more of a point. As we noted above divorce accounts for around 15,000 new households needing cheap rented housing each year. Many of these are women and children who apply to local authorities as homeless.

Another criticism of the legislation is that it encourages people to move to become homeless in London. This is not borne out by the evidence. Eighty six per cent (86%) of acceptances are of people who live in the immediate area of the local authority which accepted them.

Perhaps the most fundamental criticism of the Act is that it actually encourages people to become homeless, and that it is to blame for the enormous increase in homeless people. The Audit Commission, for example, in its examination of homelessness, made reference to the view that, 'a good proportion of the so-called homeless are intentionally on the streets perhaps to give themselves a better chance of a council house'. The Commission, however, found that most of those accepted as homeless by local authorities were on their waiting list or were eligible to be (Audit Commission 1989).

Does the homelessness legislation cause increasing homeless by encouraging people to leave home, or does the cause lie within the unequal relationship between the supply of housing and the demand for it? A sample answer to this question could not be forthcoming. However, as some argue; given the decrease in affordable housing and the increase in demand over the last twenty years it would be surprising if there was no homelessness crisis. The increase in households, particularly of those most vulnerable in the housing market and the decline of available rented housing leads inevitably to housing scarcity and homelessness. The 1977 Act's effect was limited to protecting the interests of certain types of homeless people, those with children, and those without children but who were vulnerable in specified ways.

The Act has been criticised for not being strong enough to really improve the housing chances of the households accepted as homeless, many of whom are placed in poor standard temporary accommodation for extended periods. But the Act was introduced when Government policy was to continue to substantially increase the supply of housing every year. There would have been housing resources to back up the rights given to homeless people under the Act. Those resources have been drastically reduced and it is impossible to judge the Act's effectiveness without considering that it was introduced just before a very steep decline in annual social housing production which has continued to the present time. Without the Act homeless people might have suffered even more than they have.

Perhaps because of the lack of resources to house the homeless people they accept, local authorities have not reduced the proportions of people they turned away after the Act was passed. The proportions turned away increased from just over a quarter of the homeless applying in 1971, to almost a half of those applying in 1988 (Table 2.1). The Act, in 1977, did not slow the increase in the proportions turned away.

Nor did the Act improve access by homeless households to good quality housing. The numbers in temporary accommodation has increased from 9,840 in 1983 to 30,000 in 1988 (DOE 1989). When finally allocated housing there is some evidence that homeless applicants are offered worse quality housing than that offered to waiting list applicants. Furthermore, whereas waiting list applicants normally are given three offers of accommodation, homeless applicants often only receive one offer which they have to accept.

At the time the Act was introduced it was assumed that the homeless were a marginal group whose accommodation difficulties were temporary. The Act was addressed at what was essentially a residual problem which would be eventually eradicated by increasing availability of social housing. However, it was already becoming clear, even before the Act became law that homelessness was increasing and that people were spending more and more time in temporary accommodation. Despite the Act local authorities turned away increasing numbers of homeless people.

But although the Act was deficient in many ways, it remains the best hope for large numbers of homeless people. It is likely that without the Act even more people would be on the streets. However, as the housing stock which the authorities would have used to house homeless people has decreased they have operated the legislation more restrictively. Problems which the Act was introduced to solve are now reappearing. For example, children are now once again being taken into care because of their family's homelessness or poor housing conditions. Fortunately, when it reviewed the homelessness legislation in 1989, despite pressures from some local authorities and the Association of District Councils to limit the terms of the legislation regarding residential requirements for homeless applicants, the government left the legislation intact. The government is, however, carrying out a further review of the legislation at the time of going to press. The outcome of this review will not be known for several months.

From 1977 to the present day

The second stage of the history of policy for homeless people is marked by reducing state expenditure on housing in general, and reducing rights of individuals to help of various kinds which had built up over the preceding thirty-five years under the legislation. Housing production has fallen over the ten years, breaking what had been a generally rising trend since the war. The rented sectors have particularly declined.

The local authorities fulfil their responsibilities to homeless people, both priority and non-priority, by relying heavily on voluntary sector provision by Housing Associations and voluntary organisations. Control over this provision is maintained by policy regulation, funding and other types of intervention, so that it might be more appropriate to talk of a quasi-voluntary sector rather than a voluntary one. For example many Housing Associations which are voluntary, offer 100% nominations to local authority residents, and were till 1988 funded almost entirely through government and local authority funds. They are still largely funded by public subsidy but now have to rely on raising private loans to supplement government funds.

Thus housing associations work with local authorities to provide for priority homeless people; and with voluntary organisations to provide for non-priority homeless people. Some of the larger voluntary organisations established their own Housing Associations to benefit from government funding. More recently some of the Housing Associations are directly managing their own accommodation for homeless people. Previously they would have worked with a voluntary organisation to do so.

The voluntary sector therefore provides accommodation, care, advice and assistance to homeless people. It also runs campaigns on their behalf. It provides both temporary and permanent housing for special needs groups such as those with disabilities. Voluntary provision can be seen as a response to the reducing resources available to local authorities to deal with the rapidly increasing problem of homelessness.

This latter period in policy and provision for homeless people has been marked by several positive approaches in the design and management of accommodation for single homeless people and in the expectations that all homeless people should eventually live in their own homes. However, these approaches have not been matched by a corresponding increase in resources at the appropriate levels to provide the higher standard of response for all homeless people which is expressed in policy. Indeed over this period homeless people have become much more visible and appear to be living as badly, or even worse than they were before the 1977 Housing (Homeless Persons) Act.

Thus homeless people sleeping on London's streets have become a visible embarrassment at which the government has addressed several phases of a Rough Sleeping Initiative initially with a budget of £96 million over three years. At the same time the numbers of priority homeless people in temporary accommodation waiting permanent rehousing rises. The costs of temporary accommodation are much higher than the cost of permanent accommodation. It costs twice as much to house a family in temporary accommodation for one year than it does to provide them with a permanent flat. In an attempt to stem the escalating costs of temporary accommodation, the government has introduced various Homelessness Initiatives aimed at the priority homeless, including Private Sector Leasing, the Housing Association Management Agent programme, and using private finance through the Business Incentive Scheme to provide for homeless families. The government now encourages Housing Associations to help local authorities carry out their responsibilities under the Homeless Persons Act. In the past Housing Associations were seen as complementing the local authorities' role and housing those local authorities would not house.

In this chapter macro structural tendencies have been identified as the causes of the increase in homelessness, little attention has been paid to individual causes. Each homeless person has their own story to tell and each could point to subjective reasons for their homelessness. Whilst the individual focus is a legitimate starting point for examining the causes of homelessness it is important to see how the conditions within which individuals become homeless are created by developments occurring at a much larger scale. The government response to homelessness has also been traced to show how different approaches have emerged predominantly since the Second World War.

The future is likely to be increasingly affected by the Single European Market. European markets for labour and capital will begin to have their effects in the structure of housing demand and need, and in the way housing is financed, built, allocated and managed. Migration from the poorer areas of the Community as well as from the East will ultimately affect social housing although the fact that only people in work have the right to move between member states and live in them means that it is unlikely that the UK with its relatively advanced homelessness legislation will receive large numbers of homeless people looking for help. However, the trends in housing supply and demand which have so far been contained within a national context will increasingly become European. At present social policy and housing is not part of the legislative sphere of the European legislature thus the response to homelessness will remain national in the foreseeable future. Lack of harmonisation of legislation in these areas could create problems for people moving around Europe.

The European Community is concerned to bring into sharper focus problems of homeless people in Europe. It has introduced several programmes to deal with 'excluded' or marginalised people (Drake 1991 and 1992). However, a European approach to homelessness is not possible. There is no European definition of what constitutes 'homelessness' nor any way of enumerating homeless people. Steps towards a European approach may follow from the funding of FEANTSA to monitor homelessness in all the Member States, through an observatory of homelessness. This has been running since 1991, bringing together information about homelessness in the Member States.

The trends identified in this chapter in the increase, and causes of, homelessness can be traced in other countries of the European Community and elsewhere. A study of homelessness in Australia revealed a similar, close relationship between family breakdown, ill health, institutionalisation, making certain types of households vulnerable to homelessness in conditions of housing and job scarcity (see for example, Rope et all 1984). The response to the needs of homeless people varies in the different countries. While, in the UK, the government appears to be withdrawing from state provision for homeless people, in other countries, the state has never been a provider. Thus, although the problems of homelessness in

London do have particular characteristics derived both from British legislation and the changing housing, employment, social and demographic structures in England, nonetheless these problems do reflect parallel difficulties developing throughout Europe. Understanding the nature of homelessness in London does therefore provide an important contribution

to understanding the wider significance of being without a home anywhere in Europe. 1

3 The Count: The Scale of Homelessness in London

Establishing the number and variety of people who are homeless in London is remarkably difficult. This difficulty has led to a range of estimates with little to substantiate many of them. There is however, little that can be done to address the problem of homelessness without understanding its scale, characteristics and distribution. In the attempt to unravel the many different strands of homelessness in London, six distinct sub-groups can be identified with varied qualities and problems.

1. People living 'rough' on the streets or 'skippering'.
2. People in hostels and night shelters.
3. People in bed and breakfast hotels.
4. People in squats.
5. People of no fixed abode in hospital and police cells.
6. The 'hidden homeless'.

These aspects are sufficiently different in nature to require a variety of procedures for exploration. However in day-to-day terms, these are not distinct or static, but rather make up a fluid interchange of people between settings and from homelessness to a more settled way of life.

For the purposes of this study, only the first four aspects or settings were addressed in full, with the fifth being examined in brief and the sixth not explored at all. The methods used to assess the variety and distribution for each type are to be found in the Appendix. This discussion will focus on the scale and distribution of each setting, comparing these findings with previous ones and emerging with an overview of the scale of homelessness in London at the time of the studies.

To explore the number and variety of people who are homeless in London and to examine the conditions in which they are living, the studies examined a) people sleeping rough on the streets of London b) people in hostels, c) bed and breakfast hotel accommodation d) living in squats and e) people of no fixed abode in hospital and police cells.

History of the street count

Many estimates have been made over the years as to the number of people living on the street in London and in particular boroughs. Charles Booth in 'Life and Labour in the East of London' made an estimate of 33,000 homeless people in London in 1889. This estimate was based on a census of East London and figures for the rest of London were extrapolated from these. The definition of homelessness used by Booth was that homeless people were 'Loafers, casuals, and some criminals'(Booth 1889). A further 51,000 were counted as Paupers: inmates of Workhouses, Asylums and Hospitals; 300,000 as starving: casual earnings between 18s. per week and chronic want; and 607,000 as the very poor with intermittent earnings 18s. to 21s. per week.

The history of the street survey re-emerged before the first world war when the London City Council (L.C.C.) medical officer of health made an annual census of homelessness in the County and after that the practice was revived by the L.C.C. Welfare Department which did a 'midnight survey' in Central London once a year up to 1949. At the beginning and end of November 1965 welfare staff assisted by voluntary organisations combed inner London to find 'sleepers out' (Greve 1964) (p. xiv). This National Assistance Board census of those sleeping rough came as part of their national survey of hostels and lodging houses. They found 247 people on the streets of London in 1965. In 1972 St. Mungo Community Trust carried out a survey of the streets of London and found 12,000 single homeless people with 'nowhere to go' (Tremlett 1989 p.20). However there is no documentation of the methodology involved and this figure has been taken as no more than an informed guess. Also in 1972, New Horizon estimated that there were 8,000 young people sleeping rough in London and that 20% were girls.

In 1985 a team of people was assembled by Professor John Greve to undertake a study of homelessness in London for the Greater London Council which was the local authority operating at London-wide level. The Council was abolished in 1986 leaving London with no city level government at all (Greve 1985). That study found that there were 600,000 potential and homeless people in London. These were people who were roofless; those living in hostels and hotels; and those sharing with other people, who might be expected to want their own accommodation.

Two years later, in 1986/7 The London Research Centre which was formed by many of the Greater London Council research staff, did a study of housing in London. The study found that 133 potential households, or an estimated 338,000 people, were living with other people but acutely needed their own accommodation (LRC 1989 p.32).

The London Housing Unit in 1988 estimated there were about 2,000 people sleeping in Central London alone. On a local borough level in 1987/8 the Simon Community carried out a survey of Camden and found 205 living on the street. Most recently the 1991 Census sought to include homeless people in their figures. The 1991 Census found 1,275 people sleeping rough in Greater London using a similar approach to that of the second Surrey Survey in which local organisations participated in identifying sites (OPCS 1991; see Ch.4).

Given the haze of estimates it was felt that before the present study could focus in detail on sub-groups of homeless people, some attempt should be made to establish the number, variety and distribution of people on the street, in hostels, in squats and bed and breakfast hotels through a series of counts, postal and telephone surveys and door to door visits.

While a full account of the methodology used in these surveys is provided in the Appendix, and the results are presented in full in later chapters, it is useful here to provide an overview of the approaches for each setting.

University of Surrey's counts

In 1989 a study commissioned by the Salvation Army and carried out by the University of Surrey concluded that there were 75,000 people who were visibly homeless in London. These were people living in the most basic conditions. They were living in hostels and hotels, squats (that is, illegally occupying accommodation), or sleeping on the streets, 753 were actually on the streets on a very cold April night, three times more than were found to be on the streets in 1965. Among those sleeping rough, men outnumbered women by 7 to 1. Fifty eight per cent (58%) were between the ages of 21 and 50. On the same night 10,000 people were found in a survey of 60% of London's hostels. Only 6% of hostel beds were empty, suggesting that there were likely to be 18,000 people in all London's hostels. 30,000 were estimated to be squatting, and 25,000 were estimated to be living in London's hotels, of whom a third were children.

Street

There were two street counts. The first acting as a form of pilot, concentrated on a small area of central London and involved over 100 volunteers who combed a network of streets on one cold night on November 22nd 1988. This count concentrated on noting the whereabouts and other details of people on the streets after 12am on one night. The detailed results were used to create a map of that area which is presented below (see Figure 3.1). A total of 532 people were found in this area of West Central London (271) and Waterloo and its surrounds (261).

Figure 3.1: Pilot count: map of the area

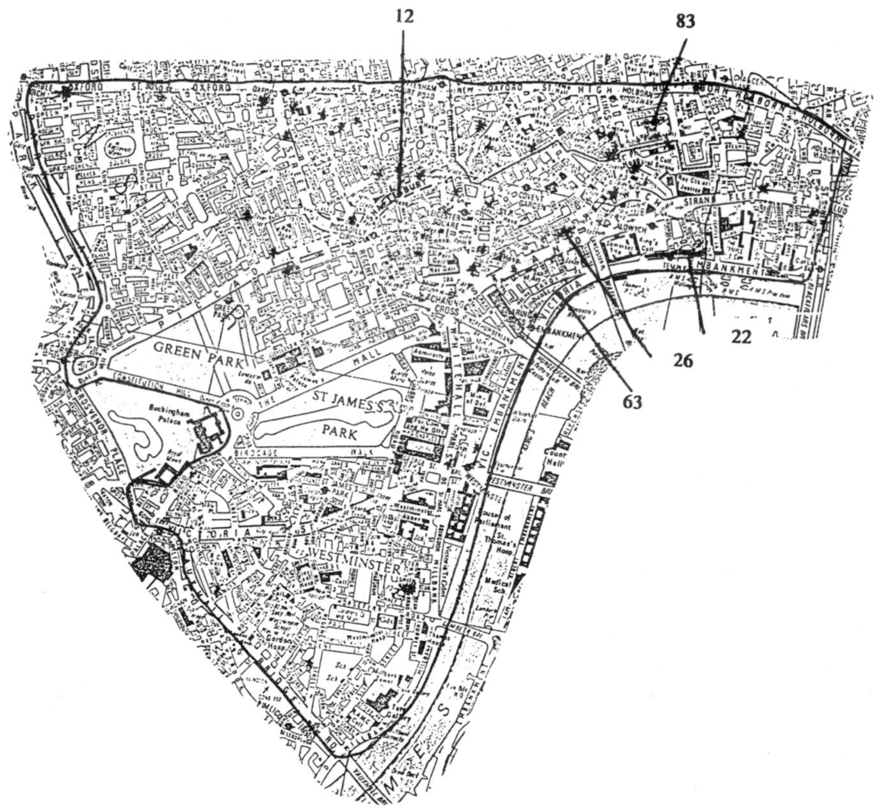

This map shows clearly the areas which were densely populated and those which contained a few 'loners'. This first count encouraged the team to organise a larger more comprehensive count of as much of London was possible. This second survey involved the help of 300 people, most of whom were familiar with homelessness in their own borough. By gaining their co-operation 17 boroughs were included in the survey on a cold night in April 1989. These were not combed as with the first count, but rather surveyors only went to places to count where they had received information about people sleeping rough. Figure 3.2 presents a map of London and the number of people found on the streets in each borough.

Figure 3.2: Pilot count: map of London

NUMBERS OF PEOPLE VISUALLY LOCATED AND SLEEPING-ROUGH
ON THE NIGHT OF TUESDAY 25 APRIL 1989

THE LONDON BOROUGHS

		Number			Number
1.	BARNET	37	9.	ISLINGTON	3
2.	BRENT	1	10.	KENSINGTON & CHELSEA	20
3.	CAMDEN	108	11.	KINGSTON UPON THAMES	2
4.	CITY OF LONDON	28	12.	LAMBETH	262
5.	CROYDON	2	13.	NEWHAM	3
6.	EALING	2	14.	RICHMOND UPON THAMES	0
7.	HACKNEY	3	15.	SOUTHWARK	19
8.	HILLINGDON	16	16.	TOWER HAMLETS	12
			17.	CITY OF WESTMINSTER	133

The second survey found 753 people sleeping openly on the streets. The National Assistance Board found 247 people on the streets of London in 1965. This three fold increase is likely to be an underestimate because the people carrying out the survey were instructed not to take any risks, such as going into derelict buildings or covered basement areas.

A comparison of the April survey with results from a similar, but more limited pilot survey conducted in November 1988 in central London, and with figures from small scale surveys carried out by voluntary organisations, revealed almost twice as many people in some areas in previous surveys. It is therefore likely that not only does the number of people on the streets fluctuate a great deal, but at least double the number of people may be hidden from obvious view. Other studies have indicated that this group overlaps with those sleeping in squats. Such illegal residences may vary from gutted buildings to reasonably comfortable accommodation.

The count of people 'on the street' was particularly notable for the fact that the people located could be divided, more or less, into two types. One was those individuals spread out, sleeping in isolation or in small groups of two or three. A second was a rather larger number of people who were sleeping in much larger groups of possibly 100 or more.

Of those described in the street survey (about a third of those found), men outnumbered women by 7 to 1. The majority of those described were young adults and middle aged, not teenagers or the elderly (58% were between the ages of 21 and 50).

Hostels

A pro-forma was sent to every hostel in London listed in the London Hostel Directory of 1988. This form or questionnaire simply asked for the number of beds in the hostel on the night of the second count, the number of empty beds and reasons for their vacancies if any. With a telephone follow-up survey, nearly two thirds of the hostels responded.

There were just under 10,000 people in 60% of London's hostels, with a 95% occupancy rate on the night. Therefore there are likely to be 18,000 people in hostel bed spaces in London. In addition to the numbers of bed spaces in hostels it was found that in the 60% of London's hostels which participated in the survey there were only 6% of total bed spaces empty, and even less for Direct Access beds, with 4% empty. Management guidelines propose that 10% vacancies are really necessary for the efficient running of hostels. The direct access bedspaces were concentrated in the centre of the city.

Bed and breakfast accommodation

Hotels were difficult to survey due in part to uncooperative hotel staff. Using a telephone survey and door to door visits a small percentage of hotels were surveyed. Almost 25,000 homeless people are estimated to be living in 710 hotels in London. 168 of these hotels were surveyed. At the time of the survey there were 5,710 residents in these hotels. Around three quarters of homeless people in hotels are living in families with children. Most of these were placed in hotels by Local Authorities. The remaining quarter are single people or childless couples who came to the hotels by their own efforts. 47% of hotels had no empty beds on the night of the survey. Nearly a third (31%) of hotel homeless were children.

Squats

Squats are notoriously difficult to count as by their very nature their inhabitants are elusive and cannot be too open about their living arrangements. By networking several key squatting organisations a rough estimate was made as to the total number in London. The information obtained suggested that the number may be near to the Advisory Service for Squatters estimation of 30,000.

Hospitals and police stations

In addition to the four homeless settings, it was thought important to try and get some figures for the number of people who described themselves as 'no fixed abode' on admittance to hospital and in temporary custody in police stations. Police and hospitals in London were contacted and asked to provide this information. This proved to be very difficult as although all hospitals obtain this information it is rarely collated and none had the resources to gather it for the purposes of the research. Only one hospital provided the information and found four patients registering as NFA. Most police stations were co-operative and indicated that there were only three people in custody on the night.

Hidden homeless

The 'hidden homeless' are those who are not in the hostels, hotels, squats or on the street, but exist by staying with friends or relatives when this has ceased to be a practical or welcome arrangement. The 'hidden homeless' are an unknown quantity, as was once 'the homeless' and it is not possible at this stage to make further distinctions between them. This research project has not attempted to assess the numbers of homeless people who may fall into this category. The London Resource Centre Housing Survey in 1986/7 estimated 133,000 people who are judged to be in need of their own accommodation in London for example, because they are staying on friends' floors.

Distribution of homeless people in London

The results show clearly that the great majority of homeless people are not visibly sleeping on the streets of London. Most are in squats, bed and breakfast accommodation or hostels. Those that are on the streets are to be found for the most part in the centre of the city, largely in groups. The total number of people estimated to be in these four settings on the 25th April 1989 was as follows:

Street	**2,000**
Hostels	**18,000**
Squats	**30,000**
Hotels	**25,000**
TOTAL	**75,000**

The figures revealed by these studies give rise to an estimate of at least 75,000 people who are overtly homeless in London. A comparison with the London Resource Centre's figures serves to emphasise that there are many different ways of experiencing homelessness and there are probably at least as many hidden homeless as overtly homeless people. Furthermore, it is apparent that there is movement between these different types of homelessness.

Any discussion of numbers with regard to homeless people must be taken with caution. It can only be used to begin to define the problem. People flow in and out of the homeless pool, sometimes for a few days, sometimes for years. The figures used from these studies reflect the spring of 1989. Some reports since then indicate small increases in those sleeping on the street. Street homelessness is potentially manageable, given the right resources and approach. The silent numbers in hotels, and on floors must also be helped and not forgotten as most of the current attention focuses on squatters and some street homeless people who may possibly be more resourceful, independent and capable than those left in unsuitable accommodation.

4 The Faces of Homelessness: An Integrated Approach

The following four chapters provide an account of each of the four faces of homelessness. The sample as a whole is discussed in this chapter with a comparison across faces in Chapter 11 to illustrate the differences.

Although varying in style and emphasis, Chapters 5 to 10 examine the setting in hand with respect to the same themes. These themes correspond closely with sections of the questionnaire used in the studies. A full account of these can be found in the Appendix.

First, the scale of each setting is addressed and further information on the counts and surveys is provided where possible.

Second, details on the characteristics of each of the populations are presented, in terms of age, gender, ethnicity, employment status etc.

Third, an account of the residential histories of the sample populations is provided and, where appropriate, comparisons are made with previous studies.

Fourth, homeless people's evaluations of the setting are provided in which key aspects of the setting are assessed in terms of their home-like qualities. This focus on evaluation by the residents emerges from previous discussion on 'hearthlessness' (Canter et al 1989), in which emphasis was made on the significance of having a roof but no domestic quality to that residence. A part of the present survey was therefore to explore the meaning of home to homeless people: those with and without a roof over their heads.

Fifth, the importance of some of these home-like qualities were assessed by the sample, and details of the results are provided in each chapter.

The nature of our data on hotels creates a different style for Chapter 9.

Chapter 10 provides an unique account of begging in London which offers a first glimpse into this growing feature of street homelessness. This phenomenon has not been discussed in any depth prior to this account and requires further study. The survey reported here consists of responses to a self-completion questionnaire. The questionnaire was developed from initial interviews and group discussions with homeless people. The focus of the questionnaire was on the experience and perceptions of those out-of-home. In total 531 people from four settings took part in the study. The numbers and distribution of the hotel homeless are described in some detail. The views, however, are more cursorily explained than the views of homeless people in hostels.

An integrated approach

This section focuses on the whole sample of homeless people, providing an overview of this varied population.

Overview of Sample

The following sections will compare our findings with other studies to illustrate the variety of homeless people in London. The sample in our study comprises 531 homeless people largely from hostels, but also from the street, squats and a very small number of hotel residents. The percentage from each setting breaks down as follows:

Figure 4.1 : Distribution of sample

Hostels	78%
Street	9%
Squats	10%
Hotels	3%
Sample	100%
Total =	531

Age

There are a number of studies of homeless people which have indicated some general trends in age. Some focused on street people (London Outreach Team 1984), others focused on hostel residents (Wingfield Digby

1976) and single homeless people in general (Drake et al 1981). It is useful to compare briefly some of these findings as summarised in Table 4.1.

Table 4.1: Age of respondents across four studies

Age	NAB 1965	Single and Homeless 1981	Out-reach 1984	Univ. Surrey 1988	Univ. Surrey 1989	Univ. Surrey 1990
	N=101 %	N=516 %	N=318 %	N=271 %	N=220 %	N=531 %
Young (1-39)	33	54	49	40	47	64
Middle Aged (40-64)	50	39	42	50	39	31
Older (Over 65)	17	7	9	10 (60+)	14	5 (70+)

The current sample has a much larger percentage of people under 39 years of age than were considered to be on the streets in the street survey in 1989 (64% as compared to 47%). However it compares more closely with the findings from Single and Homeless (54%) (Drake et al 1981).

Thus this general sample of homeless people has 7% more people under the age of 39 years than the Single and Homeless study which appears to indicate an emergence of younger homeless people in the ten years since the DOE study. However for the purpose of this report it serves to illustrate the range of ages who are homeless.

Taking the current sample and comparing ages between the different settings, the hostel sample has the oldest sample, of which 59% were under 39, as compared with the street sample (71%) and the squat sample (98%). Clearly there is a wide variation within the different homeless settings even in terms of age. With particular regard to hostels, there are more homeless people over the age of 50 in hostels than in any other setting. Twenty five per cent (117) residents of hostels are over 50. This is 21% of the total sample. Of the homeless people in our sample only four were over the age of 50 and not in a hostel. This indicates that the hostel population tends to be older than other homeless populations.

The Salvation Army hostel population (accounting for 38% of our hostel sample) tends to be older on average than the remaining sample (29% of the Salvation Army sample were over 50 years). This can be compared to

Oakley's study of Salvation Army hostel residents in which 44% were over the age of 50 years (Oakley 1980). This would suggest that on average the current Salvation Army population is a lot younger than it was ten years ago. This has implications for the type of provision suitable for this population.

Gender

Most of the previous studies on single homeless people have included a look at homeless women. Our sample was made up of only 19% women. These were mostly found in hostels, squats and hotels. This percentage is larger than that for street homeless people, for example, 92% of the sample from the London Outreach study were male (LOT 1984). Given the large number of men visibly homeless it is perhaps not surprising that most of the provision and research is aimed towards men. However there has been some work which looks directly at the particular features of homelessness among women (cf. Watson and Austerberry 1983/6 and Kennedy 1985). While it is not directly relevant to the current discussion, the indications are that women are distributed in less visible homeless settings than men. Discussion with people in the field has suggested that when provision is targeted at women, they appear as if out of nowhere, whereas they do not make demands on general provision. If one were to take their invisibility as a sign that they do not exist, it would present a false picture. Our research has not attempted to examine the invisible homelessness or the hidden homeless and as such can only refer to other work.

However existing research reminds us it is important to recognise that there are women who are homeless and that they have particular problems. Current provision for women would seem to be small. In 1981 there were approximately 760 beds available to women and over 6,000 beds for men in direct access hostels (Watson and Austerberry 1983, p.16).

Current provision tends to house more men than women. A look at the gender of the whole sample indicates that 81% were male.

Employment Status

There is little available information on the employment status of single homeless people in London. Single and Homeless indicated that 51% of its sample were unemployed (Drake et al 1981).

The sample indicates that 47% describe themselves as unemployed, with 30% in some kind of work, including 1% on Government Schemes, and 13% invalid or ill and 10% retired. Thus nearly a third of the sample are working. This group of people will have very different requirements to the retired or invalid group.

Length of Stay

A few examples of reported lengths of stay in hostels are from Wingfield Digby's study in 1976 and Oakley's study in 1980. In the former, 47% of the residents had been there longer than ten years and in the latter, 30% had stayed longer than two years. In the current survey, 30% of the sample had been where they were staying for longer than a year. It seems there is a smaller percentage of residents staying for long periods of time. However this is still nearly a third of the sample, which is quite high considering the temporary to medium stay nature of all the accommodation in the sample.

Family Status

The studies discussed here and indeed this study are focused on single homeless people due to the lack of government protection for them unless they are vulnerable under the homelessness legislation. However there are some hotel residents in this sample who are parents and who have particular housing requirements. This group is not discussed in this document, but is nonetheless in need of permanent housing. However, of interest here is the family status of the sample. In previous studies, for example, Wingfield Digby in 1972 found 63% of residents were single while in Oakley's study 67% were single.

In this study, 71% were single, 18% were divorced or separated, 3% were widowed and 8% were married or cohabiting in the total sample and 62% were single of the hostel sample. This one third of residents who were married at one time or still consider themselves married (6%), are a group who may have family ties and may not lack the support networks that others do. This is only an assumption however, as many single people have many friends and lots of support. It may be possible to assume that this third had their own family home at some point in their lives and lost it, while the single people most likely have not had this. In terms of providing suitable facilities and long-term accommodation, this difference may be important.

Place of Birth

In the current study, 62% of the sample were born in England, with 25% from Scotland, Wales and Ireland, whereas in the DOE study 30% were from Scotland etc. and 60% from England (Drake et al 1981). Thus these samples are very similar in terms of where people came from originally. In our sample there are more people from outside the British Isles and Ireland than in the DOE study ten years ago. Seventy seven per cent (77%) of the sample are White Europeans with 11% Black and 2% Asian.

Education Levels

Of this sample, 40% have no education qualifications. Thus 60% of this population has had some sort of education varying from college degrees (6%) to O-Level/GCSE (24%) to some other type such as a School Certificate (5%). The older people tended to have fewer educational qualifications.

Residential history

Last place before this one

Nearly a third of the sample came from a house or flat before coming to their current place of stay. Following this, people came mostly from hostels, the street and a room in a shared house. Table 4.2 illustrates this range of backgrounds.

Table 4.2: Last place before this one across sample

Place	%
House/Flat	31
Hostel	17
Street	10
Room in Shared House	8
Squat	8
Friend's House	6
Hotel	6
Bedsit	4
Prison	4
Other	3
Hospital/Care Institution	2
Tied Accommodation	1

Length of Stay There

Nearly a third of the sample stayed less than three months in their last place, whereas 42% stayed longer than one year.

Table 4.3: Length of stay in last place across sample

Time	%
Less 1 Month	13
1-3 Months	18
4-6 Months	13
7 Months to 1 Year	14
More 1 Year	42

Age Left Home

Table 4.4 illustrates that most of the sample left home between the ages of 16 and 25. Twenty three per cent (23%) left before they were 15 years of age.

Table 4.4: Age left home across settings

Age	%
Under 10	5
11-15	18
16-18	41
19-25	24
26-30	5
31+	7

Number of Places Have Lived In

Nearly 40% of the sample have lived in less than five places. A large proportion (22%) 117 people (out of 531) did not answer this item.

Table 4.5: Number of place have lived in across sample

Number	%
1-5	40
6-10	25
11-20	19
21-30	5
31-40	1
41+	1
Too Many to Count	9

Last Place Called Home

The largest percentage of people who answered this question (only 76% did), said that their family home or a particular place was their last home. A tenth of those who answered said they had no home.

Table 4.6: Last place called home across sample

Place	%
Family Home	24
Particular Place	23
House/Flat	13
None	10
Here	10
Other	5
Hostel	4
Marital/Cohab. Home	3
Friend's Place	2
Room in Shared House	2
Street	2
Bedsit	1
Squat	1

Where After That

Nearly a third of people said they went to a hostel when they left the last place they considered home. Nearly 20% went to a house or flat. Less than 10% went to either a hotel, a friend's house or the street.

How Long Ago

Nearly a third of the sample became homeless less than six months before our survey. For 23% of the sample, this happened six or more years ago.

Table 4.7: How long ago left last place called home across sample

Time	%
Less than 6 Months	32
7-12 Months	15
13 Months to 2 Years	16
3 to 5 Years	14
6 to 10 Years	11
11 to 20 Years	8
21+ Years	4

Area now

Eighty five (85%) of the sample were staying in Inner London when surveyed.

Prior Area

Over two thirds of the sample said that the area they were in just before this one was in London. This is not an indicator of where people originally came from, but illustrates the mobility of people among settings.

Housing List

In this sample, 57% were not on a housing waiting list. This is a high percentage of people not trying to get more permanent housing. Thus nearly two thirds of the sample were not trying to obtain more permanent accommodation through this channel. This has implications for the amount of follow on accommodation required, given that one third are using temporary accommodation as a semi-permanent home.

General Health

Background

The House of Commons Social Services Committee reporting on community care in 1985, received evidence of people leaving hospital with no support services available upon discharge, while the London Housing

Inquiry of 1988 similarly reported many incidents of long stay mental patients placed in unsuitable housing without adequate back-up. A survey of the after-care of discharged psychiatric patients in London in 1986 found that over half of the sample were unable to return to their previous accommodation or found it no longer suitable: 80% stated that their current housing was inadequate in some way. In submissions to the Committee, the Church Army reported 268 former psychiatric patients among its 1,000 hostel residents, while National Cyrenians stated that between a quarter and one third of their clients have some form of mental disorder (Thornton 1990).

A number of studies have tried to discover the incidence of mental health problems among homeless people, usually of people in hostels and on the streets. There are however, many difficulties in obtaining this information and in comparing any subsequent findings. Thus any discussion of this problem must be taken cautiously.

The National Assistance Board in 1966 found that in general, the lower the standard of accommodation from lodging house to hostel to reception centre to the street, the greater is the proportion of physically and mentally disabled people found (cited in Herzberg 1987).

There are many studies which state a high prevalence of psychiatric disturbance among various samples of homeless people, and as many which state a much lower amount. One early study of a Salvation Army hostel found 34% of the sample had been in mental hospitals at some point, and in total 84% had either a personality disorder or suffered from a psychotic illness (Crossley and Denmark 1969). Priest (1971) found evidence of schizophrenia in 32% of the residents of common lodging houses in Edinburgh, 18% alcoholics and 18% personality disorders. In a further study he compared a representative sample of lodging house residents in Edinburgh with a sample of psychiatric patients who gave lodging house addresses (Priest 1976). In this study he found a higher prevalence of schizophrenia in the random sample of lodging houses than in the clinical sample (32% and 28% respectively), but higher for personality disorders, alcoholism etc. Patch in 1971 surveyed 123 randomly selected homeless men in two Salvation Army hostels in London and found 15% of the population schizophrenic, alcoholism in 21% and personality disorders in more than 50%. Tidmarsh and Wood (1972) found a high degree of social and psychiatric morbidity among residents of the Camberwell Reception Centre. These rather high figures of prevalence have generally not been repeated in later studies.

A more recent study of a London hostel indicated that 40. Four per cent (4%) of the sample had some form of psychiatric history (Satchell 1988). A study of people sleeping rough at Christmas time found 58% of the sample had some previous history of psychiatric illness or psychopathology, and found 34% actively psychotic (Weller 1986). Herzberg (1987) carried out a retrospective study of admissions to the Psychiatric Unit at the London Hospital between 1971 and 1980 registered No Fixed Abode and provided descriptive statistics of the sample of psychiatric problems. Clearly this is a different method of exploring homeless people with psychiatric problems and is not readily comparable with looking at prevalence among homeless people generally. However, of their sample (62 men and 48 women), 25.8% men and 41.7% women were diagnosed as schizophrenic.

Research Findings

Our survey included a short version of the General Health Questionnaire which is designed to identify people with high levels of mental and emotional stress. Using the 12 item version of the GHQ and scoring using the Likert method (0-3; range 0-36), a cut off point of half-way was adopted as the most common one used in other studies such that the percentage of people who scored above that point are above average in mental stress levels. Thus statistical means were calculated and taken above a score of 18. Twenty-five (25%) of the sample had an average score that was higher than the accepted cut-off point for this questionnaire. This is put in perspective when compared with the staff sample who had an average of 21% above this point. Correlations of GHQ scores with other characteristics. Further findings suggest that those homeless people who are working full time (5%) have a lower average score than those who are unemployed (31%) or invalid/ill (43%). Similarly, the younger age groups tended to have higher average scores than the older age groups, for example those over 70 years had an average score 11% higher than is acceptable, while those between 19 and 29 had a score of 27% above this point. Fewer men than women had scores on average higher than mid-way, 24% and 35% respectively. Furthermore, those who have stayed longer than one year had an average score 14% above this mark, while those who have stayed less than one month had an average score 30% above. Those who are divorced (34%) scored higher on average than those who are single (21%).

Thus a sub-group of mentally ill homeless people do seem to exist, but not in the multitude generally discussed. There is clearly a need for accommodation for this group. This compares well with findings from other studies on psychiatric health.

Table 4.8: A comparison of GHQ 12-item scores (Likert-method) (From Banks et al 1987)
Sample A= employees in an engineering plant
Sample B= 16yr old school leavers
Sample C= unemployed men

Sample	Employed	Employed	Un-employed	Un-employed	Home-less Sample
	Sample A	Sample B	Sample B	Sample C	All Mean 13.52 SD 7.74 N= 470
Single	Mean 8.98 SD 4.08 N= 114	Mean 8.67 SD 5.07 N= 431	Mean 14.06 SD 6.79 N= 81	Mean 15.29 SD 6.85 N= 28	Mean 12.79 SD 7.36 N= 330
Female	Mean 8.53 SD 3.65 N= 83	Mean 9.71 SD 5.66 N= 190	Mean 14.25 SD 7.01 N= 44	....	Mean 15.0 SD 8.57 N= 84
Male	Mean 8.80 SD 4.02 N= 552	Mean 7.86 SD 4.26 N= 241	Mean 13.84 SD 6.61 N= 37	Mean 15.61 SD 7.82 N= 91	Mean 13.20 SD 7.52 N= 386

This table suggests that the scores from the sample of homeless people are no higher than those from samples of unemployed people from other studies. This is an important finding and would suggest that homeless people are suffering from mental stress but only in as much as other groups such as the unemployed.

Evaluation

There has been little research on how homeless people assess their place of stay apart from that by Oakley in his studies of Salvation Army hostels, and Drake (1986). This information is important in the development of any new facilities or in any development of existing facilities. The present study focuses on the evaluation of particular qualities of the various settings which people lived. Given the unique nature of this exploration there is little possibility of any comparative discussion. A series of attitudinal statements were presented to people. They were asked to agree or disagree with them. It is possible to take each amount of agreement with particular aspects as a rough guide to what homeless people think of their setting. People tend to be less critical of the aspects which are of less importance to them. A positive evaluation may not be always taken as an indication that the facility or setting is successful but that the respondent did not care about it. All reservations aside, the general evaluation across all places is still of limited general value. However a comparison across settings reveals many interesting differences between the four homeless groups.

Generally a third to half of the sample considered the place they were staying was comfortable, that they liked staying there, that others were proud of the place, that they felt safe and that they could get a good night's sleep. Generally a third of the sample disagreed.

In general approximately half the sample were reasonably satisfied with these specific aspects of where they were staying. These percentages do vary considerably across setting and this will be discussed in Chapter 11. These figures should be taken with some caution as the majority of the sample were hostel residents and many of these have stayed in the hostel longer than one year and may thus consider the hostel as their home. Only by focusing on these figures for each setting can these figures be fully understood. Many respondents evaluated the place they were in by comparing it with being on the street or in worse circumstances. Nonetheless this does provide a general picture of how people in this homeless setting consider their place of stay in the context of their homeless state.

Other aspects of life in these settings achieved differing evaluations. Only 24% of the sample agree that training for jobs was received there. In more organisational terms, 26% agreed that people there rarely argued, over 50% disagreed. The other aspects were generally considered present by just less than half the sample. Two thirds agreed that the rules were clearly understood, and 56% agreed it was well organised. In terms of helping each other, 41% agreed while 40% disagreed. Forty six per cent (46%) considered there was group spirit there.

Self Esteem and View of Others

Another set of questions were designed to examine what level of self esteem people had in terms of self esteem levels across the whole sample, 45% agreed they 'made a valuable contribution to society' and 60% that they were 'not a failure'. A third felt they did not make a 'valuable contribution to society'.

When asked about the other people staying in the same place and the general atmosphere, 43% of the sample agreed they felt 'part of a community living there' and 43% felt that the 'others there were just like them', while over a third disagreed.

Expectations

In a further section of questions explored people's expectations for the future and what aspects of home people considered important.

Generally the items considered important by the most respondents were 'having their own room' (89%), having the 'use of a kitchen' (82%), 'having a place of their own' (80%), 'living somewhere that's quiet' (75%), 'finding somewhere cheap to live' (76%), 'having somewhere where friends could stay' (71%), 'being able to decorate' (64%) and 'living in London' (56%). Thus the aspects of importance to the most people were 'having a room' and 'a place of their own' and the 'use of a kitchen'.

Explaining their situation

The final set of statements referred to people's own perceptions as to the cause of their situation and how they see the world in general. These are based on a 'Locus of Control Structure' (see Appendix), in which people see the causes of events in terms of 'chance', 'external factors' or 'personal actions'. Each statement reflects a particular cause e.g. chance.

Overall about half the sample considered that 'luck played a part in not finding somewhere to live or getting a job'. The highest percentage agreement were with items to do with external causes, such as 'I would work if offered a job' (73%) and 'the shortage of housing stops me from finding somewhere to live' (49%). Thus overall, the sample would explain their situation by the action of others or to chance and not to any personal reason.

Most of the sample did not consider personal reasons were the cause of their being without a home or job, and unsurprisingly 13% agreed they were 'too lazy to get somewhere to live'. However, 45% agreed that 'their lack of skills prevented them from getting a job' and 69% thought that 'if only they could settle down they could get a job'.

Summary

In summary, there is a wide range of people in hostels and in other homeless settings. They differ from each other in many ways and require different programmes and varied forms of accommodation. These differences should be reflected in the range and scope of the facilities provided.

This broad overview of some of the characteristics of the homeless population adds weight to the argument that there are many different groups of people who are in need of temporary and more permanent accommodation. From our study, the majority of the sample was under 39 years (64%) and only 5% over 70 years of age. This would suggest that provision should be largely aimed at this younger group, while still keeping a proportion for the smaller older group.

The study indicates that about half the sample are unemployed, with nearly a third in some kind of work. These groups as has been previously discussed, have particular requirements and the range of provision should target these specific groups.

The study further indicates that one third of the sample had been married at some point. This group have most likely had some form of family home, and would therefore have a different experience to those who have not had this. This group may thus have different housing requirements.

5 The Street

Introduction

The people sleeping on the streets have perhaps the most stressful homeless setting with which to cope. There has been little comprehensive research on their general view of the world. Neither has there been any overall focus on their distribution across London, and of course their size as a group. This present chapter provides findings from the research on the size, nature, distribution and characteristics of this population, and follows this with a discussion of the more qualitative aspects of living on the street.

Previous studies have tended to focus on particular individuals and are generally of an anecdotal type. It has been thus extremely difficult to build up a picture of who is sleeping rough, where they come from and why they are on the streets. While there have been some studies which have a local focus, few have attempted to answer these questions on a wider scale.

The study of street homelessness has tended to be included in national studies of single homelessness interviewing people in hostels and night shelters on their experience of being on the street. This is true of Single and Homeless (Drake et al 1981) but seldom taken as a subject on its own. Research has ranged in focus from the purely descriptive to the psychiatric but has failed to take an experiential approach. This project aims to explore the experience of homeless people, in order to begin to understand the kinds of decisions they are faced with and how they perceive the choices they have to make.

The first stage of our research was to discover the types, varieties and distribution of people on the street. It is clear that street homeless people are not a homogeneous group as sub-groups are identifiable. Our research, therefore, attempted to build up a picture of the different types of people on the streets. Only when this was done could further research begin to explore the experience of the different people on the street.

The information falls into two parts: the number of people visible on the street, who they are, and where it is they sleep. However, this information must first be set in context.

References to the London homeless are scattered through Victorian literature and social tracts. George Orwell before the second world war and Turner in 1960 have described life on the street in London. Further studies in the 1960's and 1970's examined the plight of the street homeless person (Edwards et al 1966), Page (1973), Moore et al. (1968). There has been a shift in the focus of studies on street homelessness from those examining life on skid row and alcoholism to those which focus on young people.

Studies by Archard (1979) and O'Connor (1963) focus on the 'down and out' on the street, taking sociological models of deviancy and social control to examine the lives of these homeless people, generally men. The old stereotype of male 'dossers' or 'winos' seems no longer to apply to the majority. The change in trend may be due to a number of reasons, reflecting in particular the large increase of young people on the street in the last few years. This in turn may have been aggravated by the Board and Lodging Rules which forced a ceiling of £7 on the amount that could be claimed for accommodation. There was also a limited claiming period of eight weeks, after which the claim is reduced by 70%.

Centrepoint, The Soho Project, Threshold and the Resource Information Service among others, have either carried out studies of the young people they are in contact with on a day to day basis or have commissioned projects. The Soho Project argued that in their annual report of 1983, that 25% of its clients were under 18 but in the first half of 1986 the proportion had risen to 87%. Centrepoint have looked at stated reasons for leaving home finding that between 1985 and 1987, 38% of young homeless people had been thrown out of home. (Centrepoint 1987) R.I.S. (1986) commissioned a study of equal opportunities for young homeless people and found it difficult to come to any firm conclusions due to the lack of adequate monitoring in emergency hostels. They did find that 35% of the young men interviewed had slept rough for at least one night, and of these 71% were black.

There have been a number of newspaper articles and television programmes which have focused on particular case studies but are still good sources of information (The Times 1987), (Independent 1987, 1988). Many other studies focus on emergency nightshelters and traditional hostels. However these findings cannot be taken as entirely representative of street homeless people as many have large numbers of long-stay residents who do not sleep on the street. Some have focused on specific aspects of street homeless people, for example projects that focus on health issues.

Dr John Balazs found that 25% of the patients he sees at a DHSS funded centre, had a serious drinking problem. He argues (Independent 1988) that drink is part of the subculture and is used as a form of anaesthetic. He sees malnutrition, infestations and 50 times the usual incidence of TB. Dr Philip Timms conducted research on a London hostel and found 30% were suffering from schizophrenia. These findings have been supported by Satchell (1988).

Brandon in 1980 conducted a study into young (street) homeless people, which was based on interviews with 107 newcomers in two nightshelters and a government reception centre. He criticised workers of having attitudes which fall within certain ideologies, such as the pathological, the spiritual, the political and individual culpability and the child model. He compared the views and attitudes of workers at two nightshelters with those of homeless people and argued that there was some dissension between the two groups.

Of direct relevance to this discussion are three studies:

1. National Assistance Board (1966) 'Homeless Single Persons'
2. London Outreach Team (1984) 'Sleeping Out'
3. Drake et al (1981) 'Single and Homeless'

The NAB first included a survey of people sleeping rough as part of their national survey of hostels and lodging houses in December 1965. This survey provided some useful information on the ages, groupings, gender and reasons given for sleeping rough of the total number found nationally (683) but not for London. In London alone they found a total of 247 people. One per cent (1%) of those found in London were women. A total of 63 people were found in Waterloo station.

Nearly 20 years later the Central London Outreach Team's (1984) report was based on informal interviews and observation of homeless people in several London locations, the Embankment, Waterloo and the Temple. etc They focused their study on three questions: who sleeps rough, why do they sleep rough and what sub-groups and patterns of sleeping rough can be distinguished? They made contact with 399 different individuals: 254 at the Embankment; 89 at Waterloo; 41 at Temple and 4 at other locations. They found some seasonal variation in numbers with one fifth less at the Embankment in winter and one third less at Waterloo. Just over a quarter were contacted in the summer and then not seen again, and about a quarter in the winter period. Almost half were contacted in both periods.

Seventy six per cent (76%) were contacted more than once. The descriptive statistics were based on 318 people. They include some general descriptions of gender, age, place of birth, employment status, sources of income, health problems, reasons for sleeping rough, and pattern/frequency of sleeping rough.

It is of interest however to discuss the reasons given for sleeping rough as well as the different patterns of rough sleepers. The London Outreach Team argued that the reasons why people sleep rough are complex, and different factors may be inter-related, suggesting that we should not be looking for a single explanation. The main reasons given were a dislike of available accommodation (24%), drinking problems (23%), financial problems (17%) and a relationship breakdown/loss (15%), eviction (5%), institutional background (7%), psychiatric problems (4%) and other factors (17%). Financial problems' and 'preference' account for considerably lower proportions of people sleeping rough than reported in the NAB survey in 1965, that is, 29% and 25% respectively.

Quite a number of those contacted on the streets were not in fact sleeping rough. 185 of the sample said they had a place to stay either in their own flat, staying with friends or in a hostel. The social aspect of the various locations were frequently described by the contacts. People indicated that they came for food or companionship. Outreach argue that if these sites are perceived as a gathering place for people on, or who have previously been on, the homelessness circuit, then this has important implications for any discussion of a solution to the problem.

Another important aspect of the report was the division of those sleeping rough into various patterns. Constant rough sleepers were defined as those who sleep rough all the time (32%). Those who regularly sleep rough to a specific pattern, that is seasonally or at weekends, were defined as regular rough sleepers (6%). Occasional sleepers were those who slept rough spasmodically (30%), and new rough sleepers were those who had started sleeping rough within the previous seven days (7%).

It is clear from the London Outreach Team's findings that the older more constant and regular rough sleepers were contacted at the Embankment more than at anywhere else. The young new rough sleepers may be found at Waterloo station as well as at the Embankment. The Embankment was the central gathering point for large numbers of all types of rough sleepers both in 1984 and today.

This type of information is vital if the varieties and distribution of people sleeping rough all over London are to be discovered. The London Outreach Team have provided a firm basis on which the studies reported here grew. Are there similar numbers and patterns of people sleeping rough outside central London? Why do people gather at one location rather than at another?

The general objectives of the Single and Homeless report were 'to provide a broadly based understanding of the characteristics, needs and housing preferences of single homeless people', and in particular for those sleeping rough information was gathered about who they were, why they sleep rough , how long they have been on the streets and where they sleep. While the results of these questions are taken from all samples (that is from different types of facility and from different parts of England) they are still worth including in this review if only because they provide not only a useful basis for comparison but put the study of those sleeping rough in context with the study of other single homeless people.

In summary 29% of the total sample had slept rough at least once with 10% having spent a year or longer on the streets. Of 122 women 16% had slept rough at least once, while of 399 men 34% had slept rough at least once. The peak age for having slept rough was between 35 and 39 years old. A comparison across places where people were found, revealed that one fifth of those who had gone to an advice centre had slept rough, while the lowest percentage of those who had gone to an advice centre came from squats, bedsits or YMCA's.

During sleeping rough periods, respondents were less likely to be employed. Of all forms of 'accommodation' sleeping rough was the one in which people were least likely to be employed. In terms of previous accommodation the highest rate of sleeping rough seems to occur after discharge from a penal institution, or to a less extent from hospital. But over a quarter of cases where respondents had slept rough after release from a penal institution, they had also been sleeping rough before going to it.

The pilot survey

The pilot survey in November 1988 indicated that it was possible to conduct a census of people sleeping rough on the street. Taking advice from the Simon Community who had successfully conducted a survey of Camden in 1988, a survey of West Central London was carried out with the help of 100 volunteers.

In total 271 people were counted in the region of West central London, North of the Thames,. This has to be taken with great caution because in a smaller area adjacent, a further 261 were counted just South of the river in the Waterloo area.

Several large groups of homeless people were found on the Embankment and at Lincoln's Inn, while many others were scattered about in ones and twos. Results suggest that there were 77 people apparently on their own, with 55 of these recognisably male, seven female and 15 unknown. There were 24 groups of two,that is 48 people in pairs, 25 of whom were noted as male, one female and 22 unknown. There were four groups of three, gender unknown and 134 in groups of four or more. The last group contains, a crowd of 71 and of 21, with three groups of five and three groups of four, one of seven and one of eight.

The count of people 'on the street' was particularly notable for the fact that the people located could be divided, more or less, into two types. One was those individuals spread out, sleeping in isolation or in small groups of two or three. A second was a rather larger number of people who were sleeping in much larger groups of possibly 100 or more.

The numbers of people found on the Pilot Survey were less than on the April Survey. In total 271 people were surveyed in the region of West central London, North of the Thames. This has to be taken with great caution because in a smaller area adjacent, a further 261 were surveyed just South of the river in the Waterloo area.

While ethnicity was not always stated, only one black person, one Turkish and one West Indian were noted. This would be in accordance with available information on the street homeless in Central London Future, see for example The London Outreach Team's report of 1984.

In only 82 cases was the age estimated, although of the 71 at the Embankment area, most were described as being between 35 and 50 years of age. This age distribution is in some ways similar to that of the homeless people contacted by the London Outreach Team.

Many counters noted the general surroundings where people not in large groups were found. In total 12 were found on shop doorways, two at theatre entrances, two on the steps of buildings and six on Church grounds; that is two in Churchyards, one in a Church doorway, one on the steps of a church, and one on a bench in a Church garden. The two largest groups of people were under the Embankment and at Lincoln's Inn.

Table 5.1: Distribution of people in pilot survey

Sites:	Lincoln's Inn	83
	Fields	63
(North)	Embankment	26
	Strand	22
	(scattered)	77
	The Temple	
	Other Locations	
(South)	Bullring	
	Festival Hall	261
	Other Locations	

While ethnicity was not always stated, only one black person, one Turkish and one West Indian were note. Further comments on the general condition of people revealed 21 found in boxes, and 21 with blankets, 13 with sleeping bags, and three with cardboard mattresses. However many homeless people included in the count were not described at all and these figures must therefore be considered with caution.

In total, counters talked to 19 homeless people in the time available. Many of these gave an account of where they have come from, or where they usually sleep, and how long they have been sleeping out. The length of time varied from seven months to 23 years. The places of origin mentioned were Ireland, Scotland, Warwickshire, and Chesterfield. Places to sleep were mentioned as the Embankment, Camberwell, and shop doorways.

Results of the survey on April 25th 1989

From a comparison between the pilot and large-scale surveys of November and April it becomes clear that the problem of street homelessness may be one for Central London to tackle and less so for the outer boroughs. Whereas on November 25th 532 visible homeless people were found on the streets of West Central London and Waterloo, 753 people were found in total on the streets of 17 boroughs on April 25th.

Table 5.2: Borough by borough

Borough	Number
Lambeth	262
Westminster	133
Camden	108
Barnet	37
City of London	28
Kensington and Chelsea	20
Southwark	19
Hillingdon	16
Tower Hamlets	12
Hackney	3
Newham	3
Islington	3
Croydon	2
Kingston	2
Ealing	2
Brent	1
Richmond	0

Total	651

A further 183 were surveyed separately in railway stations by the British Transport Police. Given the overlap between the police and the counters, approximately 102 of these were thought to be already included in the survey. This suggests 81 people, the remainder, should be added to our total to make 753 people.

This figure must be taken as the *minimum* possible number of people found on the streets on one night as it does not include those sleeping in squats or derelict buildings, nor those in inaccessible places such as parks or car parks.

Several large groups of homeless people were found in the Embankment and at Lincoln's Inn, while many others were scattered about in ones and twos. Results suggest that there were 77 people apparently on their own, with 55 of these recognisably male, seven female and 15 unknown. There were 24 groups of two, that is 48 people in pairs, 25 of whom were noted as male, one female and 22 unknown. There were four groups of three, gender unknown and 134 in groups of four or more. The last group contains, a crowd of 71 and of 21, with three groups of 5 and three groups of 4, one of 7 and one of 8.

Of the 653 individuals surveyed on the night of April 25th 1989 in 17 Boroughs of London, only 220 were described using a checklist. The total figure includes three large groups of people: 283 in Southwark and Lambeth, 108 in Camden and 133 in City of London which were mostly described in general terms.

Information is provided from the checklists, the general descriptions and by individual borough where of interest. Also included are some additional figures from the British Transport Police who surveyed the stations in the Boroughs on the night. The information gathered is based on subjective observations of counters. In many cases, it was extremely difficult to gather any information at all.

These figures are therefore to be taken as estimates only.

		Valid%
Gender:	83.0% male	(88.0%)
	11.0% female	(12.0%)
	6.0% unavailable	
Age:	1.0% under 18 years	(2.0%)
	12.0% 19 - 29	(15.0%)
	24.0% 30 - 39	(31.0%)
	18.0% 40 - 49	(22.0%)
	13.0% 50 - 59	(16.0%)

	9.0% 60 - 69	(12.0%)
	2.0% 70+	(2.0%)
	21.0% Unavailable	
Ethnicity:	60.0% White European	(88.0%)
	5.0% Afro-Caribbean	(8.0%)
	3.0% Asian	(3/0%)
	33.0% Unavailable	
Healthy:	45.0% Looks Healthy	(72.0%)
	18.0% Looks Unhealthy	(28.0%)
	37.0% Unavailable	
Asleep:	31.0% Asleep	(39.0%)
	49.0% Awake	(61.0%)
	21.0% Unavailable	
Tidy:	15.0% Looks Tidy	(33.0%)
	31.0% Untidy	(67.0%)
	54.0% Unavailable	
Behaving Strangely:	8.0% Behaving Strangely	
	92.0% Unavailable	
Groups:	52.0% On Own	(59.0%)
(Not large	24.0% In Two's	(26.0%)
groups)	10.0% In Three's	(11.0%)
	3.0% In Four's	(12.0%)
	11.0% Unavailable	

Surroundings:

Park/Open Space	30 (+ a group of 52)
Shopfront	36
Railway	29
Archway	15
Subway	14
Carpark	12
Churchyard	8
Alcove	8
Tube	8
Derelict Building	7
Bench	5
Steps	4
Alley	4
Basement	3
	-----
	181 (+52)

Many surveyors noted the general surroundings where people were found. In total 12 were found on shop doorways, two at theatre entrances, two on the steps of buildings and six on Church grounds; that is two in Churchyards, one in a Church doorway, one on the steps of a church, and one on a bench in a Church garden. The two largest groups of people were under the Embankment and at Lincoln's Inn.

There was a high proportion of people (over 60%) described as awake, between the hours of 12am and 3am in which the survey took place. Of those who were described as being awake on the night, the largest percentage were those between the ages of 30 and 39 (26.9%). Of those who were described as looking healthy, the highest percentage were aged 30 to 39 years (41.2%). Those described as looking least healthy were the over 70's followed interestingly by the under 20's.

Most 21 to 29 year olds were described as looking tidy (60%), whereas most of the other age groups were described as looking untidy.

The general feeling on the night of the survey was that there were fewer people on the street than usual. However the results of these surveys indicate that there is no 'usual' number but rather one that is prone to change in response to seasonal, weather and possibly other variations.

It is important to put this figure into perspective by comparing it with the 247 people found by the NAB in 1965. Clearly there has been a large increase in the numbers found since then. This can also be compared with William Booth's estimate of 33,000 homeless people (loafers and vagabonds) adapted from the figures given by Charles Booth in 1889 of 11,000 homeless people found in East London.

The 1991 Census found 1,275 people sleeping rough in Greater London using a similar approach to that of the second Surrey Survey in which local organisations participated in identifying sites (OPCS 1991). The figures for comparable boroughs are listed below. Although the University's figures were presented as the minimum figures for spring of 1989 and a total estimate of 2,000 was presented to give a more comprehensive picture, the figures for each borough are lower than the Census figures of Spring 1991. In other words there has been a rise in the number on the streets since these surveys, but the estimate of 2,000 would still seem to be reliable given the poor weather reported on the night. In Camden alone, there were four times as many people recorded in the Census as in the University's Survey.

Table 5.3: Comparison of survey and census: Borough by borough

Borough	Surrey Sample 1989	1991 Census (OPCS)
Camden	108	467
City of Westminster	133	297
Lambeth	262	174
City of London	28	77
Richmond Upon Thames	0	58
Barnet	37	46
Croydon	2	36
Islington	3	19
Tower Hamlets	12	19
Hackney	3	15
Kensington and Chelsea	20	14
Brent	2	10
Southwark	19	5
Kingston Upon Thames	2	3

Behavioural Mapping

A study of space use by homeless people (Chalk, Twigger, Andrews et al 1989), indicated that people sleeping rough do not use space in a haphazard way, but that there are clear rules of space use. They carried out an observational study of the private use of public space. The area which was observed over six nights was the Strand, in and around Embankment station and Charing Cross. The method used involves the careful observation and mapping of people's movements and activities over a period of time.

Researchers walked through the area at eight, nine, ten and eleven o'clock at night in February of 1989 and noted where people were and what they were doing.

A composite map of the area under study is presented in Figure 5.1. Each dot represents an occasion on which someone was observed in that location (could be an individual or the same person at a different time).

Figure 5.1: Composite map of frequency use

POSA of ex squatters moving to hostel or squat
Spread of subjects and number per point

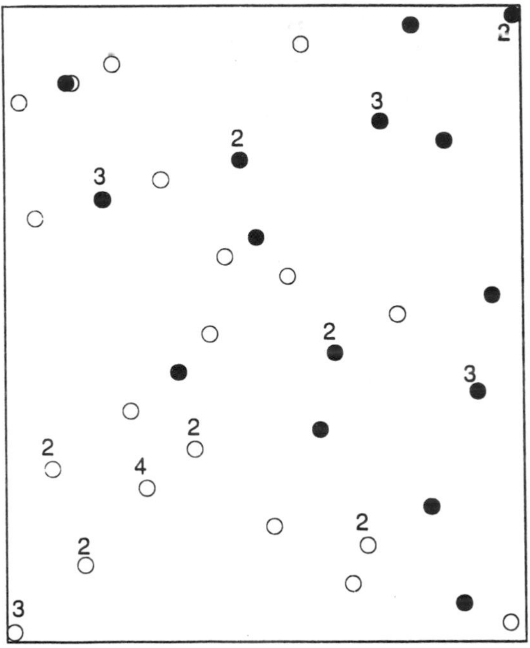

Blank circles = those who moved into hostels
Filled circles = those who moved into other squats

This figure suggests a regular pattern of use with the areas around the entrance to the station. On the basis of density of use the 11 areas marked were identified.

Furthermore, observed activities were coded into four main groups: standing, sitting, sleeping/lying and a mixture of any of these. Figure 5.2 presents these activities across the 11 areas at different times.

Figure 5.2: Mapping of Activities (from Chalk et al 1989)

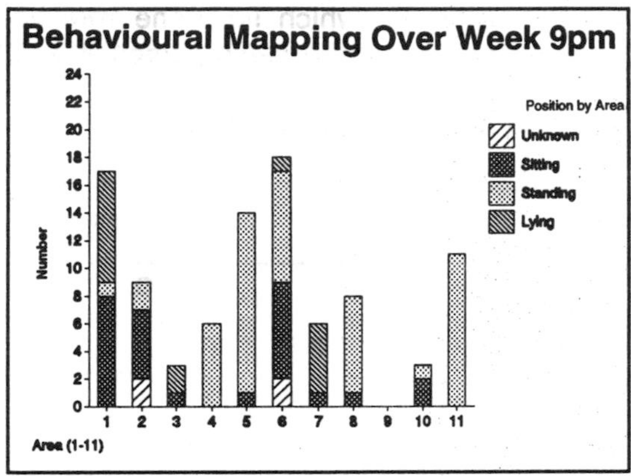

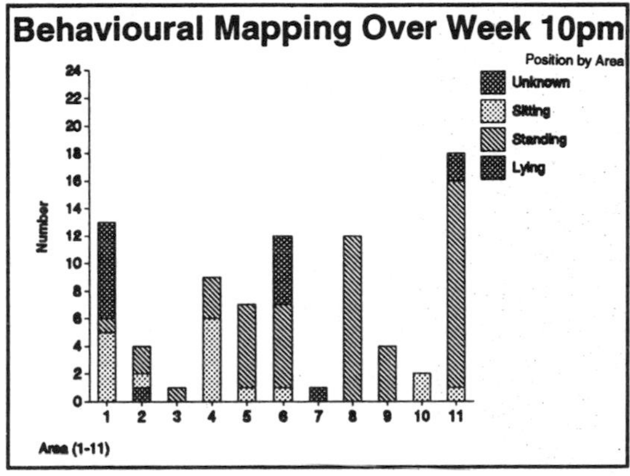

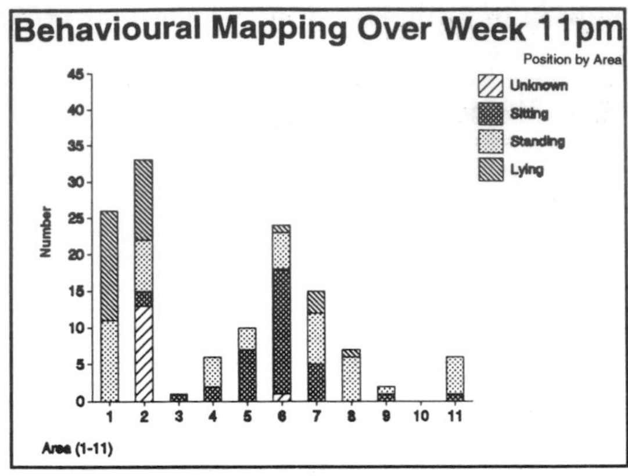

In the area around Embankment station, four groups of areas were identified as distinct 'places'. Two of these can be seen as places to stand which are in corners and where homeless people watched people pass and socialised with each other. A second area where people were standing, was more public, right in the central flow of people going to and from the tube. There was a third group of areas in which people sat or stood back. These areas were not in the main traffic flow and were removed. Finally there were three areas in which people were lying down. These areas were quieter and most secure.

The series of observations of one main street in London suggested that much of the activity observed involved the procurement and preparation of sleeping space, and activity which significantly preceded sleeping by a number of hours. Most individuals were observed to lay their bed in the same place on successive nights, suggesting a degree of territorial consensus (Chalk, Twigger, Andrews et al 1989). They further found that:

1. The chosen shop entrances have multiple usage. For the homeless they are used as places for sleep, for safety and for social interactions.

2. The actual physical form of preferred entrances is dictated by: human space requirements; security considerations, for example lighting and open space; shelter from the weather. These suggest that entrances are purposively chosen and used, on the basis that they provide relatively safe and sheltered locations for social interaction and sleeping.

Conclusion

In summary evidence was found which supported the notion that the world of the street homeless has a social structure, reflected in their use of the physical environment. Furthermore the street as a place has form and the groups in which people are staying have structure without a definite physical form.

Fluctuations

Taking examples of places covered by both surveys it is possible to see the fluctuation in numbers of people found on the streets.

1. On the night of the Pilot Survey 170 people were found in the Westminster part of the pilot area (not the whole borough) while on the night of the April Survey a total of 133 people were found.

2. In 1988 The Simon Community conducted a survey of Camden and found 205 people on the streets. They conducted a similar survey on April 25th and found only 108 people.

3. In 1988 the Vineyards Project conducted a survey of Richmond and found 37 people on the streets, but found none in the April Survey.

4. The Outreach Team of the Social Services Department of the City of London counted 50 people in 1988 but only 28 were found in the April Survey.

5. Bullring and Royal Festival Hall
   Pilot Survey: 261 people
   April Survey: 181 people

6. Lincoln's Inn Field
   Pilot Survey: 83 people
   April Survey: 52 people

As has been noted, the 1991 census produced figures that also varied considerably from these other surveys. The reasons why there are such differences are not certain. The locations themselves do, of course, change. For example, the area near Embankment Station has been re-developed so that secure covered spaces are not so readily available. But the figures do also indicate that the homeless street population is itself a fluid one. The question to be asked is where does it move to? It has been argued (LOT 1984) that rough sleepers tend to book in and out of hostels when the weather is wet and cold. They may also find shelter in derelict buildings or carparks. There is some movement between the different types of homeless settings: squats, hostels, hotels and the hidden homeless. Is it the case that there is a fixed proportion of each group which does not move, and the rest flow from one type to another? One example of this may be the notion of the homeless circuit wherein individuals move from one type of place to another. The ability of homeless people to make use of the little available to them has been already discussed. For example, Brandon (1980) argued that 'homeless people are presented by the media as more hapless and hopeless then this study would indicate'. He found them in general to be imaginative and hopeful. The individual has his/her reasons for taking shelter on any particular night in any particular way they can, or for staying on the street rather than taking a bed in a hostel.

Questionnaire survey of street homeless people

Overview

Of the 503 homeless people included in the questionnaire survey, 47 were sleeping on the streets at the time of interview. Though the sample is small, it is still possible to consider their views. The following provides a general overview of this sample, and compares it with some characteristics of the overall sample and those from other settings. It is useful to take street sleepers as a separate group, because while they share common features with the rest of the homeless people surveyed, they are a distinct group, being the only group without a roof.

This sample was largely made up of people in day centres who said they were sleeping rough, except for 20% who were interviewed on the street. There may be particular aspects of this group therefore which would differentiate between them and other rough sleepers.

Street homeless people in London according to our sample, are largely young male adults. While there are older people on the streets, they do not form the majority.

From our discussion groups and considering the whole street sample, two distinct sub-groups of people became apparent, although these are not the only ones. One subgroup was made up of mostly middle aged men. They were sleeping mostly in the Bullring and apparently resourceful, having survived without social benefits and temporary accommodation for years. Some had travelled the work circuit around England doing casual labour wherever needed. They were independent, and on the whole optimistic about the future.

They seemed to all have goals for the future in terms of places they would like to be in and jobs they would like to do, but none had detailed plans as to how they would reach their goals.

The second distinct group of those on the street were young people under 20 years who all had spent time on the streets, and most were begging around the time of the survey. Like the first group, they had survived without benefits or accommodation, but unlike them, they were pessimistic. Many gave accounts of criminal activity and convictions before they left home. Some had been in care. Most of this group who participated in the discussion group knew each other and seemed dependent on each other but on little else.

In general what seems to characterise people on the street is their desire for independence and their ability to survive outside of the formal system. There are those who do not manage to cope and who do not survive. But the majority learn how to cope and live without having to accept the rules of others. These are the people hardest to help with current provision.

Considerations of the characteristics of street homeless people

For the London Outreach Team (1984) 92% were men with only 24 women in the whole sample. For our April Count 88% of people sleeping rough were observed to be male and 12% female, showing a remarkably consistent proportion.

Eighty nine per cent (89%) of the survey street sample were male. This is the highest percentage of males in each of the four settings. Just under half of the sample of this study were under 40 years of age which is similar to the London Outreach Team's sample, the Pilot Survey of West Central London and the April survey. In the Pilot Survey in 82 cases the age was estimated, although of the 71 at the Embankment area, most were described as being between 35 and 50 years of age (see Table 4.1 p.40).

The majority of the survey sample were between the ages of 19 and 39 and were thus largely young adults. Only 4% were under 18.

Table 5.4: Age of street sample

Age	%
18 and under	4
19-29	29
30-39	38
40-49	22
50-59	7
60-69	--

Family Status

Nearly two thirds of the sample were single, with a further 29% divorced or separated.

Table 5.5: Family status for street sample

Family Status	%
Single	62
Divorced	20
Separated	9
Cohabiting	7
Married	2

Employment status and voluntary work

Table 5.6 shows that over half the sample were unemployed, but over a third were doing some form of work including casual work. A higher percentage of the street sample are working than in hostels. In terms of voluntary work, 20% of the sample said they did some. Twenty (20%) of the sample are doing voluntary work. This is a remarkably active population given the difficulties in carrying out any kind of work while living on the street.

Table 5.6: Employment status for street sample

Employment Status	%
Unemployed	53
Casual	27
Invalid/Ill	12
Full-time	4
Part-time	2
Self-employed	2

Education

Just less than half the sample had no formal educational qualifications (45%). This percentage is higher than those in hostels (41.0%) and much higher than those in squats (21%). Thirty six per cent (36%) had some trade qualifications which was the highest percentage of the four settings.

Table 5.7: Education for street sample

Education	%
None	45
CSE/GCSE	28
School Cert.	9
Degree	7
Other	7
Professional Qualification	2
A-Level	2

Birth place and ethnicity

Seventy four per cent (74%) of the sample were born in England with no-one born outside of the British Isles and the Republic of Ireland (see Table 5.7). Ninety five per cent (95%) of the sample were white with no black people in the sample.

Table 5.8: Birth place for street sample

Place of Birth	%
England	74
Scotland	21
Ireland	3
N.Ireland	2

Length of Stay

As Table 5.9 illustrates, 41% of the sample had been staying on the street longer than one year. This is the highest percentage of the four settings. The majority (59%) had been there for more than seven months.

Table 5.9: Length of stay for street sample

Length of Stay	%
More than 1 year	41
7m- 1 year	18
4-6months	9
1-3months	14
Less than 1 month	18

Use of day centres

Only 8% of the sample said they never used day centres, with 45% using them every day. This may be largely a product of the sampling method which targeted day centres for respondents.

Table 5.10: Use of day centre by street sample

Use	%
Once a Day	45
Once a Week	33
Once a Month	8
Twice a Year	6
Never	8

In summary, this sample was largely male and between the ages of 19 and 39 years and relatively active: not the stereotypical older transient 'layabout' prevalent in the recent past and still evident in the media's account of the street homeless. Many were active in some form, with a fifth doing voluntary work. There was however, the lowest educational level across the four settings. This probably has some relation to the other aspect of this sample, that there were more who left home before they reached the age of 15 than in any other setting. In addition there are no black people in this sample, with three quarters of the sample coming from England. This sample had been there the longest on average across the four settings, with 41% there longer than one year.

Residential history

There are some aspects of residential history which can be established from the survey which help to establish the flow patterns onto the street.

Last place before this one

There was a similar percentage of those whose last place before this one was the street and a house or flat (30%) (Table 5.10). Just over 10% came directly from a hostel and none from a squat. This would suggest that this population is not flowing from one clear source, that it is not hostel residents or squatters on the whole who are moving on to the street. In other words, it could be argued from this information, that the street population this reflects is made up of those first time homeless or from people coming from friends floors or from those already on the street, but not from hostels or squats.

Table 5.11: Last place before this one for street sample

Place	%
House/Flat	30
Street	30
Other	29
Hostel	11

Nearly half the sample had stayed in their last place for a year or more. This was one of the most stable settings in this sense, in terms of previous accommodation.

Table 5.12: Length of stay in last place for street sample

Length of Stay	%
More than 1 year	47
7 months to 1 year	14
4-6 months	7
1-3 months	13
Less than 1 month	19

Of those in a house, flat or shared house, over a third (35%) were rented from the council or housing association, with 21% privately renting. Eighteen per cent (18%) referred to it as owner occupied.

Age left home

A further aspect of interest is the age a person left home. For this street sample 43.1% left home under the age of 15 years. This was the highest percentage of the four settings. Figure 5.13 illustrates this pattern.

Table 5.13: Age left home for street sample

Age	%
Less than 10	9
11-15	34
16-18	32
19-25	14
26-30	4
31+	7

Number of places have lived in

Across the four settings there seems to be a similar average number of places people have lived in since they left their family home. Eighty four per cent (84%) of the sample have lived in less than 20 places. Fifty-seven (57%) of the sample have lived in less than ten places. Ten per cent (10%) have lived in more places than they could count.

Table 5.14: Number of places have lived in

Number	%
1-5	27
6-10	30
11-20	27
21-30	--
31-40	3
41+	3
Too many to count	10
Don't Know	--

Last place considered home

In terms of the last place people considered their home, as many as 24% said they had had none. This percentage was higher than that for squat dwellers or hostel residents. Three per cent (3%) considered the street their home. A further 21% mentioned a particular place as their home, such as Scotland or Brighton.

Table 5.15: Last place considered home

Place	%
None	24
A Place (named)	21
House/Flat	18
Family House	12
Other	10
Marital	9
Not Moved	3
Hostel	3

After last place called home

After they left the last place they called home, 28% went to a house or flat, and 22% went onto the street. Only 2% went to stay with friends, the lowest percentage of the four settings.

Table 5.16: After last place called home

Place	%
House/Flat	28
Street	22
Other	19
Hostel	14
Hotel	8
Squat	6
Friends	3

The majority of the sample (63%) left the last place they called home over three years ago. Ten per cent (10%) said they left over ten years ago. Less than a fifth had left the last place they considered home less than six months ago. Of the four groups this is possibly the group who have been longest homeless.

Table 5.17: Length of time since left last place called home

Time	%
3-5 Years	35
6-10 Years	18
Less than 6 months ago	17
13 months-2 years	13
11-20 years	10
7 to 12 months	7

Future Housing Status

Of the total street sample, 77% were not on a housing waiting list. This is the highest percentage across the four settings. The residential history explored here suggests that many of this sample had a stable history before they came to the street, 50% had been there for a year or more. This group is then not constantly transient. Also particular to the street homeless was that there were more of them who had left home under the age of 15 than in other settings.

Street homeless people tended to have come from the street or from houses or flats, but few came from hostels or squats. This suggests that these settings may have distinct residential patterns associated with them. This is supported further by the responses to items concerning the last place people considered home and where they went after they left there. In terms of home, a quarter said they had never had one. For those who did have a home and left it, 44% went to a house or flat and a quarter onto the street. This suggests that for the majority there is not a simple route to the street, and that there is something unique in the experience of street homeless people. They do not seem to come from hostels, that is from the formal housing system onto the streets. This supports indications from the discussion groups which suggested that those on the street are different from those in hostels in terms of how they explain their situation.

Another feature is the length of time they have been homeless, with the majority having been homeless longer than homeless people found in other settings (63% had left the last place they considered home more than three years previously).

Finally, over three quarters of street homeless people were not on a housing or housing association waiting list. This would imply this proportion will not get into semi-permanent forms of accommodation from the street.

Evaluations

The place people were staying in was evaluated by them in terms of three main aspects: social, physical and personal. These aspects encompass the broad constituents of people's experience of home (Sixsmith 1986). In other words people tend to think of places in which they live in these terms. In addition to these, organisational and financial aspects were considered. A series of attitudinal statements were presented to people regarding the place they were currently staying. People had to agree or disagree with them.

Social

Thirty six per cent (36%) of the sample staying on the street agreed 'the social life was good' there. Concerning the general social aspects of the street, nearly a third considered the people there to be 'proud of the place' and 43% felt there was 'group spirit', although 48% disagreed. Furthermore, half the sample (50%) thought people often 'helped each other', while just over a third disagreed. Nearly three quarters thought people there 'tended to hide their feelings', but over two thirds disagreed that 'personal problems were openly talked about'.

Physical/Organisational

Over a quarter of the street sample considered the street comfortable (28%), which is surprisingly high. Over a third considered they could get a good night's sleep (36%) and overall 22% said they liked staying there. When asked to consider whether or not they felt safe there, 40% said they did, the lowest percentage across the four settings.

Nearly three quarters felt they 'could leave anytime without saying where they were going'. While 44% thought people who broke the rules were punished for it. Overall, 40% thought it was 'well organised' there, with nearly half agreeing that if 'someone broke a rule he knew what would happen'. These figures are important in showing that there is a small core of street homeless people, perhaps one in five, who found it a comfortable place where they could get a good night's sleep.

Other aspects

Nearly two thirds considered the street the 'only way they could afford to live.' For people on the street, the second highest evaluation was of doing 'what I want' (59% agreed). This was higher than in the hostel sample and hotels but higher in the squats sample (75%).

Self esteem and view of others

Just over a third felt 'they made a valuable contribution to society' (38%), while 50% did not consider 'they felt a failure'. Relative to the sample from the other settings, these percentages were mid-range. Sixty per cent (60%) considered the 'other people on the street to be just like them', the highest of the four settings.

When asked to give their views on the other people on the street, generally about half the sample saw others sleeping rough as normal, healthy people capable of personal growth and development. On average, a third of the sample disagreed with all but one item. Forty five per cent (45%) considered most of the people on the street as normal people, with the same percentage disagreeing. Forty one per cent (41%) considered that most of the others were not physically or mentally ill, but 39% disagreed. Over a third considered them a threat to themselves and to society and unable to change for the better.

Expectations

Taking the social, physical and personal aspects of home, respondents were asked to give their views on things that might be important to them. The highest percentage agreement was to 'have a room of their own' (96%). Very high also, was 'having the use of a kitchen' and 'having a place of their own'. Just over a third considered 'living in London to be important', a much lower percentage, the lowest of the four settings. Also considered important were 'to live somewhere that's quiet' (77%) and 'somewhere cheap' (79%).

Table 5.17 presents the percentage importance of the eight items across the whole sample as compared with the street sample. For both samples the percentage importance was generally very high. Those on the street were no different in their views than those in the larger sample.

Table 5.18: Meaning of home: Importance
Street Sample : Percentage Importance
(Percentage Importance=those who considered the item to be very important or important).

Home	All N=531 %	Street N=47 %
Own Room	89	96
Kitchen	82	89
Own Place	80	87
Cheap	76	79
Quiet	75	77
Friends	71	65
Decorate	64	68
London	56	38

Table 5.19 presents the means and standard deviations for these items for 38 of the sample of 43 people (excluding missing values).

These statements refer to qualities of the street which people on average agreed were part of life there. These aspects which most people on the street agreed with were concerned with how they perceived themselves, their self-esteem.

Most agreed that 'I can do what I want here' and that 'the others here are just like me'. There was generally less agreement on physical items such as the comfort of the place, which are to be found at the bottom of the table. For those on the street, the items which were considered important were 'having their own room', 'the use of a kitchen' and 'a place of their own'.

Table 5.19: Mean scores for home items for street sample (Scale: 1=strongly agree; 2=agree; 3=neither; 4=strongly disagree; 5=disagree)

Item	Mean Scores	Standard Deviations
1. Afford	2.21	1.36
2. People are Like Me	2.37	1.56
3. Do What I Want	2.50	1.50
4. Not A Failure	2.76	1.55
5. Make Contribution	3.10	1.39
6. Sleep	3.18	3.66
7. Community	3.24	1.40
8. Feel Safe	3.26	1.53
9. Social Life	3.34	1.54
10. Comfortable	3.42	1.53
11. Like It Here	3.65	1.40

Table 5.20: Correlations of 'Place of My Own' with other Importance Items for Street Sample

Importance Item	Correlation
Own Room	.69
Kitchen	.64
Cheap	.57
Friends	.51
Decorate	.13
London	.04
Quiet	-.03

Table 5.20 presents some correlations between the 'place of my own' item and the other importance items, and indicates that there are four main

other items which highly positively correlate: 'having their own room', 'the use of a kitchen', 'somewhere cheap' and 'somewhere where friends can stay'. The only item which is considered important but which does not positively correlate with having a 'place of my own' is 'to live somewhere quiet'. Thus having a 'place of my own' represents the key aspects of home to street homeless people.

Explaining their situation

Half agreed they were 'stopped from finding somewhere to live by the shortage of housing in London'. Over two thirds thought they were 'just unlucky in finding somewhere else to live'. This was the highest percentage across the four settings, as it was when 71% agreed they had 'no luck in getting a job'. Furthermore, 75% thought they 'would get a job if they could settle down'. Just over half considered they were 'stopped from getting a job by a lack of skills'. Thus the emphasis is on a perceived lack of control for some, but chance for others.

Summary

Generally, the main aspect of the street which was evaluated highly was the social aspect. Half the sample thought the 'people where they lived often helped each other'. Another feature was that three quarters felt they 'could leave anytime they wanted without letting anyone know', and 59% 'felt they could do what they want'. These two aspects of social support and independence tend to characterise the street sample views. This is supported by 60% feeling the 'others there were just like them'. The street sample tended to explain their situation partly in terms of luck and chance, and partly to internal causes and not generally due to external causes.

The findings of this survey suggest that street homeless people are concerned with their independence and control of their situation as well as the social aspects of the street. This is not to say they are not concerned with other aspects or things, but these two characterise street living with regard to this sample in particular.

Furthermore, this sub-group seems to have been homeless for the longest time and generally left home at a younger age. However, there does not seem to be any substantial difference in the number of places that the street sample have lived in as compared to the samples from the other settings. This suggests there may be a different pattern of residential and other experiences which are more common to those living on the street than simply the amount of places or a transient way of life. These differences will be further explored in Chapter 11 with regard to a comparison with hostel residents and squatters, to uncover whether more distinct patterns can be discerned.

6 Hostels

The Role of hostels

The initial survey revealed that the number of people on the streets in London was greatly outnumbered by those in hostels. A further development was to survey the experiences of those hostel users. The focus was on individual residents' perception and evaluation of their hostels as a place to live, on their feelings of self-esteem what aspects of home are important to them and on their health and their relationship with staff. Observations were also carried out within hostels.

It is suggested here that provision for homeless people can be classified not only according to the size of the building, but also to the style and level of support provided to residents. Hostels are conventionally classified in these terms by the London Hostels Handbook (RIS 1991) as well as by other agencies and sources of information about hostels. Hostels range in size from small shared houses with six or eight residents to larger hostels with several hundred residents. Different types and levels of support are provided. Some hostels provide advice about income and welfare rights, some provide informal counselling, some provide counselling by a trained counsellor, others provide therapy, attendance at which can even be incorporated into a contract between the hostel and resident.

Less conventionally within the housing and homelessness fields hostels can be classified in terms of the ranges of aspects of home provided, or how far hostels facilitate the residents feeling at home. Hostels differ in the range of aspects of their design and management style which provide conditions approximating to those prevailing in a family 'home'. For example, residents may enjoy a greater or lesser freedom to behave as they wish, to bring their friends back, to cook for themselves if they wish, to decorate their room if they wish, and so on.

The survey findings reveal that residents in different hostels give quite different responses to questions dealing with their levels of self-esteem, their attitudes to whether or not a hostel provides facilities associated with a 'home', the role of staff, and their estimation of why they find themselves homeless, and perhaps unemployed. These differences might be explained by the difference in the types of residents living in the various hostels. For example some hostels may be catering for more old, and perhaps ill, residents than others. Or the differences might be explained by the atmosphere and management style prevailing in the various hostels. Some hostel management styles may be more likely to reduce resident's preparedness to exert any initiative than others. The survey findings also show some differences in the attitudes of residents and the attitudes of staff to these questions. Thus staff and residents do not always have the same understanding of the role of the hostel and its staff; nor of the levels of self-esteem of residents.

The differences between hostels on these counts have implications for policy makers and providers of facilities. The aims and objective of hostels should, of course, determine the way hostels are designed and managed. A hostel which is run for, say, recovering drinkers will have a different regime from one which is run for people who have no other problem than a lack of accommodation. This report examines hostel provision and makes suggestions about the design and management style which might best be adopted for particular resident groups.

Background to hostels

The term hostel is a blanket term which tends to cover a wide range of provision. It is usually taken to refer to organised short-term accommodation at low prices. It's upkeep is typically maintained by an organisation rather than private individuals and it usually has the barest of facilities with generally more than one bed per room. It thus differs from hotels in that a resident may be expected to share a room with a stranger. A further way to distinguish the two is that hotels are usually run privately to make a profit, whereas hostels tend to be run by charities, churches, universities,and voluntary agencies. Many facilities no longer call themselves hostels, as they argue they provide long-term accommodation for specialised groups. However for the purposes of this report, hostels shall include any facility which provides short-term accommodation at low prices (or accepts DSS claimants) and does not describe itself as a hotel.

Thomas and Niner (1989) define a hostel as 'referring to organised short-term accommodation at reasonably low prices, targeting a specific group'.

A further definition is one based on the London Hostel Directory (RIS 1992), that is, a facility is a hostel if it is in the Directory.

As discussed by RIS (1991b) a common view of hostels is that they are large buildings, offering poor quality accommodation in dormitories to homeless people, with regimes dominated by strict rules and regulations. They suggest the reality is that London has a wide range of different types of temporary accommodation and the hostels with the Victorian image make up a small proportion of total bedspaces.

The development of hostels as a type of provision for homeless people began directly in 1888 with the establishing of the first cheap food depot and shelter for men by the Salvation Army. They began to convert old warehouses and store houses into shelters to 'contain' homeless men. Other private organisations and Government Bodies then also provided this type of large direct-access hostel. The Salvation Army have replaced many of this type of hostel in Britain with new purpose-built ones, however many of the original facilities still remain in London. Hostels today embody, more than any other form of provision for single homeless people, particular social relations and specific notions about single person housing needs (Watson and Austerberry 1986).

The continuing use of hostels, now ranging from large direct-access to small and specialised, by single homeless people, is partly due to a number of factors. Firstly, the 1977 Housing (Homeless Persons) Act whilst legislating for families and single people with 'priority need', left uncatered for, the thousands of single people who are homeless. Voluntary organisations and the DHSS made provision for this group generally in the form of emergency accommodation.

Secondly, the 1974 Housing Act made funding available to Housing Associations, to build new or modernise old buildings on a large scale . Up until this time hostels were built on the basis of the maximum bedspaces for the cash available. Subsequently smaller and more specialised hostels appeared. Thus making it more economically viable to run hostels and shared housing projects.

Another important issue is the distinction between priority and non-priority single homeless. It has been argued that there are some differences in the distribution of 'priority' homelessness and single homelessness (Drake et al 1981). All districts must make some provision for priority homeless people, but there is no statutory provision for the non-priority homeless. Therefore the single homeless must seek accommodation in those areas where it is provided. This has important implications for the consideration of hostel provision, that is, the distribution of facilities does not necessarily reflect a particular 'need' in those locations. The proposed Housing Bill may have a considerable influence on non-priority single homeless people in that in order to obtain accommodation a single person may have to be labelled under one of the special need categories. However there is little certainty about the Bill's effects.

The Resource Information Service's London Hostel Directory has been produced annually since 1985 when it was started by the Piccadilly Advice Centre. It categorises hostels in the following way: emergency, short stay hostels, hostels for working people and those looking for work, semi-supportive hostels, medium stay hostels, housing schemes, supportive group houses, traditional, working people only, students, alcohol, drugs, ex-care, mental health, ex-offenders, and single parents. They can be further cross-referred in terms of ethnic groups, gays and lesbians, the physically disabled, young people, and women only (PAC 1985). A statistical overview of hostels in London produced by the Resource Information Centre provides a range of statistical information on hostels in London (RIS 1991b).

Another way to distinguish hostels is to differentiate more generally between emergency (direct access) hostels, specialised and non-specialised hostels (HSPR 1987). Watson and Austerberry (1986) argue that there are three categories of non-specialist hostels for single people: large direct-access hostels, refuges, group homes and open access hostels, and thirdly 'up-market hostels'.

The majority of direct-access hostels are run by voluntary charitable or religious organisations. Some receive statutory funding through the DSS, the DOE, the Home Office or the local authority. Others are run entirely by charities or religious bodies . According to the London Hostels Directory (1988) there were 397 separate projects in London. The 1989 Directory lists 444 separate projects and the 1991 Directory lists 452 projects with 247 of these being available to single homeless people in 'non-priority need' (RIS 1991b). RIS show that over a six year period from 1985 to 1991 there was a dramatic growth of bedspaces in the Housing Schemes category and a decline in Traditional facilities (a loss of over 2,000 beds). There was a loss of over 2,500 direct access bedspaces since 1985. Their examination of the distribution of bedspaces in London indicates that 56% are in the 14 Inner London boroughs. Outer London Boroughs are only involved significantly where specialist hostel provision is concerned. There are many other ways of classifying the facilities. In 1986 SHIL produced a report which provides information on the types of hostel and their distribution Borough by Borough. Drake et al (1985) produced a different classification system using the Directory of Hostels and some not listed there.

There are two important reports on the number, type and distribution of hostels for homeless people.

1. 1981 GLC and 1986 SHIL reports
2. Drake 1987

1. 1981 GLC and 1986 SHIL Reports

These two reports document the changes in hostel provision over a five year period. In 1981 the GLC produced a report to establish the extent of the provision for single homeless people. In 1986 SHIL set out to examine the situation five years on.

In 1981, there were 13,579 hostel bedspaces in London for adult single people. Of these, 11,500 were direct access spaces, 1,725 specialist and 330 non-specialist. There were 12 large direct access hostels providing over 6,000 bedspaces. Two thirds of these were located in Camden, Southwark, Tower Hamlets and Westminster, and one fifth in Islington, Kensington and Chelsea, Lambeth and Lewisham. There were none of this type in Barking and Dagenham, Hillingdon, Kingston-upon-Thames, Merton and Redbridge. The GLC report predicted 4,000 of these bedspaces in large hostels would be gone within five years. The total number of bedspaces was 13,579 in 1981 and 10,078 in 1985/6. There was a drastic reduction in bedspaces in direct access hostels from 6,106 in 1981 to 2,583 in 1985 indicating the almost total lack of progress to date in their development. However altogether there has been an increase of more than 5,000 bedspaces in new hostels, mainly small, good standard non-specialist provision (SHIL 1986).

A Salvation Army study referred to in the report argued that 70% of residents in their direct access hostels were there on a long-term basis, thus filling a permanent housing role. It is argued therefore that in practice at a maximum, only 30% of direct access bedspaces (max.) are available as true emergency spaces.

SHIL argue that no more than 1,000 bedspaces should be provided in direct-access-type hostels. Furthermore it is argued in the 1985 report that 83% of the move-on accommodation needed by residents of hostel and shared housing projects run by the voluntary sector is not met either by housing associations or the local authority. This is highlighted by the fact that approximatly 90% of the hostel and shared housing accommodation in Greater London is provided by the voluntary sector. The 1986 report includes a number of tables illustrating the distribution of bedspaces in London for single homeless women, ethnic minorities, unmet housing requirements, and single homeless with mental disabilities, physical disabilities or mental illness.

In summary these two reports are important, in that they focus directly on single homeless people, who would seem to be the main residents of London hostels. They describe the kinds of facility available and where these can be found as well as tracing the changes in the provision of these facilities over a five year period.

2. Drake (1987)

The importance of this report is its classification of hostels. This report listed 692 hostels. The 1988 Hostels Directory listed 397 projects and hostels. This difference may be accountable by the exclusion in 1988 of student hostels.

The Census of hostels: Pilot stage

The pilot survey of hostels and nightshelters took place on November 22nd. 1988. The hostels which fell within the pilot area were identified and each sent a form, which asked the number of residents on that night and the number of empty beds. It was decided that the minimum of information should be requested in the pilot survey in order to get the maximum response.

There were in total 16 hostels in the pilot area which cater for homeless people, varying in degrees, 14 of which provided the required information. In total there were 1,349 residents and 48 empty beds on the night which suggests there were 3.4% empty beds. However 22 of these beds belonged to one hostel which is closing soon and while people are not being turned away, they are only offering short-term accommodation. The sample includes a large, student hostel, believed to take homeless people. This hostel had 307 residents on the night and 12 empty beds. It was decided also to consider even those residents who have lived in the same hostel for ten years or more, as they are still technically homeless.

It is also important to note that three of the hostels were either being refurbished, and thus partially closed; in the process of closing down completely and thus not accepting new residents and displacing the existing residents, or in the case of one hostel in the area, already completely closed. In total 3% of the total beds were empty and available, which is well below the figures needed to run a hostel efficiently. It clearly falls within the margin of error, and thus effectively, the hostels were full. However the information gathered was insufficient to clarify reasons for empty beds, or revealing differences between types of hostel. The subsequent April Count attempted to obtain more information than the November study for these reasons.

Given the good response rate from the pilot survey a London-wide postal survey was organised as part of the Survey of April 25th 1989. Due to the range of information already collected by the Research Information Service on all aspects of hostel provision for the 1989 Directory, it was decided to focus on simply the number of residents and empty beds in hostels listed in the London Hostel Directory on the night of the survey. To clarify this information the hostel staff were asked if the hostel kept beds open for any reason, whether or not the empty beds (if any) were available for use, and whether or not the hostels were direct access or not (See Appendix). To supplement the postal survey, a telephone survey was conducted on the 26th April in which 100 Traditional, Emergency and Short Stay hostels were phoned and asked to respond to the questions regarding the previous night.

Table 6.1: Results summary

Total number of Hostels in London in 1989 (all contacted):	444
Number of Hostels who participated by post and by phone:	267 (60%)

The total figure includes all the hostels listed in the London Hostel Directory 1989. The directory lists student and working people's hostels which may take homeless people, thus the figures below should represent the maximum number of hostel bedspaces available in London for homeless people.

Table 6.2: Hostel occupany - April 1989

Number of Residents:	10,115 (100,084 adults and 31 children
Total number of Empty Beds: (Includes those out of use for refurbishment or repairs: 120, or those that have been booked and paid for: 17)	756
This leaves:	
A) Valid Empties: (Beds which can be used)	630
B) Open Access Empties: (Excludes quotas, for example Equal Opportunity, or kept for Social Services, or emergency beds)	438
Number of beds held for quota reasons=	192
% Empty Beds: Valid Empties --------------- =	630 --- = 5.8
Number of Residents + Valid Empties	10,745
This can be represented as the percentage occupancy rate which is 94.2%.	
This does not take into account those beds which are out of use for technical or administrative reasons. Taking these into account (137) reduces the percentage occupancy rate to 93.	
Number of Direct Access Hostels	75
% D/A of total 267	28%
Number of Residents in Direct Access Hostels:	4,745
Number of Empty Beds in Direct Access Hostels:	
A) Valid Empties:	186
B) Open Access (excludes emergency beds and beds held for court use:17)	172
% Direct Access Empty Beds: 186 --- 4,745 + 186 = 4,932	= 3.7%
Percentage direct access occupancy rate is 96.3%	

Variety and significance of hostel accommodation

Hostel types

Table 6.3 presents the hostels in the London Hostel Directory 1989. The Directory classifies the hostels according to eight main types and seven subsidiary types and these are used to subdivide the hostels included in the Survey. The table shows firstly the total number of each type of hostel as listed in the directory, the number which participated in the survey and the percentage these are of the total. Secondly the table shows the number of residents and empty beds in each type of hostel and thus the total number of bedspaces for each type. Empties here are those beds which are available for use, that is they are not being refurbished or are out of service, but they include those beds which are being kept free for specific groups or that the Local Authority may wish to use.

Thirdly, there is the predicted number of bedspaces for each type in London based on the number of hostels in the survey as a proportion of the total number in the Directory.

Summary of hostel survey results

Table 6.3: Summary of hostel residents (A)

Type of Hostel	Total	Survey	%	Resid.	Empties	Beds	Predic.
Traditional	22	22	100	2105	113	2218	2218
Emergency	11	8	73	616	24	640	876
Medium Stay	39	31	79	385	63	448	567
Short Stay	53	32	60	460	22	482	803
Working People	77	42	54	3363	151	3814	6507
Housing Schemes	38	15	39	833	82	915	2346
Group Houses	11	4	36	69	3	72	200
VS	7	5	71	84	7	93	131
Students	28	7	25	647	11	658	2632
TOTAL A	286	166	58%	8562	476	9040	16,281

Table 6.4: Summary of hostel residents (B)

Figures for those hostels which target each type. **Bold** = Figures for those hostels not included in A., that is hostels which are not also one of the types listed above.

Type of Hostel	Total		Survey		%		Resid.		Empties		**Beds**	Beds	Predic.
Students	33	**32**	7	**7**	21	**22**	647		11		658	**658**	2991
Alcoholics	20	**13**	15	**11**	75	**85**	259	**174**	29	**14**	288	**188**	221
Ex-Offenders	54	**31**	34	**21**	63	**64**	633	**257**	75	**30**	708	**287**	448
Young People Leaving Care	27	**15**	13	**5**	48	**33**	115	**30**	29	**12**	144	**42**	127
Drug Users	15	**7**	8	**5**	53	**71**	86	**45**	18	**17**	104	**62**	87
Single Parents	12	**10**	7	**6**	58	**60**	64	**51**	3	**3**	67	**56**	93
Mental Health	54	**40**	54	**16**	100	**40**	365	**231**	45	**39**	410	**270**	675
TOTAL B	215	**148**	138	**71**	%		2169	**1435**	210	**126**	2379	**1563**	4642
TOTAL A & B	473	**406**	298	**231**	--		10,094	**9,360**	679	595	11,419	**9957**	**18,281**

1. Empties= Those beds which are available for use,that is they are not being refurbished or are out of service for some reason. These figures also include beds which are being kept free for specific groups or local authority.

Table 6.4 presents the results from the April Survey for those types of hostels which have not previously been included as one of the types in Table 6.3. On the left side of each column is the total number of hostels, residents, or empty beds which are described as being for a particular type of homeless need. The right hand column, in bold, contains the figures for each type of hostel that is not already in Table 6.3, that is, is not also one of the main types of hostels as described in the Directory. The necessity for this is due to the classification system used in the Directory which has emerged from the way in which the staff of the facilities themselves describe their function and service.

Using this table, it is possible to count the number of hostels which cater for each specific group as well as indicate the total number of residents and empty beds in all the facilities. For example, there are 20 hostels which target alcoholics as listed in the Directory, 13 of which are not at the same time described as any other type of facility. This information allows a total figure to be established of the number of bedspaces in the survey and predicted to be in London, which does not include duplications.

From Table 6.4 it is possible to see that there were 9,998 residents and 208 empties in 223 separate facilities on the night of the Survey. This indicates that there were 9862 bedspaces in 60% of the facilities listed in the Directory. Using this percentage the estimated number of bedspaces in London is 18,281. See Table 6.3 for a detailed breakdown of this estimate.

Table 6.5 Estimated number of hostel bedspaces in London

Working People	6507
Students	2991
Housing Schemes	2346
Traditional	2218
Emergency	876
Short Stay	803
Mental Health	675
Medium Stay	567
Ex-Offenders	448
Alcoholics	221
Group Houses	200
Young People	
Leaving Care	127
Very Short Stay	122
Single Parents	93
Drug Users	87

Estimated Number of Hostel bedspaces in London	18,281

Hostel bedspaces: A comparison

The full results from the hostel survey can be compared with the Shil 1986 report which suggested there were 10,078 bedspaces in London. The figure estimated here of 18,281 is a maximum figure which includes all the large hostels. The comparisons made with the NAB study (1965) and Wingfield Digby (1972) have to be taken cautiously as lodging houses no longer exist in London and thus these studies referred to a different type of provision. Indeed none of the studies have collected information on exactly the same types of hostels. Wherever possible in making comparisons below these differences will be pointed out.

The April Survey figures do not include those beds which are out of use, whereas Shil (1986) acknowledge that the number of empty beds and total bedspaces figures do include those out of use due to refurbishing or other reasons, thus their figures are larger than they would be if this had been taken into account.

Bearing this in mind, the percentage occupancy rates for London hostel bedspaces from 1983 to 1985 were presented for women and for men and ranged from 79% to 92% for women and 84% to 93% for men (Shil 1986). This compared with the 93% found in the April Survey, indicating that the occupancy rate has not declined, but that on the night of the survey it was as high as that revealed by Shil in 1986 based on the GLC figures taken over a five year period from 1981 to 1985.

Wingfield Digby (1972) argued that there had been a reduction in the number of hostel bedspaces in the Greater London Area by 13% from 1965 to 1972. There was no account of direct access bedspaces at this time. He noted the growth in numbers of small hostels (+27%) and the decline of large hostels with over 200 beds (-33%) nationally. (Since that time, there is a guideline of 30 beds maximum placed upon the building of new hostels in London.) The number of hostels and lodging house bedspaces in the Greater London Area in 1965 was 12,212. This had declined to 10,692 in 1972.

Salvation army

Of the eight Salvation Army hostels listed in the London Hostel Directory, seven were included in the April Survey. These included six traditional hostels and one which targets people with alcohol abuse problems. On the night of the survey, these hostels had 808 residents and 39 empty beds. The percentage of empty beds was 4.6%, which is lower than the overall sample (5.6%). This is a 95.4% occupancy rate as there were no beds out of use. Although four of the seven hostels in the survey are direct access hostels, the percentage of empty beds in direct access hostels was lower (3.7%). This would indicate that these hostels had a higher percentage of empty beds on the night than did all the direct access hostels.

These figures can be compared with those found nationally by Wingfield Digby in 1972 and with the National Assistance Board in 1965. In 1972, the total occupancy rate was 86% which was very similar to that found in the NAB 1966 survey. Of particular interest here is the rate for Salvation Army hostels nationally which was 93% which is only marginally less than the 95.4% found for Salvation Army hostels in London.

Direct access

Shil (1986) argued there were 4,885 direct access bedspaces in nine boroughs in London. The April Survey revealed 4,931 direct access bedspaces in those hostels which participated. Given that this survey considered as direct access any hostel which described itself as one, it is impossible to predict what this figure would be for all direct access hostels. It is most likely however, that most direct access hostels were included in the survey, as the telephone survey targeted traditional, emergency and short stay facilities which have tended to operate as direct access.

Table 6.6: A Comparison of hostel bedspaces

Direct Access Bedspaces in London		
GLC	1981	9,751
Shil	1986	4,885
Univ. Surrey (Not all of London)		4,931

It is useful to compare the occupancy rate of the Direct Access Hostels in the April Count with the percentage occupancy of hostels in the November Pilot Count which was 97% (3% empty beds). The hostels included in the pilot count were generally large direct access facilities, and thus a comparison with the percentage of direct access empties is appropriate. For the November Survey this was 3.4% and for the direct access beds in the April Survey it was 3.7%. Clearly this would indicate that there has been little change in the percentage of empty beds in direct access facilities from November to April.

Discussion

The administration of hostels does require the availability of space capacity to allow both for maintenance and the possible upsurges in demand at particular times of the year. These very high occupancy rates therefore strongly suggest that there is an under-provision of hostel beds in London and that at crucial times it will be very difficult indeed for everyone who wants a bed to be able to find one.

There are however a large number of beds which are being held for target groups, or an agency or local authority. Perhaps this is a reflection of the legislation which tends to cater for those in special need and therefore funds projects which do not cater for single homeless people. It is possible that these beds are being consistently underused and are therefore not being as effective as they could be in providing facilities for homeless people. Other issues may be the improvement of some referral systems, or the lowering of a standard of admittance.

Hostel Residents: Who Are They? A summary of research on the characteristics of hostel residents.

Many studies have been done to discover who is in hostels, and most of them have focused on some or all of the following pieces of information: age, sex, marital status, place of origin, last place of residence, reason left home, length of stay, whether had slept rough or not, and whether had been in institutions or not. The second type of information gathered was on attitudes to the hostel in question and preferred type of accommodation. There have been many such studies over the last twenty years culminating in the largest and most influential: Single and Homeless in 1981.

This review will focus only on the main ones of this kind,attempting to give a general overview.

1. Early studies

In 1966 the National Assistance Board made the first attempt to obtain statistics on hostel residents on a national level. It also included people in government reception centres and those sleeping rough. Although the figures apply nationally, there were a few results directly relevant to the London situation. Thirty one point five per cent (31.5%) of the total number of beds for men and 34.4% of the total for women were provided in the London regions. This was out of a total of 597 'common lodging houses' investigated.

In 1978 Lodge Patch conducted a national survey of hostels which focused on the evidence of mental health problems among residents. It is of interest here due to its comparison of hostel numbers with the NAB study in 1965. The changes in the number of establishments and beds in the GLC between 1965 and 1972, demonstrated an overall reduction of 13% in number of beds. There are further national figures which are not directly relevant here. This was followed in 1976 by a survey by Wingfield Digby for the DHSS taking in a random sample of hostels and lodging houses and the residents therein. From 1965-1972 Wingfield Digby conducted research in hostels and lodging houses with a sample of 2,000 residents. The occupancy rate, of those hostels in the study was 86%. He argued that single people were using hostels and lodgings as permanent accommodation. Of the middle aged residents, one in three had been in one particular hostel for longer than two years. About one third had slept rough. In all the hostels about 47% of the residents had been there for longer than ten years. On reasons for leaving home, 75% stated family or marital reasons; 30% physical, mental or social problems; 49% employment reasons; and 54% accommodation reasons. In general 63% were single, 16% separated, 9% widowed and 12% divorced.

On accommodation preference, 43% stated they liked living where they were, and 50% said they would prefer to live somewhere else. Of the female population, generally younger than their male counterparts, 43% had been in the same establishment for longer than two years. On places of preference 50% 'liked it there', while 36% would prefer somewhere else.

This study was very influential in the 1970's, and documented some of the worst conditions. He argued that 'the nature of their accommodation seriously undermines their opportunity to get better accommodation'. (Wingfield Digby 1976:p.52)

Other small 'in-house' studies have been conducted which contribute to the wide-ranging body of information on residents' characteristics. One of which was conducted by the Look Ahead Housing Association (Beacon Hostels) in 1980, another by Terry Burke for the Salvation Army in 1981.

Ray Oakley carried out research on profiles and perspectives of the residents of Salvation Army hostels in London. He found a number of similar points of information about hostel residents. Forty four per cent (44%) were over the age of 50; 67% were single; 30% of residents had stayed longer than two years; 59% said they had slept rough. Oakley compares this to the findings of a 1976 OPCS survey where 57% of those in Salvation Army hostels and 54% of those in all hostels had previously slept rough. Oakley's study had wider aims than providing characteristics of residents; he also sought to discover the many purposes of hostels. He recommended a wider range of accommodation options and argues that 'the need in hostels is to recognise the heterogeneity of the population and to provide the wide range of environments suitable for them'. His further work has contributed to new hostel designs which will be discussed further on.

2. Single and homeless (Drake et al 1981)

The most influential study on the characteristics of hostel residents and on single homelessness in general was the Department of the Environment's 1981 study Single and Homeless. The study funded by the DOE set up in 1976 to provide ' a broadly based understanding of the housing needs and preferences of the single homeless'. The report examines homelessness 'both in terms of individuals and in terms of their social, economic and residential environments' (Drake et al 1981, p.13). The research is important as it documented clearly the heterogeneous nature of homeless people, refuting stereotypes of old men with health or social problems. The research took three years to complete.The study took the form of one large-scale survey and two desk-top studies. The survey included interviews with 521 people in seven local authority districts: Manchester, Stoke-on Trent, Bedford, Brighton, and the London Boroughs of Camden, Tower Hamlets and Haringey. The first desk survey was of the clients of a national referral agency (sample size 6,531) and the second a survey of the users of an East London Night Shelter over a six month period (308 people).

Single and Homeless gives a profile of single homeless people in terms of age, sex, place of origin and last place of residence. Some of the findings are summarised here.

1. In the general survey 40% were over 45 years of age. In fact the age distribution of males in the survey was similar to that of the general population. The females in the study were younger than the general population, and in general younger than the men. Young people were more likely to be found at advice centres, the intermediate age groups in hostels and night shelters, the elderly in large hostels.

2. Large numbers from all three samples, especially the nightshelter sample came from Scotland and Ireland.

3. The longer respondents had been homeless the less likely they were to have any education beyond school leaving age. Two fifths had education beyond school leaving age.

4. Forty nine per cent (49%) of the sample had spent time in institutions.

5. The majority of the sample wanted independence in furnished accommodation, that is, flats, houses or bedsits.

The general picture was that younger people (under 30) in the main had few social or medical problems, but where they did they tended to be social ones. Interim groups (30-49) reported high rates of alcoholism and mental illness, while older people (over 50) suffered mainly from physical illness or disability.

The research found that homelessness is clearly associated with loss of employment. When they had had a home only 12% were unemployed and the main type of employment was regular. At the time of the survey 51% were unemployed and even those who were employed only had casual work. The longer people had been homeless the more likely they were to suffer from social and medical problems. In addition other processes included loss of social and familial support and also associated with homelessness was reliance on lower standard accommodation. The longer people had been homeless the more likely they were to be living in night shelters or large hostels or sleeping rough.

The respondents were asked their last settled base or permanent home, their last sleeping place, and the accommodation at the time they were interviewed. For the last settled base, the majority of people were living in mainstream housing with most living as dependents with parents, relatives or spouse. For the last sleeping place, only one third have cited mainstream accommodation; two fifths said they were staying in hostels, nightshelters, boarding houses and lodging houses. Just under one eighth had slept rough. More than a quarter of the whole sample had some experience of sleeping rough.

The vast majority of the single homeless expressed a preference for accommodation in houses, flats, or bedsits (85%). Most were staying in hostels, the majority preferring furnished accommodation. One third said they would prefer not to share accommodation. One twentieth would prefer hostel accommodation. They conclude that about 'two thirds of the single homeless require ordinary mainstream accommodation with little more than sensitive help and advice from the housing management'.

The report makes several recommendations, the first being that at the point at which people leave home, appropriate accommodation advice and support should be available which might help preserve existing social networks and prevent individuals from becoming long-term homeless. Secondly, attention is needed to improve the standards of much of the existing accommodation used by the homeless. Thirdly , there is a continuing need for general purpose hostels. Fourthly that after care provision should include co-ordinated activity so that no-one is discharged homeless or to inappropriate accommodation. Fifthly, there is a need for more supportive hostels for those falling in between hospitalisation and independent living. Sixthly, factors such as willingness to share should be considered when agencies are providing accommodation for single homeless people. Seventhly, provision at the local authority level requires co-operation and co-ordination of agencies offering advice, accommodation, cash and social and medical support. Finally, programmes of re-housing should be extended and encouraged.

3. Lodge Patch (1978)

Having considered the most influential studies on hostel residents, it is important to note two surveys conducted in the 1970's by two psychiatrists, Lodge Patch (1978) and Tidmarsh (1978). Based on interviews with residents in two Salvation Army hostels, Lodge Patch concluded that high numbers of homeless men had personality disorders (50.4%), schizophrenia (14.6%), depression (8.1%), and mental subnormality (11.4%). Only four men (11.4%) were considered 'normal'. He concludes that:

> To regard the homeless man as a blight, however is to miss the cardinal point that he is not simply one who happens not to have a home, he is also a man who is incapable of sustaining one, and may be incapable of any other way of life than that which he has adopted (Lodge Patch 1978).

Studies such as Single and Homeless succeeded in banishing this image of the homeless man, pointing out the heterogeneity of single homeless people. However it could be argued that some hostels have a more homogeneous population, such as some of the Salvation Army, and the St. Mungo hostels and that there are large numbers of homeless people who do need assistance and care.

Tidmarsh (1978) carried out a study of the Camberwell Reception Centre and argued that the homeless men had 'usually come from backgrounds of considerable social disadvantage and that psychiatric illness, alcoholism and personality disorders were unduly common'.

4. While much of the reviewed research mentions in passing information on gender, ethnicity, ex-psychiatric patients, the physically disabled, there are a few studies which have focused directly on these groups. For the purposes of this research some of these will be discussed and others just mentioned. This section is not intended as a complete literature review as many new studies/reports are emerging which examine these as well as other groups in relation to hostels, for example those with HIV/Aids and young people leaving care.

Women

While women have been included in some of the research already mentioned, there are a few studies which focus directly on homeless women. Watson and Austerberry have taken a feminist perspective to women's housing problems producing a guide to women's hostels (1982), research on single women's housing problems and a feminist perspective on homelessness (1986). In London there were approximately 760 beds for women (Watson and Austerberry 1983, p.16)and over 6,000 beds for men (GLC and LBA, 1981, p.16) in direct access hostels. There were five women only and 34 mixed, small open-access hostels providing 55 beds for young women and 114 beds with no age restriction (Austerberry and Watson 1983). There were approximately 8,000 beds for women in 60 women-only and 95 mixed hostels (ibid.). The Women's Housing Handbook for London (1988) provides a wide range of information on housing for women, including a descriptive list of hostels that cater for women.

In the hostel research, 70 women were interviewed in open access hostels. They found only nine of the 70 were working. Noted in particular was a sense of social isolation. Watson and Austerberry (1986) explore the cultural and social history of homelessness, arguing that homelessness is an historically and culturally specific concept (Watson and Austerberry 1986). More directly relevant to the examination of hostels are the interviews conducted with 160 single homeless women . Some of the key findings were that approximately one third of women had been treated for mental problems, the majority of whom were living in the direct-access hostels. Only a small proportion of the women were Asian, African or West Indians. Thirty eight per cent (38%) had had children at some time in their lives. Over one third of the women interviewed lost housing due to marital dispute. In terms of housing preference, more than half the women wanted to live alone; 17% per cent wanted to live with a husband/boyfriend or children or both and 23% wanted to live with friends. The book provides open ended responses to a number of questions and in this way gives some further insight into the experience of being homeless and living in a hostel. A Report on Homelessness Amongst Women by the Women's National Commission (1983) gives an overview of the homeless situation for women including a look at the literature on hostels. They argue that women make different demands on homelessness provision and are differently provided for. They further argue that the present provision is neither adequate nor appropriate for them.

Ethnic groups

There has been little research into the experience of black homeless people and none on the experience of hostels. There are no facts available on whether emergency housing projects are providing an equal and accessible service for young black people (R.I.S. 1987). SHIL created an anti-racist group to discover how much information was available on the extent of black and other ethnic minority homelessness and housing need. They conducted research mainly on local authorities. While not directly relevant to this review it is important in that it provides useful information on the extent of black homelessness in a number of London boroughs. It also lists housing projects aimed at specific ethnic groups, as well as the number of boroughs which have commissioned studies of their own.

Cara produced a report on Irish Homelessness in 1988 which was based on a study of 17 hostels in the City of Westminster. This involved a census over two nights in 1986 and some in-depth interviews with the most representative sections of Irish people found in the hostels. They noted 1,094 respondents in June 1986 and 1218 in November 1986. They found 26% of all hostel occupants were Irish. They argue for specialist housing for Irish homeless people as existing facilities fail to understand the cultural forces operating within Irish homelessness. Furthermore UJIMA's Housing Association produce an annual report which provides information on black homeless people.

Gays and Lesbians

No published studies have yet been found addressing directly the quality or accessibility of hostels for gays and lesbians, although the directories do list hostels who specifically encourage them as residents. Also the Housing

Advice Switchboard conducted a telephone survey of callers on their sexual orientation, noting 25% of the calls were from gay and lesbians.

Young people

It is important to mention the Centrepoint Night Shelter studies on the experience of its young residents (Randall 1988). This study suggested that there may be over 50,000 young people in temporary accommodation in London. Centrepoint annually houses about 2,000 young people. The GLC in 1984 did a study of hostels for young people in London. At that time there were 27,693 bedspaces and 567 hostels. Of these less than 10% were specifically for young people. The hostels were mainly small in size, and concentrated in Inner London. In recent years there has been a strong research emphasis on them and young people (Stockley 1993).

Ex-psychiatric patients

While 'history of mental illness' has been researched in some of the studies already discussed, one recent study is of special note. Dr. Timms conducted research in a London hostel and found 30% were suffering from schizophrenia. These findings were supported by Satchell (1988) who conducted a survey of a housing association that houses homeless men. Taking into account that many ex-psychiatric patients would be referred to his hostel, he found 59 out of the 146 had some form of psychiatric history (40.4%).

Summary

The homeless population is a fluid, heterogeneous one. The characteristics of residents are not consistent. Indeed the largest and broadest piece of research, 'Single and Homeless', presents a younger population on average, one which was quite highly educated, and one which had less respondents who had spent time sleeping rough. It may be that the smaller pieces of research have documented pockets of single homeless people in particular settings, and therefore cannot be generalised to describe other homeless groups. Or it may be that taking a representative sample of homeless people from different areas, types of setting and different facilities is not a satisfactory way of discovering more about particular homeless groups, for example, London hostel residents.

Resettlement

There have been a few studies on rehousing and resettlement, many by government departments, (DHSS 1986),(DOE 1983). The Department of the Environment's study on rehoused hostel residents indicated some of the common areas in the resettlement debate. 517 respondents were interviewed from a range of establishments. Seventy per cent (70%) were in houses, 105 in bedsits, 6% in other hostels. There was an ambivalence in attitudes to hostel life. While many liked the companionship of the hostel, the comfort, staff and entertainment, many disliked the type of people, the dirt, the rowdy behaviour and the food. Eighty one per cent (81%) of the respondents like the independence. Fifty per cent (50%) were judged to be living 'successfully'.

Design

The design of hostels has not been much of a subject of discourse with some exceptions (Drake et al 1981, Oakley 1973, 1981, HMSO, Garside et al 1990) outside the work of the Salvation Army's staff architect, Ray Oakley. Some of the latest Salvation Army hostels outside of London have been developed according to the staff architect of the Salvation Army, Major Oakley's rehabilitative aim, basing his design on the individual growth therapeutic model. This design 'theme' has been well documented in a number of unpublished reports (Oakley 1973, 1980). It is important to note here the existence of this work. 'Single and Homeless' suggests various types of accommodation which would be appropriate as for 'ordinary' single people, ranging from purpose built schemes to flats or houses in the existing stock, given as they argue that two thirds of the single homeless require mainstream accommodation (Drake et al 1981).

Management

On the management of hostels, the National Federation of Housing Associations produced a report for discussion (Drake et al 1987). It is specifically aimed at those providing accommodation for single homeless people and covers key issues in management, such as defining realistic goals, the relationship between worker and resident, stress, need for clear referral criteria, resettlement, rules and regulations, resident participation, and worker management.

Salvation army sample

The survey of hostels, hotels, squatters and those on the streets consisted of 515 'resident' questionnaires completed and 100 staff questionnaires. These questionnaires were distributed to samples of residents and staff from 35 different 'settings'.

This section presents some central descriptive aspects of the Salvation Army sample. In total 154 residents from Salvation Army hostels were interviewed from all seven hostels in London. In addition 30 staff across the hostels were included in the survey. Further information was obtained from all seven hostels regarding the gender, age, ethnic origin and length of stay of all residents. In general terms the survey sample approximates in distribution the ages and length of stay of the total sample in our studies. From Table 6.7 it can be seen that the survey sample has a higher percentage of younger residents than does the total sample, and in Figure 6.8 a smaller percentage of residents who had been in the hostel for more than a year.

Table 6.7: Age of Salvation Army hostel residents

Age	%
19-29	38
30-39	16
40-49	15
60-69	11
50-50	10
70+	5
Under 18	5

Table 6.8: Length of stay of Salvation Army hostel residents

Length	%
More than 1 year	28
Less than 1 month	22
1-3 months	21
4-6 months	15
7 months to 1 year	14

However these percentage differences are not large and given the nature of the survey may be unavoidable. The comparison would thus suggest, that the survey sample is a representative one as far as this is possible.

The sample of residents are made up largely of older men, and residents who have stayed in the hostel more than seven months. Over two thirds of the sample were born in England with over 10% Irish and 10% Scottish. Less than a quarter of the sample were in any kind of employment with over half either retired or registered invalid/ill. Comparing those not on a housing waiting list with samples from other hostels, it is clear that a high percentage of the resident sample are not actively seeking alternative accommodation. In addition the percentage of residents from the sample who came from either another homeless setting or an institution was over 50%.

Evaluation of Salvation Army hostels

This section provides an overview of the residents' evaluation of the hostel in which they were staying in at the time of interview. A number of statements regarding physical, social and personal aspects of the hostel were posed to residents who had to agree or disagree with each one. In this way it is possible to view the responses as the amount of satisfaction residents have with these aspects of hostel life. These differences in 'satisfaction' reveal something about the goals of the residents to the extent that satisfaction is considered here to be a measure of the extent to which aspects of a place are meeting the goals of the residents.

More residents agree that 'Being in the hostel is the only way I can afford to live' than to any other aspect. Considering the decrease in percentage agreement down to 'I can do what I want here', it is possible to see the physical aspects of the hostel are those which residents agree are present more than the social or personal aspects. They are less satisfied with those aspects of home which are not simply provided by somewhere cheap, safe and where they can get a good night's sleep. To explore the relationship between the items it is necessary to examine the correlations as presented in Table 6.9.

Table 6.9: Rank order correlations of meaning of home items: Salvation Army residents

Satisfaction With Place	Q.6 Overall I like staying here.
Q.3 I think this is a comfortable place to be in.	.67
Q.1 The social life is good here.	.60
Q.4 1 can get a good night's sleep.	.53
Q.5 Being here is the only way I can afford to live.	.46
Q.2 I can do what I want here.	.41
Q.11 I feel safe here.	.40

It is clear that those who like staying in the hostel also think it is a comfortable place to be in and a place in which the social life is good. For those who like staying in the hostel it seems the social and personal aspects of home are not distinct from the physical aspects. It becomes more 'homelike' in the physical, social and personal senses of home for this subject .

Exploring this further it would seem that there are people who feel differently about the hostel, for example there are those for whom sleeping and feeling safe are aspects which are satisfactory and others who are more satisfied with being social. Thus there are several different types of people in Salvation Army hostels who have different goals and aspirations.

Varieties of Salvation Army Residents

Two particular groups of residents have been identified who have several attributes in common. The first group are those residents in the sample who are over 60 years of age, are unemployed, retired or invalid/ill and who have been in the hostel for over a year (N=40). The second group are those who are under 60 years of age, employed in some capacity and who have been at the hostel less than one year (N=25).

It is useful to compare how these two groups responded to questions which focused on aspects of home which are important to the respondents. Group 1 would seem to be less concerned with having their own place, the use of a kitchen and a place where friends can stay than Group 2, but more concerned with being in London. This indicates the younger Group 2 think the domestic, social aspects of home are important, whereas for the older Group 2, what is most important is staying in London. This may be due simply to having lived longer in London and being more committed to it as a place than the younger group. For the evaluation section, more of Group 1 feel safe, and get a good night's sleep than Group 2. These groups may be seen as having different goals, i.e. the older group's aspirations being more to do with being elderly and requiring somewhere safe and restful and the younger's to do with being social. Far more of the older group felt they were part of a community in the hostel than did the younger group and fewer felt a failure.

Table 6.10: Comparison of two groups of residents:Salvation Army

Statement	Group 1 Older	Group 2 Younger
	Percentage agreement	
Importance of London	88%	47%
I feel safe here	83%	67%
I can get a good night's sleep		
Only way I can afford to live	78%	58%
Friends can stay		
	76%	52%
Importance of use of kitchen	52%	80%
Importance of own place		
Importance of somewhere where	50%	88%
friends can stay		
The social life is good here	40%	80%
	20%	42%
I can do what I want here	15%	29%
I feel a failure	13%	38%

Salvation Army: Differences between the hostels

A section of the questionnaire (Section B) focuses on some of the organisational issues in each hostel: staff and resident relationships, rules, control etc. From these items it is possible to present a preliminary profile of each hostel according to the views of staff and residents together. In this section the general item 'Generally people here are proud of this place' is correlated with the other items in the section to discover which aspects of the hostel milieu are considered to be a positive part of being proud of the place. In summary those aspects of the hostel environment not included in the highest correlations are generally to do with support, spontaneity and involvement.

The variety and range of homeless people in London has been illustrated by the existence of at least two groups of people within Salvation Army hostels who may have different experiences, short and long-term goals. These differences have implications for the kinds of provision the Salvation Army provides. The differences between the hostels indicate that each hostel has a particular 'milieu' or environment which needs to be understood and taken account of in any future policy decisions and in the development of new designs.

Hostel sample as a whole

Similar sub-groups were found in all hostels. To explore this population further, two sub-groups of hostel residents were selected and their responses to the questionnaire are presented in Table 6.11. The first sub-group was made up of those residents under 50 years of age, who were working in some capacity and who had stayed less than one year. The older group was made up of those over 50 years who were retired, unemployed or invalid/ill and who had stayed for longer than one year.

Table 6.9 presents the responses to the evaluation section of the questionnaire and places the items in order of their chi squared results. This illustrates those items which differed significantly between these two sub-groups.

Of interest in this table is the different aspects of home which are positively evaluated by the two sub-groups. For the younger, working group who have stayed less than a year in the hostel, the aspects evaluated most positively were the physical aspects:getting a good night's sleep, how comfortable it was and how safe they feel. For the older group who are retired, unemployed or invalid/ill the aspect of safety is evaluated highly by more of them than any other aspect. Getting a good night's sleep was also positively evaluated as well as being the only place they could afford to live.

Overall, the hostels were evaluated positively by more of the older group than the younger. For example, 71% of this group liked staying there overall, as compared with 47% of the younger group.

Four aspects of home were found to be significantly different between the two groups: 'social life', 'like it here', comfort and safety. These aspects were highly evaluated by more of the older group than the younger. The varied experience and goals of these groups can be illustrated by these four aspects and could form the basis of the meaning of home to older hostel residents.

Table 6.11: Percentage agreement to meaning of home items: hostel sample

Aspect of Home	Younger Group (180) F	Older Group (48) F	Chi-Square >/ 5.991 sign.level =0.05 df=2
Social Life	44% (80)	66% (30)	8.742 significant
Like It Here	47% (84)	71% (34)	8.4789 significant
Comfort	58% (104)	79% (36)	7.445 significant
Safe	57% (90)	81% (25)	6.766 significant
Afford	57% (111)	75% (36)	5.333 not significant
Good Night's Sleep	60% (107)	75% (36)	3.746 not significant
Do What I Want	36% (64)	47% (21)	2.548 not significant

Table 6.12: Percentage agreement to importance items: hostel sample

Aspects of Home	Younger Group (180) F	Older Group (48) F	Chi-square signif >/5.991 0.05 level df=2
Kitchen	82% (130)	40% (12)	32.075 significant
Decorate	71% (125)	32% (15)	25.52 significant
Own Place	86% (152)	55% (25)	25.409 significant
Friends Back	75% (134)	37% (17)	19.9146 significant
Cheap	76% (137)	54% (25)	17.472 significant
London	52% (82)	84% (26)	11.06 significant
Quiet	70% (125)	83% (40)	7.310 significant
Own Room	85% (135)	87% (26)	.2671 not significant

Clearly there is one aspect which is agreed important by large percentages of both groups, which is 'having a room of one's own'. However after that there is little similarity in emphasis. Important to more of the younger group was to 'have a place of their own', 'own room', 'the use of a kitchen' and 'having friends back'. Of importance to fewer of this group was 'living in London'. Many of the other group of older residents considered 'living in London' and 'living somewhere that's quiet' important as well as their 'own room'. These aspects would seem to reflect the age of this group: a concern for quiet and continuing to reside in the same place. Of importance to fewer of this group in general were 'being able to decorate', 'having friends back' and 'having the use of a kitchen', things associated with the young, social adult. The largest significant difference was for 'having the use of a kitchen' which was important to more young people than old.

These differences in both evaluation and aspects which are considered important can and have been developed into more concrete models of provision. By focusing on the meaning of home in this way, and exploring the views of the variety of homeless people, the significance of home can be made more explicit.

Hostel Residents

As in the previous chapter, the results from the survey are presented for hostel residents largest sample of homeless people were from hostels, with 415 residents taking part in the survey. (Details of this sample and of the selection of hostels used in the study are to be found in the Appendix).

The size of this sample of hostel residents allows more generalisations to be made than were possible with the other smaller samples. This particular sample formed the basis for later analysis and for the resulting typology of hostels.

The following provides a highlighted account of the biographical details of hostel residents.

Biographical Details

Gender

Although mostly male, the hostel sample contained a higher proportion of women than did the street sample.

Age

Those in hostels were both younger with 38% between the ages of 19 and 29, and older with 26% over 50 years of age. This was unlike the street which had more between the ages of 30 to 39 and fewer over the age of 50.

Table 6:13: Age of hostel residents

Age	%
18 and under	5
19-29	38
30-39	16
40-49	15
50-59	10
60-69	11
70+	5

Family Status

There were slightly more single people as compared to married, divorced or separated people in hostels than on the street (72%). There were more divorced or separated people on the street than in hostels.

Table 6:14: Family status of hostel residents

Family Status	%
Single	72
Widowed	4
Married	4
Co-habiting	3
Divorced	13
Separated	4

Employment status and voluntary work

Forty five per cent (45%) of those in hostels sample were unemployed, almost 10% less than on the streets. More people in hostels were in full time work (12%), part time work (5%) but 20% fewer doing casual work (7% as compared with 27% on the streets). There was a high percentage of the hostel sample who were retired (12%) or invalid/ill (16%). In fact, a smaller percentage of hostel residents work in some form than on the streets. Furthermore a smaller percentage do voluntary work in hostels (17%) than on the streets (20%).

Table 6:15: Employment status of hostel residents

Employment Status	%
Full-time	12
Part-time	5
Retired	12
Casual	7
Unemployed	45
Self-Employed	2
Government Scheme	1
Ill	16

Education

Forty one per cent (41%) of those in hostels said they received no formal education. This percentage was lower than on the street as more people obtained A Levels and professional qualifications. Thirty per cent (30%) of the sample had some trade qualifications, which is lower than the street sample.

Table 6.16: Educational qualifications of hostel residents

Qualifications	%
Degree	4
Professional	5
A-Level	7
CSE/GCSE	24
Other	13
None	41
Not Known	6

Birth Place and Ethnicity

Sixty one per cent (61%) of hostel residents were born in England, with 13% born in Ireland (the highest percentage across the settings) and 13% from Europe and other places. Thirteen per cent (13%) were black with 75% white European. There were more black people staying in hostels than other settings, except hotels.

Table 6.17: Country of origin of hostel residents

	%
England	61
Scotland	8
Wales	2
Ireland	13
Europe	1
Other	12
N.I.	3

Table 6.18: Ethnicity of hostel residents

	%
White Europeans	75
Asian	2
Black	13
White Other	8
Other	2

Length of stay

Those in hostels who had stayed less than three months in the hostel, which is about 10% higher than on the street. Also there was a smaller percentage in hostels who had stayed longer than one year (28%) as compared with the street (41%) and squats (35%).

Table 6.19: Length of stay of hostel residents

Length of Stay	%
Less than 1 month	22
1-3 months	21
4-6 months	16
7 months-1 year	13
More than 1 year	28

Use of day centres

Nearly two thirds of the hostel residents never used day centres (63%). Nine per cent (9%) said they used them once a day. This compares with 67% of those who never used them.

Table 6.20: Use of day centres

Use (At least)	%
Once a Day	9
Once a week	15
Once a month	8
Twice a year	5
Never	63

Summary

The hostel sample contains a wider range of people in terms of age, employment status and length of stay than in the other settings.

Residential history

The residential history of hostel residents is important.

Last place before this one

Twenty seven per cent (27%) of the sample came from a house or flat to the hostel. This is slightly less than in the street sample. A further 19% came from another hostel. Only 9% came from the street. Two per cent (2%) said they had come from a hospital or care institution and 5% from prison. Forty four per cent (44%) of the sample had spent more than a year in their last place, with 31% having stayed less than three months.

Of those in rented accommodation, a third rented from the council or from a housing association, and 20% from a private landlord. Fifteen per cent (15%) of the places had been owner occupied.

Age Left Home

Forty one per cent (41%) of hostel residents left home between the ages of 16 and 18; 16% left home between 11 and 15. A higher proportion of hostel residents left home at an older age than those on the street. Sixteen per cent (16%) of hostel residents left home between the age of 11 and 15 as compared with 34% of those on the streets.

Table 6.21: Age that hostel residents left home

Age	%
Less than 10 years	5
11-15	16
16-18	41
19-25	24
26-30	6
31+	8

Number of Places Have Lived In

Sixty five per cent (65%) of the sample had lived in 10 or less places. This compares with 57% of those on the street. More of those on the street had lived in many different places than those in hostels.

Table 6.22: Number of places hostel residents have lived in

Number	%
1-5	43
6-10	22
11-20	18
21-30	5
31-40	1
41+	0
Too many to count	10
Didn't Know	1

Last place called home

Twenty six per cent (26%) of hostel residents considered their family home as their home, with a further 22% referring to a named place such as Manchester or Ireland, for example. Only 9% said they never had a home. Twenty four per cent (24%) of those on the street said they had never had a home.

After they left their last home, 37% went to a hostel. Sixteen per cent (16%) went into a house or flat, while 7% went onto the streets. Thirty per cent (30%) of the accommodation was rented from the council or housing association, while 21% was privately rented.

Thirty two per cent (32%) left the last place they called home less than six months ago and 62% left less than two years ago. This sample is thus a comparatively newer homeless group than those in the street sample on one level, taking the meaning of being homeless as having no home.

Housing waiting list

Fifty six per cent (56%) of the hostel sample were not on a housing waiting list. Less than a third said they were.

Table 6.23: Hostel residents on housing waiting list

	%
Yes	32
No	56
Don't Know	12

Summary

The residential history of the hostel sample suggests that in general they are more settled than those from the street. This is illustrated by the finding that one third of the sample had come straight from a house or flat and a further 19% from another hostel. This is the highest percentage across the settings of people coming from housing. Furthermore the sample who had left home were older than in other settings and overall lived in fewer places.

Evaluations[1]

The qualities of each setting were examined by a series of attitudinal statements. These referred to the overall evaluation of the hostel, the way the residents thought about themselves and the other residents and how they see the world. In terms of the experience of staying in a hostel 59% of hostel residents thought they were comfortable places. Sixty one per cent (61%) thought they could get a good night's sleep.

Social

These percentages decrease when the residents comment on the obviously social qualities of the hostel.

Forty four per cent (44%) of the hostel residents considered the social life to be good there, the second highest across the settings. Thirty eight per cent (38%) thought that generally people were proud of the place. Nearly half thought there was little group spirit, while 30% disagreed. Roughly equal percentages felt people helped each other as did not help. Over two thirds of the sample agreed people tended to hide their feelings. Over half disagreed that personal problems were openly talked about.

[1]See Appendix for details of the questionnaire used.

Table 6.24: Evaluation of qualities of the hostel

	% Agreement
Sleep	61
Only Way can Afford to live	61
Comfortable	59
Safe	59
Like it Here	51
Social Life	44
Do What I Want	37

Physical/Organisational

The highest percentage across the four settings agreed that hostels were comfortable (59%), and that one could get a good night's sleep there (61%). Half agreed they liked staying there. The physical aspects are evaluated highly by more of the sample than any other aspect and more than in any other setting. Closely linked to the physical aspects of hostel life, are the organisational aspects. When asked if they felt safe, 59% agreed they did, which was not as high as those in squats and hotels.

About half considered they could leave any time without saying where they were going, while 65% felt that those who broke the rules were punished for it, the highest across the settings. Sixty per cent (60%) thought it was well organised there, second highest to hotels. While 72% agreed that when someone broke a rule he knew what would happen.

Other aspects

Sixty one per cent (61%) felt living in hostels was the only way they could afford to live. Only just over a third (37%) felt they could do what they wanted.

Summary

In general the hostel sample tended to positively evaluate the physical aspects such as comfort and good sleep, and the social life but not the personal aspects such as independence.

Self esteem and view of other residents[2]

A series of statements relating to people's levels of self esteem were included in the questionnaire. In response to these statements, 43% felt they 'made a valuable contribution to society', while 58% disagreed they 'felt a failure'. Forty per cent (40%) considered the 'others there to be just like them', second lowest to hotels. When asked to consider the others in the hostel in general, the highest percentage agreed that they required some kind of support. Half thought they were generally 'able to return to society' and 'capable of change' and 'not a threat to themselves or to society'. Over a third didn't consider them to be 'normal people' and 'considered them to be physically or mentally ill'.

Expectations

Residents were asked to assess the importance of further aspects of home. The highest percentage of the hostel sample agreed that having their own room (87%) was important, followed by having a place of their own (79%) and somewhere cheap to live (79%).

Having the use of a kitchen was also considered important by 78% of the sample, and somewhere quiet by 77% (the highest percentage across the settings for this item). Of importance to fewer residents was having somewhere where friends could stay (68%) and living in London (58%).

[2] See the Appendix for a detailed account of the questionnaire.

Table 6.25: Percentage importance of aspects of home for hostel sample

Aspects	%
Own Room	87
Own Place	79
Cheap	79
Kitchen	78
Quiet	77
Friends	68
Decorate	61
London	58

Explaining their situation

Nearly half the residents agreed that they were 'stopped from finding somewhere to live by the shortage of housing in London' and that they've just been 'unlucky in finding somewhere to live'. Seventy six per cent (76%) agreed they were 'not too lazy to find somewhere to live'.

In terms of getting a job, 73% agreed they 'would work if offered a job', and 69% agreed that 'if they could just settle down they could get one'. Forty three per cent (43%) thought they had 'no luck in finding a job', while 44% agreed. Forty six per cent (46%) disagreed that they 'can't get a job because of a lack of skills'.

Table 6.26: Percentage agreement to locus of control for hostel sample

Aspect of Control	%
'Not lazy in finding somewhere to live'	76
'Would work if offered a job'	73
'If settled-would get a job'	69
'The shortage of housing stops me from finding somewhere to live'	47
'Lack of skills-stops me from getting a job'	46
'Unlucky in finding somewhere to live'	46
'No luck in getting a job'	43

Summary

Overall, the interesting aspects of these items are that most of the hostel residents do not think the others there are just like them, that they are different. This may be due to the finding that there is a wide range of people of different ages, and of different employment status. The other aspect to note is that hostel residents consider the use of a kitchen to be highly important.

Hostel staff

Staff and residents: A profile of differences

The focus on the differences in view of residents and staff emerges from the recognition that staff and residents have different roles within a hostel and therefore perceive their environment in different ways (cf. Canter 1977). These differences are fodder to the development of design ideas and solutions that are effective for staff and residents alike. Several sections of the questionnaire reveal interesting differences between residents and staff both in terms of how staff perceive residents to be and how they both perceive the hostel.

First attitudinal questionnaire

While much of the content of the first survey concerns demographic information, some attitudinal questions were included to begin the exploration of values and attitudes which formed the next stage of research. As part of the telephone survey, some attitudinal questions were posed to managers and staff of hostels on certain aspects of hostel life. These questions focused on the social and physical aspects of hostel life for staff and for residents. Two further questions were included which explored attitudes to homeless people in general. Eighty five hostel staff participated in telephone interviews which form the basis of the following discussion. The structure or mapping sentence used to construct the first four questions was:

The extent to which (x) agrees that		[social] [physical]	aspects of the
[hotel] [hostel]	help/hinder	[residents] [staff]	agrees -----> disagrees

where (x) is a member of staff of a London hostel/hotel.

These questions were put to hotel staff for comparison purposes. This is discussed in Chapter 9. Staff were simply asked to either agree or disagree which many did not find an easy task. It should be noted that there are some difficulties with asking attitudinal questions over the phone. The statements were sometimes reworded to clarify what was being asked of the hostel worker, which may of course lead to different responses. Furthermore the agree-disagree responses do not form a scale and so do not allow room for degrees of agreement. However, the results are still interesting indicato of particular attitudes among hostel staff which were followed up in the second survey.

The percentages as listed include those for agree, disagree and missing values, and also listed are the valid percentages which give the percentage agreement and disagreement of those who were described.

Table 6.27: Attitudes towards hostels

Question	Hostels (**sample 85**)	Valid
Q.1 This hostel is well designed for cleaning and supervision.	72% Agree 22% Disagree 6% Missing	(76%) (24%)

Q2. This hostel is a friendly place to work.	77% Agree 18% Disagree 5% Missing	(81%) (19%)
Q3. Residents have enough space (and privacy) to everyday needs.	58% Agree 39% Disagree 3% Missing	(60%) (40%)
Q4. This hostel is a sociable place where residents can get to know each other.	93% Agree 4% Disagree 3% Missing	(96%) (4%)
Q5. Homeless people are just normal people who have hit on hard times.	71% Agree 20% Disagree 9% Missing	(78%) (22%)
Q6. Homeless people could not find themselves somewhere to live if they wanted to.	88% Agree 5% Disagree 7% Missing	(95%) (5%)

Most hostel staff agreed with the statement that homeless people 'could not find themselves somewhere to live if they wanted to' (95% valid).

Table 6.28: Correlations between selected questions: Hostels

			Hostel
Q2. Q4.	Friendly Place to Work Sociable For Residents	))	.80
Q1. Q4.	Well Designed for Cleaning Sociable For Residents	))	-1.00
Q5. Q4.	Homeless People just Normal People Sociable For Residents	))	-1.00
Q1. Q6.	Well Designed For Cleaning Homeless people could not find themselves somewhere to live if they wanted to.	))	.22

Q5.	Homeless People Just Normal People	)	.46
Q6.	Homeless people could not find themselves somewhere to live if they wanted to.	)	

Table 6.16 presents the correlations between selected questions.

A perfect positive correlation is one which suggests that Q2 & Q4 are highly positively correlated at .80.

Several issues emerge from these results. There are difficulties staff face in terms of reconciling their views of the people they look after and the facility they work in. Staff have a work role in that they have various duties they must perform, and they also have a relationship with the residents as people and often these do not easily accord. For example, those staff who view residents as normal people, do not think the hostel is a sociable place for them. Furthermore, those who consider the hostel to be 'well designed for cleaning and supervision', do not think 'it is sociable for residents'. However on one level the two concur in that staff generally agreed that a 'friendly place to work' was also 'a place that was sociable for residents'. So on the social level at least the two roles complement each other.

A further example of this is provided by the finding that all (100%) of those who disagreed that homeless people 'could not find somewhere to live if they wanted to' (that is agreed that they could), agreed that it was a 'friendly place to work'.

Furthermore, of the 95% who agree the hostel 'is a sociable place for residents', 77.8% also agree that homeless people are 'normal people'. However all of those who disagree with the hostel being 'a sociable place' (5%) agree that homeless people are 'just normal people'. Eighty three per cent (83%) who agree homeless people are 'normal people who have hit on hard times', 85% thought it was a friendly place to work.

These findings could be interpreted as an example of cognitive dissonance (Festinger 1962), in that it seems that for staff to find the hostel a friendly place to work they have to think positively of the residents, or it may be that dealing with different types of residents has implications for how staff view their working life. Neither can be supported from these results as there can be no cause attributed from correlations or cross-tabulations.

These positive views tend to be consistent for example, of the 95% who agree that homeless people could not find somewhere, 77% of these think that homeless people are just normal people. Similarly, of the 80% who agree that homeless people could not find somewhere, 90.8% of these think that homeless people are just normal people.

Differences between types of hostel

There were some differences between types of hostel. The hostels which were focused on in the telephone survey, were emergency, traditional, short-stay and medium stay hostels. Table 6.17 shows the type of hostel in which staff agreed the most and the least with the statements presented describing particular qualities of the hostel.

Table 6.29: Attitudinal questionnaire: Differences between hostels

	Highest	Lowest
	Semi-Supportive	**Emergency**
Q.1 This hostel is well designed for cleaning and supervision.	81% Agree 15% Disagree 4% No response	62% Agree 38% Disagree
	Traditional	**Emergency**
Q2. This hostel is a friendly place to work.	95% Agree 5% Disagree	50% Agree 12% Disagree 38% No response
	Short-Stay	**Emergency**
Q3. Residents have enough space (and privacy) to everyday needs.	100% Agree 0% Disagree	25% Agree 75% Disagree
	Traditional	**Short-Stay**
Q4. This hostel is a sociable place where residents can get to know each other.	95% Agree 0% Disagree 5% No Response	67% Agree 33% Disagree 0% Missing
	Semi-Supportive	**Emergency**
Q5. Homeless people are just normal people who have hit on hard times.	85% Agree 11% Disagree 4% Missing	25% Agree 75% Disagree 0% Missing

	Emergency/Short	Traditional
Q6. Homeless people could not find themselves somewhere to live if they tried	100% Agree 0% Disagree 0% Missing	67% Agree 5% Disagree 28% Missing

Comparing these types of hostel in terms of whether or not staff agreed with the statement that homeless people are just normal people who have hit on hard times, it is clear that 75% of those in emergency hostels don't think so, while 85% of those in semi-supportive hostels do agree. This is a large difference highlighted by the fact that the second lowest percentage agreement is 50%.

More staff at traditional hostels think they are sociable places for residents (95%) than those in short-stay hostels (67%). Staff at traditional hostels (67%) did not agree as highly as those at emergency and short-stay hostels (100%) that homeless people could not find somewhere to live if they wanted to.

Few staff at emergency hostels thought that residents had enough space for their everyday needs (25%) compared to those at short stay hostels who all thought they had enough space (100%).

Half of them thought that their emergency hostel was a friendly place to work (50%) compared to short-stay hostels in which 95% thought their hostel was one.

Second survey

In the second survey 86 hostel staff completed a separate questionnaire to the residents. This questionnaire contained the same sub-sections as the resident one but asked staff to answer the items in different ways. Staff were asked to indicate how they thought the residents would answer the statements. In this way it is possible to compare how the views of residents and staff differ and to use this information in the development of models of hostel care.

Firstly however the staff sample can be discussed in terms of their background and general views of the residents.

The staff sample were both male and female with slightly more men in the sample (55% male). Forty four per cent (44%) were under the age of 30 years and over half were single (54%). The sample was selected across the organisation so that 42% were management, 36% auxiliary staff and 19% were care staff.

Most of the staff had worked in the hostel for more than six months (76%), with 29% of these being there for over two years. Seventy seven per cent (77%) of the sample were white Europeans and 12% were black. The majority (60%) were born in England with 7% born in Ireland. Their education was mixed also with 31% of the staff having degrees and 48% having either A levels or professional qualifications.

It is useful to compare their residential history with those of the hostel residents. Fifty six per cent (56%) of the staff sample had lived in 1 to 5 places in their lifetime whereas 65% of the sample of residents had lived in 10 or less places.

There were also differences in terms of how staff viewed the residents and how they imagined residents would evaluate the hostel and what might be important to them.

Firstly, in terms of how staff viewed the residents it is useful to compare them directly with how residents viewed other residents. Table 6.18 presents this comparison with percentage agreements to a series of statements reflecting a variety of therapeutic models, for example, a normalisation model which has a view of the person as normal and ordinary or the prosthetic model which has a view of the person as someone who needs support.

This compares favourably with the first survey in which 71% of the staff considered homeless people to be 'normal people who have hit on hard times'. From these findings it would appear that staff have a more positive view of residents than do the residents: more of the staff think of the residents as 'not a threat', normal people, able to change for the better, and able to go back into society. However more staff than residents considered that they require some kind of support. The staff may not have been as honest in their responses as the residents, or the staff may genuinely view the residents in a better light than each of the individual residents who after all have less choice in being there than the staff.

Table 6.30: View of residents by staff and residents

Statement	Staff	Hostel Residents
'Normal people'	63%	45%
'Not ill'	43%	40%
'Able to change for the better'	67%	50%
'Not a threat'	73%	48%
'Require some support'	90%	71%
'Able to go back into Society'	67%	51%

Locus of control

A further comparison of differing views of residents is provided by the locus of control section of statements illustrated in Table 6.31. These are the statements which are aimed to examine how people view the world and how they explain their situation. These have been generated on the basis of personal action, chance, external factors in relation to jobs and housing.

Table 6.31: Perceived control of residents' actions

Statement	Staff	Hostel Residents
'Unlucky in finding somewhere to live'.	35%	46%
'Too lazy to find somewhere to live'.	13%	14%
'Shortage of housing stops me finding somewhere to live'.	74%	47%
'Would work if offered a job'.	49%	74%
'Had no luck in finding a job'.	27%	43%
'A lack of skills stops me from getting a job'.	58%	44%
'If could settle down could get a job'.	62%	69%

For staff homeless people's inability to obtain work and housing were explained in terms 'of a lack of skills' (58%) and a 'general shortage of housing' (74%), whereas more residents would see it in terms of 'bad luck' (43%) and 'not being offered a job' (74%). Fewer staff (49%) think residents 'would work if offered a job than do residents' (74%).

Evaluation of hostel

Generally staff and residents had different views about the facilities as well, both in terms of their roles and the general organisational climate. These are presented in terms of a table of means, whose comparison across residents and staff were found to be statistically significant.

Table 6.32: Table of significance (T-test <0.05. 2 tail probability) means across staff and residents (1=strongly agree to 5=strongly disagree)

Item	Staff Mean	SD	Residents Mean	SD
Social Life	3.15	1.06	2.94	1.40
Do What I Want	3.48	1.07	3.16	3.16
Afford	2.49	1.10	2.44	1.41
Like It Here	2.43	1.05	2.83	1.42
Safe	2.06	0.91	2.51	1.35
Community	2.75	1.12	2.99	1.40

The staff means are generally higher than the residents for these items with greater variance for residents. This suggests that staff have a poorer view of residents' views of hostel life than do residents. Linking this with the previous discussion it seems that staff hold a more positive view of residents than do residents but consider that they are more critical of the hostel than they actually are. The exceptions to this are that residents in general feel less 'safe', less 'part of a community' and 'like staying there' less than staff think they do. In general staff consider the hostel to be 'more comfortable' and 'safer' to residents than do residents.

In terms of personal characteristics, there are further interesting differences between residents and staff's views. Table 6.33 compares further means which are significantly different.

Table 6.33: Self esteem of residents by staff and residents

Item	Staff Means	SD	Residents Means	SD
Community	2.75	1.11	2.99	1.40
Failure	3.08	1.11	3.63	1.44
Make Contribution	3.32	1.13	2.87	1.37

From these items, residents have a higher self-esteem than staff consider the residents think they have. In other words, residents are less hard on themselves than staff think they are, but staff think they feel part of a community more than they actually do.

In terms of what is important to residents, most staff were close in their assessment, but differed on the items shown in Table 6.34.

Table 6.34: Importance of home for residents

Item	Staff Means	Staff SD	Residents Means	Residents SD
Decorate	2.54	1.19	2.31	1.43
Own Place	1.73	0.99	1.79	1.26
Friends	2.12	1.08	2.14	1.40
London	2.09	0.93	2.40	1.41
Cheap	1.49	0.69	1.99	1.26

Staff consider that living in London is more important to residents than their responses suggest it actually is. In general, the staff underestimated how important these items were to residents.

Conclusions

There is as great a variety of staff as there is hostels. However there are some clear differences in their perspectives of the residents and those of the residents themselves. Staff and residents have different roles within a hostel, and this would suggest that they think of that environment in different ways. Staff tend to have a more positive view of the residents' than they do themselves. Perhaps this reflects an honesty in residents responses which is lacking in the staff's as they may have been wary about giving a poor impression. There is the hint of 'politically sound' responses on occasion and not entirely honest ones. However it may also be true to say that people are often more critical of their own situation and actions than observers and this may also go some way to explaining these differences.

Role of staff

Residents and staff were asked to evaluate staff's role in the hostels. Table 6.35 presents the means and standard deviations for these items. The significant items are marked with *.

Staff clearly see their role as one of providing practical advice, spiritual help and care and support, while residents see it more as caretaking the building, providing care and support and supervising the residents. Thus while 90% of staff think they are providing practical advice, just over half the residents agree.

Table 6.35: Role of staff in hostels. Significant (T-test <0.05. 2 tail probability) means across staff and residents (1=strongly agree to 5=strongly disagree).

Item	Staff Means	Staff SD	Residents Means	Residents SD
Provide care and support *	1.76	.63	2.28	1.26
Supervise *	2.59	1.06	2.57	1.29
Give housing advice	2.22	1.15	2.59	1.34
Caretake the building*	2.11	0.95	2.32	1.23
Offer practical help *	1.74	0.89	2.42	1.28
Give spiritual help	2.78	1.34	2.85	1.42

Both staff and residents were asked to consider these roles in terms of what 'should' be done. Table 6.35 presents these results.

Table 6.36: Desired role of staff in hostels. Significant* (T-test <0.05. 2 tail probability) means across staff and residents (1=strongly agree to 5=strongly disagree)

Item	Staff Means	Staff SD	Residents Means	Residents SD
Should provide care and support *	1.56	.78	1.96	1.08
Should supervise	2.55	1.24	2.49	1.27
Should give housing advice *	1.88	0.92	1.91	1.13
Should caretake the building	2.19	1.19	2.06	1.15
Should offer practical help *	1.53	0.75	1.86	0.99
Should give spiritual help	2.63	1.38	2.47	1.34

The desired role of staff is very similar for residents and staff with slightly less involvement desired by residents in general. Thus both share a view about how staff should be within a hostel setting, but the reality is perceived differently.

Conclusions from hostel survey

Overall, a number of important points emerge from the study of the experience of hostel residents and staff. Hostels are crowded, busy places, with virtually no spare capacity. They are in a situation in which it is difficult to improve and develop facilities except by building new hostels. This has been the general trend throughout the 1980's, to change from the general purpose, open access hostel to purpose built provision for special needs. Along the way this has greatly reduced the provision of open access accommodation.

The move towards more specialist facilities has probably also increased the variations in types of hostel available with the consequent variations in the type of people who are found in those hostels. Amongst this range it is clear that there are those for whom the hostel is experienced as a home and those for whom it is a direct reflection of their homelessness. The older, retired residents tend to be in the former category and the younger, active ones in the latter.

Across these range of experiences there does appear to be a broadly positive view of hostels combined with a reasonable positive self image held by residents in general. Certainly the picture of a very highly institutionalised set of facilities in which staff have an overbearing, paternalistic attitude towards residents is not borne out by these results. The only points of disquiet are that although staff's views of the residents are moderately optimistic, they still overestimate the help they give them and underestimate the residents' own desires to be independent.

The central message then, is the need to understand more fully the different types of provision that exist and how each of these types may be improved and developed.

7 Design and Development of Hostels

Approach to designs for therapeutic environments

Therapeutic environments can be any one of a range of facilities offering different levels of support. By exploring and evaluating a number of therapeutic environments and exploring the therapeutic models in use therein, design criteria have emerged which help to shape a wide range of different types of environments.

There have been many approaches to providing facilities for homeless people. Traditionally the Salvation Army and other organisations used converted warehouses which symbolised the passive help in crisis and custodial support role of the providing organisation. More recently there has been a move towards facilities which symbolise and facilitate individual development. While these models of therapeutic care have been discussed elsewhere (Canter and Canter 1979), it is important to mention them in that they serve to illustrate the many changes in the style, development and use of facilities for homeless people. This change is ongoing and necessary as homeless people themselves change and become more varied in their experiences and expectations.

There is a general movement away from institutional settings. Designs have reflected an emphasis on care and support. However what actually makes a building or a facility institutionalised is still unclear. Many have discussed the constituents of an institution, for example Goffman 1961, who painted a vivid picture of a total institution from the perspective of the 'inmates', and King, Raynes and Tizard (1971) who developed an institutional scale on which facilities can be placed. It seems it is not simply a matter of size or of regime, but is a combination of physical, social and organisational aspects.

Each model of therapeutic care has design implications which have been discussed by Canter and Canter (1979), by Oakley (1980) and Moore (1989). The 'social' models have been adopted by the Salvation Army in the design of facilities outside of London. It is important to note here that the key to the design theory or theme is the model of man adopted by the designer and the organisation and the goal of the facility. If the facility's aim is to provide a setting for personal development, and therefore that the user (homeless person) is capable of growth and development, there are clear design implications.

These are some general principles in the design of residential/ therapeutic environments which have emerged over the last ten years. Primarily there is a growing recognition in the importance of relating design to the particular goals of the organisation and the people who will use the facility as well as the activities that will go on there. This principle has its roots in the whole on environmental psychological approach to design, which is firstly, that goals/aims of the facility have to be made explicit and secondly, that the organisational structure and ideology has to be understood and accommodated in the design solution. The physical context both facilitates and symbolises the interactions which take place within it. Buildings are part of an organisational system and as such may help or hinder it in achieving its goals.

A Place Theory approach is used in this research, in which the individual's experience is considered within a particular physical and social context and is not solely a product of the society or determined by his or her own actions. A further consideration in the design of facilities is that people with different roles have different perspectives and conceptualisations of the environment. In this case there is thus the necessity to consider both the views of staff and residents, and on the larger level, the designer, policy makers, financiers and publicists.

Furthermore there is recognition that the organisation and designer have to share common models or goals for a facility if it is to operate as intended (Rivlin and Wolfe 1979, Moore 1989).

Thus in the development of design themes for new facilities, the research has involved the views of the residents and staff of hostels in London and other members of the Salvation Army organisation. This has integrated the study of therapeutic environments with the investigation into homelessness in London and in particular a detailed focus on hostels. This overall perspective has resulted in some general design themes for facilities which aim to help and support. Each of these will be discussed firstly in terms of some of the issues other studies have raised.

Size

Many recent studies have focused on the size of facilities, arguing that large facilities reduce the effectiveness of programmes (Ittelson 1974). It has been argued that as buildings grow larger it becomes more difficult to maintain them as 'strong programme' buildings where most of what happens is specified by explicit rules. However, further studies have suggested that size itself is not the issue, but some aspect of the organisational structure which size reflects (Mazis and Canter 1979).

It therefore appears to be the case, that the size of the facilities can vary but that with each size, there are organisational implications which must be acknowledged. In other words the size while neither intrinsically good nor bad, does have organisational implications. It is argued here that larger hostels, for example, are more suited to one kind of service than another. In the discussion of each type of facility, the issue of size will be further explored.

Location

Traditionally, many institutions were located away from the community. This symbolised the purpose of the facility, which was to remove the individual from society. The symbol of location should not be underestimated. Places have different meanings to people, and residents and staff will associate different things with particular locations. The chosen locations should reflect the different types of residents for which the facility is designed. Indications from the research were that different groups of people required different things from their location. Young people tended to see their centrality in the community as very important, that is, being close to shops, services, transport and facilities, whereas older people tended to care more about the internal features of the hostel and less exactly where it was situated. Each location of each type of facility would have to be carefully chosen in this respect.

Layout

The layout of older hospitals and other early institutions was blamed by many for creating an institutional atmosphere with long corridors in big, compact buildings. However there has been surprisingly little evaluation of layout per se. What has emerged is the approach to design outlined above, which stresses the importance of considering the variety of perspectives of those who will use the building, the goals of the organisation and the aim of the facility. In addition some general ingredients have been identified which are flexibility, variety and character.

In general, though, the most fruitful way of considering overall layout is whether it provides a formal hierarchical system of related spaces, thereby supporting a structured organisation, or whether the contact between spaces is more complex and network-like, supporting more informal, social forms of interactions. Different facilities will require different approaches to layout.

Any flexibility of a layout is only beneficial if used as such by the staff and residents: its varied use has to be an integral part of the organisation. If left to chance, it can be misused and thus have an unintended effect.

While the layout of the rooms, lounges, staff rooms and so on, have an important part to play in the functioning of a facility, perhaps the most important is the position of the kitchen.

The kitchen

Access to and position of the kitchen, has been found to be a major distinguisher between institutions and non-institutions. A number of authors, Gunzburg (1970) and Rivlin and Wolfe (1979), have pointed to the significance of the kitchen in an institutional setting (Mazis and Canter 1979).

In many institutional contexts, and generally always in domestic homes, the kitchen can be a stimulating and interesting place. Where a kitchen is placed can significantly influence the facility generally. If placed centrally it creates a different atmosphere than if placed in a separate building or far away. Mazis and Canter found that the kitchen being close to the living room facilities as in most homes, is a key factor in non-institutionalised facilities (Mazis and Canter 1979). One way of looking at this is in terms of the importance of the 'hearth'. The hearth with its associated ideas of food preparation, family gathering and warmth, signifies the domestic feel or the core of home and thus the kitchen and its location is very important. The position of the kitchen will be discussed for each type of facility.

Sleeping accommodation

Separate rooms have consistently been shown to provide the most supportive and satisfactory accommodation for the great majority of residents in institutions, with integral sanitation as a great additional benefit. For a small proportion, double rooms will have some advantages and so this type of provision should also be included.

Other non-institutional features

Mazis and Canter (1979) found a number of other features which were significant in the distinction between institutionalised and non-institutionalised settings. These were, after the kitchen, the number of people in and size of the sleeping areas; adequate toilet facilities and the ease of control over environmental elements. This fourth factor is perhaps one of the most important factors in the development of large facilities that are not at the same time institutions in the old sense. A facility in which the residents have some control and are not dependent upon the services, the heat and light and the position of the furniture for example, is less likely to be regarded as non-institutional. Also the interior quality is important in the form of the details: vivid colours, differentiation of decorations from one space to another, pictures and personal belongings.

Summary

Each type of facility has design suggestions and possibilities. However the overall approach would be to develop varied facilities in size, layout and design which had different distinguishing features. This variety reflects the many types of facilities found in the survey and in addition reflects the variety of homeless people in London.

A TYPOLOGY OF HOSTELS

General introduction

Hostels vary in terms of the views of the residents and their psychological characteristics. Each hostel has a different profile: the sample of residents are different and each hostel has a different 'feel'.

The views of the residents form an important part of evaluating the success of a facility. By exploring how 'satisfied' residents are with a range of aspects of hostel life, and comparing the average views for each hostel, it becomes possible to directly compare hostels in terms of the perceived service they provide to residents. The focus of the environmental psychology approach is on the experience of the individual and how that can be incorporated into the design process, in this instance, the discussion of types of future provision for homeless people in London. It is thus integral to this study that the views of residents be taken seriously and used to shape future provision.

Towards a typology of hostels

Organisational issues in the study of hostel life

This section explores the salient features of hostel organisation as considered by the residents of the facilities in the study. Thirty five items were selected from the questionnaire for discussion and analysis in this section (see Figure 7.1 for a list of these items). These items consist of the

MOOS Community Oriented Program Evaluation Scale (Moos 1974), a section of the Meaning of Home questionnaire and a section of the Perceived Role of Staff section. These items concern the organisation of the hostels.

Taking the questionnaire responses for residents from hostels, it was possible to establish the mean or average score for each facility. If a person agreed with a statement, they would have a score of '4' for that question, '5' if they strongly agreed, or '1' or '2' if they disagreed. In this way it was possible to compare these items in terms of how each facility responded to them.

Figure 7.1 lists the items used in this section and provides an illustration of a Smallest Space Analysis which shows their relationship (Lingoes 1973). The SSA inter-correlates every item with every other i.e. provides a measure of their relationship, and produces a spatial representation of this relationship (See Appendix for details). In this way the closer any two items are in space, the more highly correlated they are, that is, the stronger their relationship. For example, two items very close in this illustration are training (item 15) and spiritual help (item 34). This indicates that those respondents who tended to agree that training for new kinds of jobs is provided also agreed that the staff provide spiritual help. In other words these two items are positively correlated. Thus this SSA may be taken as a visual summary to the relationship between all these items for the resident sample across the hostels. It can be examined to reveal the major themes that distinguish between different hostels.

In examining the plot, three themes can be identified by the formation of three groupings. The first grouping, to the right of the plot, are items concerned with the running of the hostel, for example, 'staff here supervise residents', and 'people who break the rules are punished for it'. These items are mostly to do with order and organisation of the hostel. The second grouping on the left hand side of the plot contains items more to do with the other residents in the hostel and the general atmosphere:'there is group spirit here' and 'people here often help each other'. The central grouping of items on this side include 'I feel safe here', 'The social life is good here' and 'I can get a good night's sleep here'.

In examining this relationship, three constituents of hostel life emerged. Taking some items as examples and as the focus the three broad areas are marked A,B and C. The first constituent A is the central region of the plot and indicates the items which residents considered to be the greatest constituent of hostel life and contains items which refer to preferences. These items are important in that they show how residents see their current circumstances, whether or not they feel wanted or accepted in that place and how much they feel a part of the social group. These are seen to be the central issues to residents across the facilities.

The second constituent B consists of items to do with care of staff and group support. The emphasis in this aspect of hostel life is on the extent to

Figure 7.1: SSA of hostel evaluation

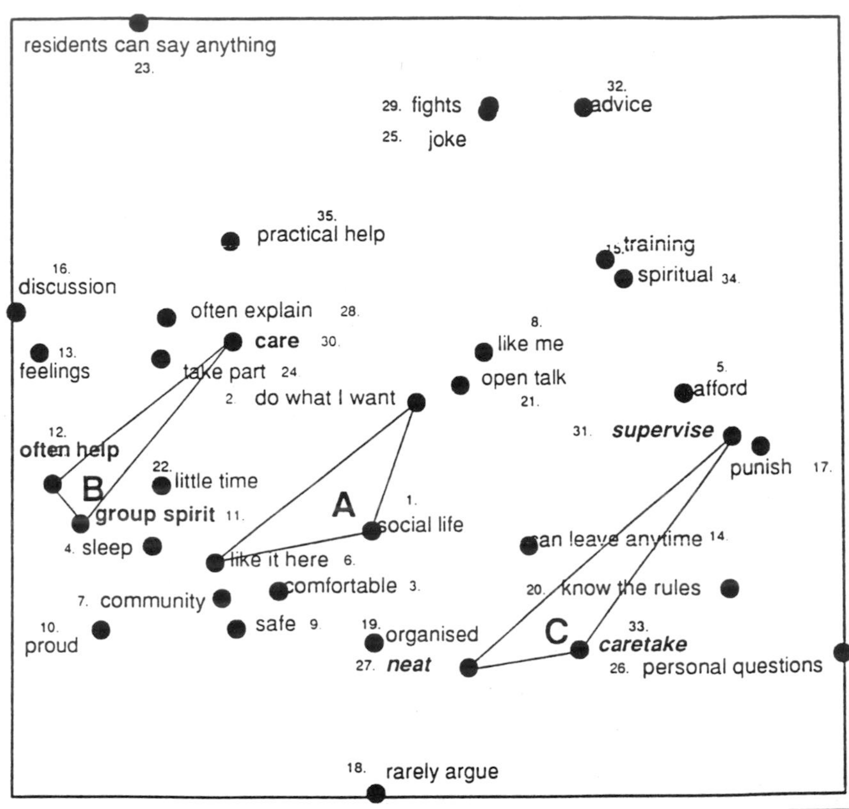

1. The social life is good here.
2. I can do what I want here.
3. I think this is a comfortable place to be in.
4. I can get a good night's sleep here.
5. Being here is the only way I can afford to live.
6. Overall I like staying here.
7. I feel part of a community living here.
8. The people here are just like me.
9. I feel safe here.
10. Generally people here are very proud of this place.
11. There is group spirit here.
12. People here often help each other.
13. The people here do not hide their feelings for one another.
14. The people here can leave anytime without saying where they are going.
15. Training for new kinds of jobs is highlighted here.
16. There is discussion about what people will do after they leave here.
17. People who break the rules are punished for it.
18. The people here rarely argue.
19. It's well organised here.
20. If someone breaks a rule he knows what will happen.
21. Personal problems are openly talked about.
22. Staff have little time to encourage residents.
23. Residents say anything they want to the staff.
24. Residents are expected to take part in things here.
25. Residents often criticise or joke about the staff.
26. Residents are rarely asked personal questions by the staff.
27. The staff make sure this place is always neat.
28. Staff often give an explanation about what this place is all about.
29. If someone fights with someone else here he won't get into real trouble with the staff.
30. Staff here provide care and support to residents.
31. Staff here supervise residents.
32. Staff here offer a housing advice service.
33. Staff here caretake the building.
34. Staff here provide spiritual help to residents.
35. Staff here offer practical advice.

which residents are helpful and supportive to each other and how supportive the staff is towards the residents.

The third constituent C comprises supervision and order primarily. These items are to do with the role of staff being to maintain order and how the place looks.

These three themes would seem to distil the essence of residents' views of the places in which they were staying at the time of interview. Thus together they provide the main points of the profiles which characterise hostels in general.

Differences between the hostels

Taking these three constituents of hostel life, the question arises, can the hostels be characterised in terms of how strongly the average sample of residents for each hostel agreed they were present? Are some hostels more concerned with supervision and control than with providing care and support, or is there more group spirit than supervision?

In order to explore how these three constituents vary across facilities, a Partial Order Scalogram Analysis was carried out on the nine items which typified each of the groups, A,B and C (see Appendix for details).

The POSA takes the profile of responses for each hostel and organises them in an order from highest to lowest. In this case, the highest number a hostel could score was 4 (high average agreement with an item) and the lowest 1 (low average agreement with an item), thus a high profile across the nine items would be 444334434 and a low profile would be 11221121. The analysis puts these profiles in order from the highest to the lowest and in this way can illustrate the differences between hostels in terms of their overall profiles across these items (the total score across these 9 items). In addition to this order from highest to lowest total score, the analysis looks at a further order or scale, one in which each profile has the same overall score (is quantitatively the same) but has higher scores for some items and lower for others. Figure 7.2 is thus an illustration of all the hostels in terms of how they score on these items.

Figure 7.2: POSA of hostels

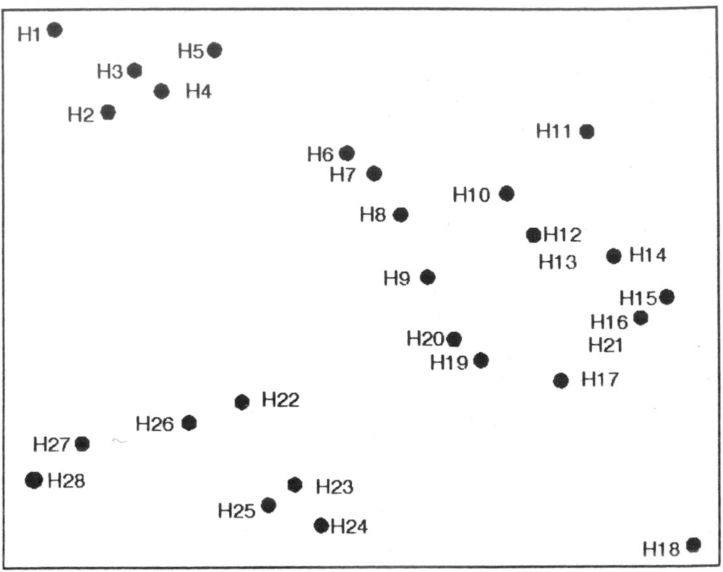

To take an example, H11 is at the top right hand corner of the plot. It has a profile of 323344444 which means that on average the residents strongly agreed with each of these items. This places H11 highest overall. On the other hand, H28 for example, has a score of 111121322 which places it at the bottom left of this plot. On average therefore the residents gave the hostel a low score on these items. Thus from top right to bottom left lies an ordering from highest to lowest profile for these items. Thus the hostels that fall along this diagonal/axis can be seen to be high or low overall. The items which are particularly high on the top of this axis and low at the bottom are overall I like staying here; the social life is good here and I can do what I want here: the constituent labelled A on Figure 7.3.

Another example is H1 which has a profile of 434442422 which places it at the top left of the plot, while H18 is to be found at the bottom right with a profile of 433224444. This indicates that both hostels have the same overall quantitative score (4+3+3+2+2+4+4+4+4) but each hostel had a different emphasis i.e. the hostels differ qualitatively. H1 scores higher on the items to do with group spirit and care and support than does H18 which scores higher on items to do with supervision and order, but both hostels score the same overall. Thus a second diagonal/axis can be drawn from hostels high on supervision and low on group spirit to those high on group

Figure 7.3: Typology of hostels

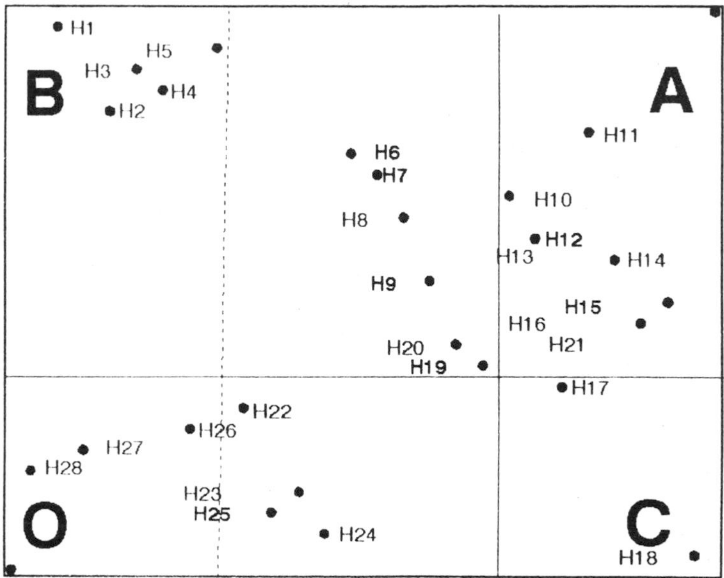

spirit and low on supervision. In this way there is a quantitative *and* a different qualitative sequence across the plot.

Framework for a typology of hostels

Types

Figure 7.3 is a proposed model of the relationship between the hostels found in Figure 7.2. It is only a framework for an emerging typology and therefore contains aspects which need to be further explored and developed. However as a framework, it presents a fruitful way of discussing the differences between hostels.

This figure represents a typology of hostels based on the average views of the sample of residents in each hostel. It is argued here that A, B and C
may be considered to be successful types of facility based on this criteria, that is they score highly on one or all of the three constituents. Within Type B there is a strong sub-section of hostels which will be discussed separately. Type O scores low on all criteria. There is a range within each type to include those hostels which are also pulling in the direction of

another type. For example within Type A is one facility which is fully a member of that type and three which are pulling towards Type C. In this way the hostels can be discussed within this framework.

Properties of types

This model presents four distinguishable types of hostels. Although not totally discrete they do offer a way of discussing the hostels in terms of their strengths and weaknesses. Each type has particular features or properties which contribute to its position on the plot. This section will focus on the general properties of hostels within each type, taking into consideration additional information on both the facility and the resident population. The facilities will be discussed in terms of their size, organisational and management style while the resident sample will be discussed in terms of their average self esteem, health scores and how they view the other residents in their hostel.

Facilities

Size and levels of access

Figure 7.4 is an illustration of the POSA of hostels with an indication of their size. The Type B hostels are all hostels with less than 40 beds, while Type A, C and O hostels are on the whole, large facilities as an indicator of the access and privileges within a facility. Figure 7.4 shows that most of the hostels which have these three things are Type B hostels. This indicates that this group is quite a distinct one and shares a number of common features considering curfew, no kitchen access and no visitors being allowed in a resident's room.

Other organisational aspects:

A number of other aspects were explored to see whether or not they contributed to the typology in any way but were found to spread across all types. These were direct access or not, levels of staffing, whether they have their own move-on accommodation or access to some within the local borough and whether the hostel offers single rooms, a variety of rooms or dormitories. Thus these do not seem part of the defining features for each type.

Residents

To describe the average of each sample of residents, some of the psychological attributes were taken from the survey (see Appendix for details of questionnaire sections).

Figure 7.4: Size of and access to hostels

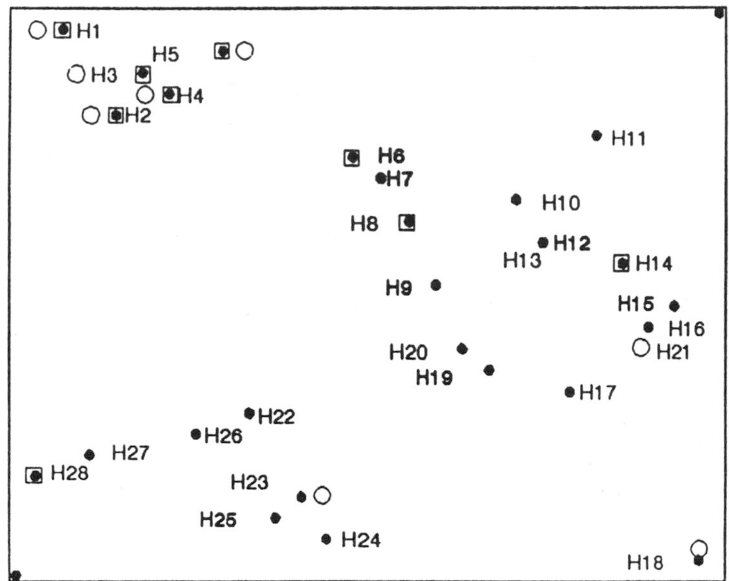

Hostels marked with □ are hostels with less than 40 beds.
Hostels marked with ○ are hostels which allow visitors around the hostel, allow access to kitchen and do not have a curfew.

In addition to these three psychological aspects, there is the concept of control. Focusing on the axis from B to C, that is from group spirit to supervision, it is possible to consider this as an axis from maximum personal control to maximum external control. In this way hostels which score highly on supervision may be considered to be high on external control and hostels which score highly on group spirit may be considered to be high on personal control. This builds on the properties of Type B in that as well as some high self esteem and good health the residents may also feel in control.

It is important to stress here that these cannot be explored independently of the hostels. The good health of Type B hostel residents and low in Type O hostels may be a reflection of the admission policies of the hostels. It may be that residents with a high self esteem and good health form a more positive view of their environment than those who do not. This suggests a hostel which offers a supportive environment will sustain individuals with a positive view of themselves and not have a negative effect. It is bound to be the case that there is an interaction between the person and the environment and that the psychological characteristics of residents interact with the type of provision. The important thing is to match individuals with facilities more effectively.

Summary for each type

This typology has been developed from the questionnaires received from residents from 28 facilities in London. The information gathered indicates that there are broadly four types of facilities. There are three which are essentially good practice and one type which includes hostels not evaluated positively on any of the criteria presented to residents.

The types could form part of an integrated system of hostel accommodation in London. On its own one particular type can only satisfy the needs or respond to one group of homeless people. This is a development of a range of facilities which complement each other in terms of the service they provide, so that residents have a choice and the co-ordinators have a choice in where they place people. Though these types differ in their particular characteristics they share basic elements.

1. They are all varying forms of temporary accommodation or in some instances, transitional housing, that is they should be designed to accommodate people only on a short to medium-term level.

2. There is movement between types and out of the system to more permanent accommodation.

3. There should be high levels of staff care in all types which should take various forms and styles.

4. In terms of design, there should be individual rooms available to all with some shared accommodation if desired.

5. It should be possible to obtain a good night's sleep, some privacy, a wash and food: the basic necessities in any facility.

6. All types should have a standard level of comfort and basic characteristics such as a varied style.

7. Whatever the rules in each facility, they should be made explicit and be clearly understood by staff and residents.

Type A

Type A is divided into A1 and A2. These types of facility are similar on all variables but cater for different groups of residents and therefore have some different organisational aspects. The discussion of Type A facilities will therefore include both A1 and A2. Type A hostels were those which residents evaluated as places where the social life was good, they could do what they want there, there was supervision, care and support: all nine issues within the satisfaction questionnaire were considered present in these hostels.

There were few facilities in this type and it may be that being positively scored on all aspects of hostel life is not normally possible. This becomes clear when you consider that an emphasis on supervision and control may reduce an emphasis on group spirit and residents helping each other.

In addition to these constituents, other aspects of Type A facilities were revealed. These facilities are mostly large hostels (greater than 40 beds), they do not allow complete access to visitors and there is little access to the kitchen.

The residents of these facilities were on average, middle aged to young adults with one exception of a facility which caters for older residents. The residents on average had very high self esteem, a positive view of the other residents in the hostel and had a high overall evaluation of the hostel as a place which had social, physical and personal aspects of home.

There is only one hostel which is a distinct member of Type A. This hostel scores positively on all items. It is a large hostel and has many common features to the other hostels in A and C. It caters for a very specific group. The other hostels in A are generally large, with high self esteem.

Type A is divided into A1 and A2. These types of facility are the same on all levels but cater for different groups of residents and therefore have some different organisational aspects.

Type A1

The positive qualities of Type A facilities can be summarised in the form of broad recommendations.

Size

This type of facility should be large to medium in size. This particular size would allow for a YMCA feel to the facility: a roomy, busy, organised facility.

Services

A range of services should be available, and these should be well publicised. The key to this type of facility is that information should be freely available and on offer, but that an individual can choose not to make use of these services and still stay. This facility should be a short to medium length of stay. Kitchens should be available for use and there should be a restaurant service in addition.

Staff

From the residents' perspective they are places in which the staff have time for the residents but rarely ask personal questions. Staff should be available and around at fixed times (not necessarily live-in). Staff would have a caretaking role and a care and support role, providing help when requested.

Design suggestions

These facilities should be comfortable, large places with single rooms and shared spaces.

Layout

This type of facility should have clusters of rooms with lounges and shared spaces. The staff rooms should be quite central and accessible to all. Kitchens should be available, but there should also be a restaurant service. This type of facility would need a main reception area.

Location

There is no particular need for this type of facility to be in central London.

People

This group of people should be more diverse than in B. They are mostly individuals who are still in the workforce or if not, should be encouraged to return.

Type A2

This type should be very similar in design and layout to type A1. The organisation should be similar. The difference for Type A2 is that it should be targeted at those people out of the workforce permanently: the elderly and invalid/ill (but who do not require high levels of care). There would be activities on offer though highly structured and open to all. They should be aimed more at the older age group and at people without other support networks.

Type B

Type B facilities were hostels which were well liked as places to stay overall, and had a particular emphasis on group spirit, residents helping each other and the care and support of staff. There was little emphasis placed on supervision and order.

A range of facilities were in this type, some more clearly Type B's than others. These hostels were all small facilities, had kitchen facilities which residents were allowed access to, allowed visitors around the hostel and did not operate a curfew. These hostels shared a community feel about them, in which residents tended to cook for the group. There was a great reliance on peer support. Staff were not so obviously present as 'staff' but generally tended to live in and act as live-in workers.

There were facilities in this type whose residents had both high and low levels of self esteem, that is, there was a mixture of facilities whose average esteem varied from high to low. All facilities had on average residents who had a positive view of the other residents and who had generally high (positive) health scores. This type of facility had on average the highest evaluation of residents of the homelike aspects of the hostel, and also had the highest levels of aspirations, that is, residents in this type on average considered a range of items to do with aspects of home to be important. This indicates that these residents aspired to more than those residents who scored low on this aspect.

The grouping of hostels in the top left of the plot, the sub-section of Type B are all small hostels, with less than 40 residents. They offer a range of services including, follow-on accommodation, kitchen facilities, have no visitor restrictions and do not operate a curfew. This type consists of hostels which score highly on group spirit and care and support. The social life is good and residents believed they could do what they want there. In addition the sample of residents are not apparently suffering from any mental health problems. The three other hostels in Type B share the same properties but share some similarities with Type C, that is, they are concerned with supervision and order more than the other members of Type B. Overall Type B hostels seem to be small, caring places with strong group and staff support.

In terms of general recommendations the strengths of Type B facilities can be summarised as follows:

Size

Type B facilities should be small facilities, less than 40 beds. This small scale should help create a domestic feel to the places.

Services

As small places, Type B's should have a central shared kitchen and living room. Group and self catering should be encouraged. Residents should be able to come and go as they please and have their own key. The facility should be aimed at providing for people for a medium length of stay.

Staff

There should be minimum direct supervision by staff but rather, constant and informal staff presence. There should be a recognition that all the people in the group need support and help. Staff should have a care and support role. Residents should be encouraged to support each other and a sense of community should be developed.

Design suggestions

This facility should have a very domestic theme with individual rooms and varied interiors. It should have lots of shared space and if possible, a garden.

Layout

The size of this facility should allow for a domestic arrangement with kitchen as the hearth; the centre. There should be a small office for staff and a small reception area.

Location

This type of facility should not be in central London but should be quite close. It should be close to mainline travel and other general facilities such as shops and recreation.

People

The people in this group should be as homogeneous as possible: eg. young people or street people. While this type of facility does provide medium levels of care, it is important that the residents can exercise some degree of independence.

Type C

Type C facilities were hostels where the residents evaluated them as places they like staying in; places concerned with supervision, less with group spirit and residents helping each other. These hostels were some of the largest facilities on the whole, with basic accommodation and services. The supervision, building caretaking role of staff was emphasised by residents as was the good social life.

The residents tended to have low self esteem, and generally low health scores and a poor view of the other residents. These facilities offered a basic service to a mixed group of people. They tended to have low levels of aspirations and generally evaluated the facility as not having any homely aspects.

There is one hostel in Type C which has more of the properties of this type than the others. It is concerned with supervision and neatness. This high scoring on supervision and order is matched with quite high scoring on 'liking it here' and 'social life'. Other hostels of this type share these properties but are pulled towards being all-rounders, that is towards Type A and to some extent towards Type B. The residents seem to have even incidence of good health and mental stress and a mixture of low and high self esteem. This type of hostel is no less caring than Type B but the emphasis is on supervision and order.

If such facilities are to be provided their strengths would lie in the following points:

Size

Type C facilities should be direct access emergency accommodation. The size of this type may vary. This type of provision may be most effective sub-divided into a number of small (ten beds) units which would be attached to other types of facility. In addition there may be separate Type C facilities on their own. This type should however, be organised as one large facility which happens to be physically located in different places. Each of these units would be separate from the rest of the facility to which it is attached, and should be managed accordingly.

Services

This type of facility should be a set of busy and active places. They should be well organised and neat and should work on the basis of being a short stay facility where help is available if needed. People should be moved on from here in a short space of time. The services of the facility to which this type is attached should be available to these residents, including a restaurant service.

Staff

Staff should have a mainly supervisory role, but should also offer care and support. The monitoring and communication between units would be very important for this type of facility.

Design suggestions

This facility as discussed already in terms of size, should provide basic, comfortable accommodation for a short stay. The accommodation should be both individual rooms and some shared rooms. This type of facility would vary in the amount of autonomy it would have, some being separate distinct buildings, while others being attached to other facilities.

Layout

The layout type may vary, however there should be some communal areas, some access to a kitchen, and in particular ample office accommodation to interview and assess incoming residents.

People

The people who are in this type of hostel are the most diverse, requiring a first step in the housing system. Their diversity makes the supervisory role of staff very important.

Location

This type of facility would seem to be best located in central London.

Type O

This type of hostel scored low on all items and may be considered to be unsuccessful. There is a range within this type from those hostels which are clearly Type O's to those which are similar to A B and C types. Generally the hostels are large facilities with low levels of access. The resident sample on average has low self esteem, low health scores indicating mental stress and a low view of the other residents in the hostel. The hostels of this type include a range of facilities which have particular features the other hostels do not have such as catering for people in care or those on probation. These particular features and roles necessitate caution in making recommendations. For example, it might be unfair to expect a probation hostel to be well liked as a place to stay.

This type of facility tended to score low on all items evaluated by the residents. There was a range within this type from those hostels which were clearly Type O's and had no apparent redeeming features and those which were borderline B's and C's.

Generally the hostels were some of the largest facilities in the sample and offered very basic accommodation and services. There was no access to the kitchen, little access to visitors and they operated a curfew. The most agreed feature of Type O's was the possibility of getting a good night's sleep.

The residents generally have low self esteem, low health scores and tended to have a negative view of the other residents. The staff did not seem to have any apparent role to the residents, nor did the residents seem to support each other or have group spirit. These were facilities which would benefit from change. In comparing these with Type C's and B's it seems that what differentiates between them is that in the other types there is a generally higher level of appraisal by residents across all the items, that is the hostels are scored better across all the items, and in addition, there is some particular emphasis which makes B's and C's shine, for example supervision.

There is clearly a factor which is important and that is the residents in type O facilities. They seem to score the lowest across most aspects. It may be that these facilities have to cope with a particularly demanding range of residents. This is important to consider, as any approach to an integrated system requires careful assessment selection of clients. By targeting a facility towards the particular needs of some group, rather than one facility taking the people which no other organisation will take, there is a detrimental effect on the clients as they do not get the specific help they require, on the staff and management who have to be all things to all people, and on the organisation who may not be able to develop strategies to cope with this group or find ways to change the situation.

Placing facilities

It is impossible for any one facility to be a type A, B and C at the same time. It may be desirable to focus on one type and shape the facility to move in that direction. In focusing on the successful hostels, those which fit into one of the three types, two strong features emerge.

Firstly, the hostels which form strong members of a type for example, H11 target a specific group of individuals who by and large form a fairly homogeneous group. The success of H1 may also reflect the consistent type of person the project accepts. This homogeneity may be a key factor to having a successful facility. This homogeneity can be developed on the basis of many characteristics. The examples provided by the hostels here such as age, nationality or on the basis of some psychological characteristics including health or self esteem may be just the starting point.

Secondly, to have a clear role within this framework, that is to be identifiable as one type of facility with a strong direction, helping to clarify the goals of the facility and thus target more effectively a particular section of the homeless population. The benefits of having clearly defined goals and directions in the design of hostels has been discussed elsewhere

(Oakley 1980 and Moore 1989) and accords with the general management principles that clear objectives are essential to effective management.

The framework outlined here can also be used by existing hostel management to help them clarify and focus their goals and models. For example, the peripheral members of Types A, B and C are places which can move towards a more clearly defined type of provision. H19 and H20 could move towards becoming Type C hostels which may be large, but they can be run effectively by focusing on what they do best, which is providing short-term accommodation with minimum support, but supervised, where people are looked-after. By providing the follow-on accommodation to make this possible, these hostels could have a strong and important role to play in the general framework.

Type B hostels provide care and support on a small scale and cater for specific groups. Hostels such as H6 and H7 could move further in this direction and thus become more effective. It may be that by focusing too much on supervision and order these hostels are hindering the move into being a distinct Type B.

H27 would seem to require a major change in direction on every aspect. In the exploration of why H21 is a Type O, it became clear that the sample of residents responded in a very diverse way. It may be that by housing a homogeneous group the hostel could move in a clear direction towards A,B or C.

Types of programme provision

Each type of facility provides a particular range of services. However although the range of programmes should be available to all, a framework for assignment of people to programmes needs to be developed and monitored. Four areas of help have emerged from our studies as significant:

Employment

Links should be developed between the local Job Centres and the facilities to encourage people to make contact. In addition, information on benefits and allowances should be provided.

Housing

There should be frequently updated information available to all, on the range of agencies and what they offer as well as their referral procedure and entrance requirements. In some instances this information is left for day centres to provide. From our survey, 64% of hostel residents never use day centres. Thus to provide this range of information to residents where they are staying ensures they can take advantage of it.

Counselling and interpersonal skills

A range of counselling, social programmes that focus on helping residents 'change' particular aspects of behaviour, social problems, alcohol and substance abuse would be of value in many hostels.

As revealed from our survey, there is a range of people who become homeless who have different levels of self esteem and health. These people should be offered basic guidance and help in whatever type of facility they are accommodated. Clearly in addition to this general help, specific programmes should be developed for particular facilities.

Domestic and financial skills

A range of courses would be available on general domestic, social and financial skills, offering money guidance courses, interpersonal skills, cooking, cleaning, and returning to the workforce.

While our research did not focus directly on the levels of interpersonal and domestic skills homeless people have, many expressed their need for help in learning how to manage their finances and develop domestic skills. Many men in particular who have left their family home are not equipped to cope with the running of their own home. These courses should be offered to all.

Implications for resident selection and staff training

A framework has been proposed which uses the views of residents to differentiate between facilities. In this way it draws attention to the successful features of hostels and some of the weaknesses. Clearly it is intended to focus discussion and identify possible directions and not be used as a league table of hostels. What is most striking from this information is that both large and small hostels can be equally liked by residents. This adds weight to the argument that there is need for a range of provision targeting different groups and with different management styles. The indications from successful facilities in each type, are that a main ingredient for success is to select homogeneous groups for each facility. These may be similar in terms of a number of different criteria: age, employment status, health, and coping skills. By targeting a particular group the facility can provide a focused service, and can manage the facility with greater ease and more direct help. Residents would be selected in this way from the general pool of homeless people who would flow through the direct access emergency provisions. This system would work, depending on the flow of people through the system, being able to offer a range of facilities to an individual and on the co-operation between the other agencies and facilities in London.

It is very important not only to develop design theories and goals and aims of facilities, but that staff share these aims and are equipped to help carry these through. A number of studies have demonstrated that even with clear design goals and carefully researched buildings, unless the staff share the same therapeutic models as the designer the result will be not be effective (Rivlin and Wolfe 1979, Moore 1989).

Each type of facility has particular requirements. While these are directed largely at managers, all staff should share a common approach and a common goal for the facility.

Type A facilities should have staff and management that can adopt a caretaking role and a care and support role. They should therefore have these appropriate skills, while not having a strong supervisory role.

Type B facilities demand a more integrating and participatory role of staff in that they should be capable of fitting into and creating a community in the facility.

Type C facilities require a strong supervisory role from staff, while obviously still providing care and support to residents.

Management and monitoring of facilities

Proper management of the system is vital if the various types of facilities are to be effective. A central body should manage the flow of people through the system, so that whatever type of facility a person is in, their movement through will be carefully monitored.

It is proposed that a general management and support committee is created to facilitate and monitor the changes and movements in people. This committee should oversee the following functions, possibly with at least one person for each function:

1. Employment opportunities for hostel residents.
2. Move on accommodation.
3. Counselling and personal skills programmes.
4. Domestic and financial skills programmes.
5. Monitoring of hostel utilisation and the throughput of people.

Each type of facility has particular roles for staff and management which have been already discussed. Drake et al (1987) produced a report on the management of hostels which was aimed at those providing accommodation for single homeless people. It covers key issues in management such as, defining realistic goals, the relationship between worker and resident, stress, the need for clear referral criteria, rules and regulations and resident participation. Generally the system's rules and procedures for referral and selection of residents should be clearly defined. The goals for each type of provision should be made explicit and form an integral part of deciding the approach of management to that type of hostel.

Once established, the system of facilities would need constant monitoring. The system should be a flexible evolving network of facilities which develop from constant feedback from the hostels' performance. Criteria should be agreed upon by which to measure each facility's success. In parallel, the progress of each resident should be monitored and there should be regular communication between the central strategic management and the hostel management. The management and support committee would also enable the system of hostels to help each other directly.

Management of the facilities should be easier and more effective than possible at present. Each type of facility has clear objectives and also the residents would be more homogeneous. This would enable managers to manage the staff and residents more directly and more effectively.

The need for follow on accommodation

The success of the proposed system is dependent on the availability of more permanent accommodation. Residents should see a system that facilitates their progression to independent housing or sheltered accommodation and not one which shelters them in unsuitable facilities indefinitely. There is general agreement within the field of homelessness that more long-term accommodation is badly needed for many homeless people. Often the efforts of such organisations are frustrated by the fact that though they may provide excellent short stay accommodation, their hostels are being used as long stay housing, and as such are unsuccessful. If a facility is designed and managed as a short stay facility it must be allowed to act as such or it becomes inefficient.

The provision of move on accommodation should take two forms. Firstly, the development of independent flats in which people take up tenancy agreements and live independently. Secondly, there should be a range of sheltered accommodation in which people who do not feel they can live independently can find a more permanent base, but can also find assistance if required. The development of these two types of accommodation in addition to the proposed system of hostels would seem to be an effective strategy for the provision for homeless people in London as in any large city.

The examination of a variety of hostels has been valuable in identifying the broad types of hostel that exist. This identification has shown that there is one group, large general purpose hostels, that are broadly unsuccessful in psychological terms. Most of these are the older facilities that are now being closed down and replaced with very different types of provision.

The success of the three other, very different types of provision is an important finding. It shows that the general government policy of making facilities for homeless people more clearly targeted to specific needs has much to recommend it. However, some of those needs include single people in crisis who have no other obvious vulnerability. This need is provided for at present, quite well in certain types of facility and it is important that it is not lost with increasing specialisation of provision.

The different types of successful hostel do complement each other. There is no one kind of hostel that all should aim to be. Cities like London need an integrated range of provisions that can help the wide variety of people who find themselves homeless.

8 Squatting in London

Introduction

This chapter draws together the findings of the research into single homelessness in London as they relate to the characteristics of squatters. It describes the personal background of squatters, their biographical history, their evaluation of places in which they have lived. It further explores their perception of hostels, workers and themselves, as well as the aspects of home they consider important. In the final study, squatters formed just under 10% of the overall sample of 531 homeless people.

Despite the fact that there has been, at times, a high level of media interest in squatters, little research has been carried out. There may be a number of possible reasons for this, primarily its semi-illegal nature may place the participants upon the fringes of society and official organizations may be reluctant to co-operate in anything they see as legitimising it. Furthermore squatters may be suspicious of research as they fear the information will be given to the authorities. In addition, many individual squatters stay in one situation only for a short time before moving to another location either voluntarily or through legal action. The basic problem in studying squatting, though, is its essentially informal nature which makes the identification and questioning of squatters a difficult and time-consuming process.

There is no one definition of 'squatting' and the degree of its legality varies from the criminal, when forced entry has been obtained to live in a briefly vacant property and any available services used without payment through to the quasi-legal situation of people being given keys to an empty house on the understanding that they have no tenure. The present study covers the less criminal end of this range. There is, a dearth of literature on squatting and what is available consists mostly of newspaper and magazine articles. Out of 70 references in a recent bibliography, no less than 54 consist of magazine or newspaper articles. This source dried up after the mid 1970's until recently. About a dozen other references are concerned with specialised topics such as squatting and the law. 'Underground' and anarchist magazines defend squatters and present a political account of the activity. The main work on squatting is Bailey (1973) which describes the radical squatting movement of the 1960's. Another work from the same period is Wates; (1976). It is an account of a group of community associations, tenants' groups, students and squatters who opposed schemes for redevelopment in North London. It has one chapter on squatters' involvement with the opposition against the redevelopment scheme, but gives very little information regarding their way of life. More recently there was a section on squatting in 'Access to Housing' published by the London Research Centre in 1988, but this provided little more than an estimate of the number of squats and squatters and some basic information about them. One publication which should not be ignored is the Squatters Handbook which states the legal position of squatters, provides advice to the squatters and generally encourages people to this form of self help.

Number of squatters and squatted properties

The London Housing Survey (London Research Centre 1986/87) suggested that up to 40% of squatted dwellings were owned by other than local authorities while an unpublished study on the Docklands area suggested that the percentage was even higher. Three figures have been quoted for the total number of people squatting in Greater London, figures of 30,000 by the Advisory Service for Squatters (ASS 1987), and 40,000 in 1990. The London Research Centre gave an estimate of 12,500 1986/7. However calculating the number of people squatting is fraught with difficulties for a number of reasons: lack of reliable data; mobility of squatters; squatters' reluctance to give information and political embarrassment.

1. The lack of reliable data

The only official figures are the Housing Investment Programme (HIP) Returns which gives the number of each London Local Authority (LA) properties that are squatted. Some LA Housing Departments indicate, informally, that they could be an underestimation by as much as 30%. The criteria for inclusion in the returns are not always the same. One Local Authority apparently deletes the property from the list as soon as it obtains a court order but another one will wait until it has evicted the squatters before excluding it and in addition there is a lapse of times before the Local Authority becomes aware of a property being squatted and this will vary from Local Authority to Local Authority.

2. Mobility of squatters

Because of the precarious nature of squatting many squatters are highly mobile and on eviction will move from one squat to another or stay with friends in other squats for a short while.

3. Squatters' reluctance to give information

Considerable suspicion was encountered from some squatters during the field work although the suspicion decreased in some cases as the research progressed. There was a desire to know the purpose the answers were being used for and on more than one occasion the question was asked whether information would be given to the Local Authority concerned. Squatters argued that universities were part of the 'establishment' and therefore would be likely to distort any information given. Thus there was often an unwillingness to give details of other squats and whilst some squatters co-operated in completing questionnaires others refused to do so. In about one quarter of the visits to squats it was made clear that the author was unwelcome and no further visit was made, although on the opposite end several visits were made to some squats and in one case the squat became a base from which further work could be carried out. Government, Local Authorities, and even some Voluntary organisations, have painted squatting in as bad a light as possible and that few squatters, want to assist the Local Authority in finding out details of the squats. Squatters are generally portrayed by the authorities as 'vandals' 'layabouts' 'freeloaders' 'criminals'. As will be seen, while some squatters fit the popular image, many others are ordinary people requiring somewhere to live and willing to carry out improvements and repairs to their properties. Squatting has recently been made a criminal offence.

4. Political embarrassment

Squatting has a high political profile and there can be political embarrassment if the number of squatted properties is high. In this way there may be political mileage in ensuring that the figure is presented as low as possible. Any estimate of the number of squatters must be treated with a degree of caution and may also change from time to time.

Research sample

Unlike the other faces of homelessness, there was very little existing work on which the present study could be based. Enquiries to local housing or homelessness organisations produced either no information or merely hearsay and therefore initially there had to be reliance upon the squatting organizations and individual contacts with the hope that some sort of network could be built up. However, too great a reliance upon the former was not desired as not all squatters find accommodation through the squatting organizations.

In London there are seven local 'squatting groups' according to the ASS some more active than others, giving advice on squatting, on court and legal procedure, and often able to direct homeless people to potential squats. In other areas there are informal networks of 'people in the know' who can direct people to empty properties. There is also a degree of entrepreneurial activity centred around local squatters, bookshops, vegetarian restaurants, and food co-operatives.

Research studies

The first pilot study was carried out in the London Borough of Lambeth where the local squatting group, which ran a bookshop and advice centre in a squatted building, was approached and after initial suspicion a good co-operative relationship was formed. Two main methods of research were used; participant observation and questionnaire. A total of four weeks was spent in field work living in squats. The researcher returned to the squats several times. A number of unstructured interviews were carried out with squatters.

The second pilot study centred on a large squat in South London opened by a group of church people. Some of the people staying there appeared to alternate between staying in squats, or somewhere else under cover, and sleeping rough on the streets. It was decided, partly for reasons of safety, that participant observation was not appropriate so a questionnaire, including an attitudinal section was administered. Respondents were asked to mark a statement somewhere on a seven point scale ranging from 'very strongly agree' to 'very strongly disagree' and unstructured interviews were carried out immediately after the questionnaire had been completed. Several of the squatters were known to the researcher and he was able to continue gaining data over a longer period. One result of this approach was the recognition of the danger of receiving inaccurate information from respondents when only one method was used.

The third pilot study was carried out in the London Borough of Ealing which had no squatting organisation so the first objective was to identify the squats. This was time consuming and difficult but there was an important finding. A local church was convinced that there was a high level of squatting in the borough but despite numerous visits and conversations with workers and two squatters and three ex-squatters little evidence could be found for that belief. It is possible that squatters themselves exaggerated the number of squats partly for strategic reasons since if the borough could be made to appear to be a good squatting area then that would attract other squatters resulting in a self fulfilling prophecy. On the other hand a few squats may have become highly visible so resulting in an exaggerated notion of their numbers. There is no data for this pilot study.

In the main study two visits were made to a squatting organisation in South London, once by two research assistants and once by the researcher, in order that the questionnaire could be completed. The time chosen coincided with a 'drive' by the local authority, in whose area the squatting organisation worked, to evict as many squatters as possible. This resulted in a large number of squatters coming to the organisation for advice and assistance so that it is likely that the researcher was able to survey squatters who would not be normally found there. Visits to the organisations were continued after the data collection. Visits, including several over night stays, were made to squats known to the researcher in a North London Borough. Entry was also gained to a moderately large squat in the centre of London which accommodated about 20 young squatters. One over night stay was made at that squat.

In addition to the above, note was taken of any of the other respondents in the main study who referred to 'squat' as their last place of stay. They formed a separate group which was compared to the remainder of the squatters in the analysis. In addition, four interviews were carried out with officials and representatives of voluntary organisations.

The squats

In the first pilot study questions were asked about the condition of the squats in which squatters lived. Although the numbers are small, from subsequent observation and experience, they appeared typical of squats in general. Visits were made to squats including stays for up to a week at a number of squats.

In the 28 dwellings a total of 105 people resided, a mean of 4.2 (sd = 1.33) per dwelling. In only one instance was the dwelling occupied by a single squatter. It was thought by other squatters that both dwellings owned privately and by housing associations were over represented. There was a general perception by squatters that for security reasons it was rare for one person only to occupy a squat, and this was supported by observation.

Table 8.1: Ownership

Ownership	Number	%
Local Authority	17	61
Housing Associations	5	17
Privately owned	3	11
Don't know	3	11
Total	28	100%

Table 8.2: Types of dwelling

Type of Dwelling	Number	%
Terraced House	16	57
High rise flat	8	29
Semi-detached house	3	11
Flat above shop	1	3
Total	28	100%

Almost all of the 28 dwellings in the first study had one or more utility. Table 8.3 shows the access to utilities.

Table 8.3: Utilities

Utility	Yes	No	% Yes
Water	25	3	89
Gas	20	8	71
Electricity	24	4	86
Telephone	6	22	21

The 3 'squats' without water were in semi derelict properties possessing no other utility and in one of the dwellings without electricity the occupants were waiting for it to be connected. In addition respondents were asked to assess the physical condition of their squat. Whilst the answers are of a subjective nature there is no reason to suppose that anyone would describe the physical condition of a derelict or semi derelict squat as excellent. Of the 28 squats, 23 were described as fair, poor or bad and from the researcher's own observation most of the properties seen by him required some kind of repair or renovation. There was no evidence of squatters taking over homes temporally unoccupied because residents were away on holiday or at work.

In many cases the squatters had decorated their homes, sometimes in a very off beat way and the various motifs, colour schemes, pictures would be an interesting subject for study. In only two cases, not included in this study, was there evidence that the squatters had vandalised the properties.

Description of squatters

The proportion of female respondents is probably on the low side since there were a number of 'woman only' squats unable to be included in the studies which were either formally declared as such or had developed naturally. The second study excludes one 'no response'. In the first study one girl was pregnant and two were pregnant in the second study. In the first two studies the mean age of squatters could be determined.

Table 8.4: Gender

Gender	1st study	2nd study	Final study	Total
Male	29 (78%)	34 (83%)	33 (73%)	96 (79%)
Female	8 (22%)	6 (15%)	12 (27%)	26 (21%)
Missing		1 (2%)		
Total	37	41	45	122

The under 16s in the first study included three children of parents living in the squat and two were runaways, one from a children's home and the other from a foster home. In the second study all were runaways. A different age range was apparent in the final study.

The squatters were mainly young people. In the two pilot studies just over 83% were aged 35 or under while in the final study approximately 73% were aged under 30 compared to 46% in the overall Sample (N=531). There may be a number of reasons for this: younger people may be more resourceful or less respectful of property rights; the younger people may attract more
people of similar age or older people may be more inclined to use hostels,

because the squatting group was younger than the overall homeless sample. It is possible that the differences between the squatters and those in hostels for example, is primarily to do with age.

Table 8.5: Mean ages in first two studies

	1st study	2nd study	Overall
Mean	21.8	23.7	22.8
SD	6.4	7.7	6.5
N	37	41	78

Table 8.6: Age in final study

Age	Number	%
Under 18	13	29
19 to 29	20	44
30 to 39	11	25
40 to 49	1	2
Total	45	100

According to Table 8.7 in all studies divorced and separated people form only a very small proportion of the squatters.

Table 8.7: Marital status

	First study	Second Study	Final study	Total
Single	29 (78%)	37 (90%)	32 (71%)	98 (80%)
Married/ Cohabiting	4 (11%)	1 (2%)	7 (17%)	12 (10%)
Divorced	1 (3%)	3 (8%)	2 (4%)	6 (5%)
Separated	1 (3%)	-	2 (4%)	3 (2%)
No Response	2 (5%)		2 (4%)	4 (3%)
Total	37 (100%)	41 (100%)	45 (100%)	123 (100%)

As regards the occupations of squatters, some of the work was related to self help within the squatting community; for example one person classed himself as self employed and acted as a furniture remover for other squatters. If there was going to be a repossession the squatters used his services to ensure that they were able to remove their belongings to safety before the bailiffs came.

Another example was a squatter who ran a small vegetarian restaurant (without planning permission) at which other squatters regularly met, while another ran a printing business for other squatters assisted by the Government's Business Enterprise Scheme. What the bare figures do not show is the thriving entrepreneurial activity that was in evidence amongst many of the squatters. Most of the businesses were 'legitimate', undeclared. There was the occasional dealings in drugs although most of it was on a mutual reciprocal basis, where people sometimes acted as suppliers to a network of friends and associates. Two major drugs suppliers known indirectly to the researcher moved into squats as a temporary measure in order not to incriminate their own home, moving out as soon as the deal was completed.

Table 8.8: Employment status

	1st study	2nd study	Final study	Overall
Unemployed	9 (24%)	38 (93%)	16 (36%)	63 (51%)
Employed	13 (35%)	3 (7%)	22 (49%)	38 (32%)
Self Employed	5 (14%)	-	4 (9%)	9 (8%)
Government Scheme	4 (11%)	-	-	4 (3%)
Student	3 (8%)	-	2 (4%)	5 (4%)
No Response	3 (8%)	-	-	3 (2%)
Missing	-	-	1 (2%)	1 (0%)
Total	37 (100%)	41 (100%)	45 (100%)	123 (100%)

The sample was also asked if they took part in voluntary work. Some worked in squatting organisations, taking part in various activities in the running of the hospital squat.

Table 8.9: Voluntary work

	1st study	2nd study	Final study	Overall
Yes	7 (19%)	14 (34%)	14 (31%)	35 (28%)
No	28 (76%)	27 (66%)	27 (60%)	82 (67%)
Missing	2 (5%)		4 (9%)	6 (5%)
Total	37 (100%)	41 (100%)	45 (100%)	123 (100%)

Respondents in the second and final studies were asked to state both their ethnicity and their country of origin and although the question was worded slightly differently in the two stages they are still comparable. As can be seen there are some differences between the two groups for the country of origin, a higher proportion came from Ireland in the final study whereas a greater proportion came from Scotland in the 2nd study. However, the final group of squatters contain far more white Europeans than the other group.

Table 8.10: Ethnicity

Ethnicity	2nd study	Final study
White/European	25 (61%)	38 (84.4%)
Afro/Caribbean	2 (5%)	2 (4.4%)
Other	4 (9.75%)	2 (4.4%)
Black Asian	2 (5%)	2 (4.4%)
Don't know	4 (9.75%)	
Missing	4 (9.75%)	1 (2.2%)
Total	41 (100%)	45 (100%)

The overwhelming majority of squatters in the first group were white Europeans. It is likely that Afro Caribbean squatters were under represented in this study. In the first and final studies there were a few younger people from the continent, Australia and New Zealand who were using squatting as a means of cheap accommodation while visiting Britain.

Table 8.11: Country of origin

Country of Origin	2nd study	final study
England	23 (56%)	27 (60%)
Scotland	7 (17%)	3 (7%)
N. Ireland	1 (2%)	6 (13%)
Great Britain	3 (7%)	-
United Kingdom	1 (3%)	-
Commonwealth	2 (5%)	-
Europe	-	2 (4%)
Other	-	4 (9%)
Missing	4 (10%)	3 (7%)
Total	41 (100%)	45 (100%)

Respondents were asked to give their educational qualifications in all studies but only in the final two stages were questions asked about trade qualifications.

Table 8.12: Education

Educational Level	1st study	2nd study	Final study	Overall
Degree	5 (14%)	-	7 (16%)	12 (10%)
Professional	-	1 (2%)	6 (13%)	7 (6%)
A Level	13 (35%)	5 (12%)	9 (20%)	27 (22%)
O Level/CSE	10 (27%)	9 (22%)	13 (29%)	32 (26%)
None	7 (19%)	24 (59%)	10 (22%)	41 (33%)
Missing	2 (5%)	2 (5%)	-	4 (3%)
Total	37 (100%)	41 (100%)	45 (100%)	123 (100%)

A larger proportion of the hospital squatters possessed trade qualifications and sometimes the nature of the trade qualifications were stated which included:

City & Guilds Carpentry & Joinery
Dog Trainer (Armed Forces)
City & Guilds Painter & Decorator
Painter & Decorator
City & Guilds Bricklaying
Joinery & Graphic Design
Welding & Marine Engineering
City & Guilds Horticulture
Bargeman
City & Guilds unspecified.

The skills, therefore, are generally in the fields of manual work.

Table 8.13: Trade qualifications

	2nd study	Final study	Overall
With Trade Qualifications	12 (29%)	8 (18%)	20 (23%)
Without Trade Qualifications	29 (71%)	31 (69%)	60 (70%)
Missing		6 (13%)	6 (7%)
Total	41 (100%)	45(100%)	86 (100%)

Except in a few cases, the squatters in the first and final studies formed near traditional households, which had been initiated on an individual level. However, the hospital squatters formed a communal squat with, at the beginning, a strong peer group leadership exercised at first by the older men. Most of the hospital squatters who took part in voluntary work did so within the squat itself in which they saw their contribution to the running of the squat as a voluntary activity. These activities could include cooking, cleaning, security duties and general maintenance.

Discussions with the non-hospital squatters suggested that they often took part in jobs below their capabilities or educational achievement, e.g. one person with a degree worked as a hospital porter and another as a painter. Some indicated that this was by choice, that such occupations enabled them to avoid what was known as the 'rat race'. It is difficult not to conclude that the distinction between the hospital squatters and the remainder is one that is based to some extent upon class supported by the educational level attained. Certainly the older men who formed the leadership in the hospital squat appeared to have worked in manual working class jobs and the leadership that was exerted was authoritarian and directive. However the proportion of squatters who had squatted before were similar in both groups, nearly 64% of the hospital group had as compared with 69% of the first group. Although, the first group had squatted more times than the hospital group had done so.

Table 8.14: Average number of times squatted previously

	1st Study	2nd Study
Mean	2.71	2.13
SD	2.30	2.21

Summary

The great majority of the squatters were young, single, white males. There are strong differences between the squatters in the second study and those in the other two. The hospital squatters had a slightly higher mean age but a wider distribution than the other two, have a higher proportion of single and unemployed people and had a markedly different level of educational achievement. More people in the hospital study were disabled but there were more with trade qualifications.

Accommodation history

Another comparison arises if being on a housing waiting list is taken to signify at least some ability and willingness to use the official agencies.

Table 8.15: Housing waiting lists

	1st Study	2nd Study	Final Study	Total
Yes	16 (43%)	10 (24%)	17 (38%)	43 (35%)
No	19 (51%)	30 (73%)	22 (49%)	71 (58%)
Missing	2 (6%)	1 (3%)	6 (13%)	9 (7%)
Total	37 (100%)	41 (100%)	45 (100%)	123 (100%)

The clear distinction between the hospital squatters and the remainder is further emphasised. By far the lowest percentage on a housing waiting list is found in the second study. Whilst it is easy to put this down to personal attributes or lack of them, there may be more general reasons why this is so which may be discovered by examining their accommodation history.

Since the hospital squat had only been opened for just over two months, respondents were not asked how long they had been in the squat, perhaps on reflection a mistake, since one may well have distinguished differences in attitudes between those who had been there since the beginning and those who had recently entered it. However although the range of times was larger for the first study than for the final, the two can still be compared and this is done in Table 8.16.

Table 8.16: Length of stay in squat

Length of Stay	1st Study	Final Study	Total
Under 3 months	5 (14%)	14 (31%)	19 (23%)
3 to 6 months	10 (27%)	4 (9%)	14 (17%)
7 to 12 months	11 (30%)	8 (18%)	19 (23%)
Over 1 year	9 (24%)	18 (40%)	27 (33%)
Missing	2 (5%)	1 (2%)	3 (4%)
Total	37	45 (100%)	82 (100%)

Despite the fact that respondents are squatting there is a remarkable degree of stability in the time spent in the same place. Over half, (56%) had stayed in the same place for more than six months. In the final study there was a high correlation, 0.61 between the length of stay in the current place and the length of time squatters had stayed in their previous place. But since the mean length of time hospital squatters had been squatting must be less than two months the evidence suggests that one group of squatters have experienced a more stable life style than another group. The squats were more likely to be better furnished and the squatters more likely to be working.

Table 8.17 supports the distinction between the two groups of squatters. In the second group (the hospital group) there is a far higher incidence of living on the street than in the first one.

Table 8.17: Types of previous three tenures (Studies 1 & 2 only)

Nature of last 3 tenure(s)	1st Study	2nd Study
All squats	8	0
Last two squats	7	3
Last one squat	6	5
Squatted previous in last 3	6	6
Last 3 local authority	2	0
Last 2 local authority	0	1
Last 1 local authority	0	4
Last 1 lived in hostel	0	4
Last 1 privately rented	12	2
Last 1 lived on street	1	12 *
Lived on street in last 3	3	8

** these are in addition to those who lived on street in last 3 tenures.*

It can be suggested that broadly speaking the overall number of squatters can be divided into three basic groups: a sub-group where squatting was seen not only as a response to homelessness but also as a political statement, a sub-group for whom squatting was seen, if not wholly as desirable, then as appropriate: while another group used the squats as a response to a critical situation. Only for the first group was squatting seen as wholly a positive action. For the other two sub-groups, it was suggested, squatting is seen as both a positive and negative act although in varying degrees.

Fifty one per cent of the squatters in the first study had moved from a squat to their squat and this is close to the percentage in the final study, 46%.

The first group, the non hospital squatters, were focused on the same area with 65% having moved within the same area from their last place to their present squat, as compared with 29% of the hospital squat (Table 8.18). On the other hand, 32% of the hospital squatters had moved to Greater London from another part of the UK recently, compared to 19% for the first group of squatters. Table 8.18 suggests that more people in the hospital group had recently moved to London or the area in which the squat was situated. It is possible that this is one of the reasons why there were less people on a housing waiting list, they may be more recent arrivals. The 'pull' factors of the possibility that there is more work to be found in London may be one of the reasons for their greater recent mobility. Against this the argument can be raised that they could have been put on a housing waiting list in their home towns or areas, but in those areas there may be no emphasis upon the importance of being registered.

Table 8.18: Area of last three tenures

Last Three Areas	1st Study	2nd Study
Last three same area	9	6
Last two same area	7	2
Last one same area	8	4
Last three Greater London	1	8
Last two Greater London	1	3
Last one Greater London	1	1
Last one in other part of UK	4	3
In same area previously	1	2
Other part of UK in last 3	3	10

The first study indicated that 24% of those squatting heard of the squat from a squatters group. None of those in hospital squat heard of the squat this way.

Table 8.19: How squatters heard of squat

How heard of Squat	1st Study	2nd study
Squatters group	9 (24%)	0
Friends	16 (43%)	11 (27%)
Present Occupants	9 (24%)	17 (41%)
Self	3 (9%)	6 (15%)
Missing		7 (17%)
Total	37 (100%)	41 (100%)

Non hospital squatters were far more optimistic about their ability to keep off the street. Squatters responded on a five point scale to the question 'How likely is it that you will end up end living on the street?' Discussions implied that this optimism came from confidence that they could deal with any situation rather than confidence in the results of being on housing waiting lists. Through follow up and ordinary social contact it was found that out of seven people only one person was on the street within a year. All the others were either still in squats or had become licensees. However, as will be seen, several squatters moved from the hospital squat directly to the street.

Table 8.20: On the street within six months

(5= 'No chance at all' to 1= 'Almost certainly')

	1st study	2nd Study
Mean	3.97	2.51
SD	1.03	1.31

Reasons for squatting

Squatting in the 1960's and early 1970's was marked by a strong commitment to radical left politics and present day squatting organisations themselves are sometimes marked by a similar political outlook. A question arises as to whether the political values of the activists are reflected by the mass of the squatters.

One way of seeing if this is so is to ask their reasons for squatting. In the first study an open ended question was asked. Most people gave more than one answer. A total of 38 different reasons were given which from a content analysis were formed into five separate categories. Only in three instances did the respondent indicate that s/he was unable to return home. A further content analysis was carried out in order to see if 'other' reasons could be subsumed under specific reasons. In six cases, the 'other' reason on examination could be seen in more specific terms. An ideological commitment was the second least frequent reason although approximately 30% suggested that ideological reasons or principle played a part. But in only two instances was this given without any other reason at all.

Table 8.21: Reasons for squatting

First study

Reasons for squatting	Number of Times Mentioned
Need for a home	30
Cheapness or money	23
Ideology or principle	16
Friendship or relationship	18
Other reasons	10

Both groups were asked what resources were needed to improve their quality of life. Because of the open ended nature of the question each answer involved a number of resources and another content analysis was carried out in order to form a number of primary resources.

Table 8.22: Resources needed

Primary Resource	1st Study	2nd Study
Home or own home	16	31
Money	12	19
Good job	4	7
Security	7	2
Facilities for squat, e.g. heating	11	1
Desire for greater co-operation with other squatters	9	0
Political factors e.g. no poll tax	2	4

It is noteworthy that there were only two responses which are overtly politically orientated in their responses in the first study and only four in the second, although the desire for better co-operation between squatters could be interpreted in a political manner. There is an air of conformity about the responses from the squatters, most resources required are no different from those required by any people of a similar age. However there are marked differences between the two groups, the resources required by the hospital squatters are far more basic than those by the other groups. Without a basic home and job the other resources are irrelevant. It should be noted that in the first group only seven of the squatters were unemployed which accounts for the low number who required a job.

Sometimes, especially in the hospital group, emphasis was laid upon their inability to obtain these resources because of their past life or their present circumstances.

> I want what anybody else wants, a home, a family, a decent job and some money to spare but with the state I'm in at present that's a big order.
>
> (Male 24: Hospital squat).

> If you've been in care or in trouble employers and other people mark you out and you have to be ten times as good as anyone else to get a decent job.
>
> (Male aged 18: Hospital squat).

Yet even the last saw his life developing positively for he added;

> but that means you've got to fight ten times as hard and I'm doing that.

> I came off of smack six months ago smack really cracked me up then and still is now so that makes it even more difficult.
>
> (Male 21: Hospital squat).

The hospital squat

From the responses to the open ended question of the first study a series of closed questions were formulated for the second pilot study, the hospital squat, with a seven point response scale ranging from 'very strongly agree' (score = 7) 'to very strongly disagree' (score = 1). Table 8.23 shows the mean scores and standard deviations for the hospital squatters.

One group of squatters saw themselves as able to offer employers skills in an interesting work activity whilst another group saw themselves as having few worthwhile work skills only able to obtain boring jobs. Once again the optimistic group consisted mainly of younger people. There was a strong hostility to hostels with only six squatters disagreeing with the statement 'I definitely intend to keep out of hostels.' This too was strongly correlated with items 4 (0.62) 7 (0.53) and 1 (0.51). Reasons given in interviews included the lack of freedom in hostels, too much intrusion into one's private life and criticism of other residents especially if they gave evidence of psychiatric problems. Nearly 50% agreed to a greater or lesser

Table 8.23: Evaluation of squats and views of squatters

ITEM	Mean	SD
1. Getting a home of my own is important to me.	6.2	1.2
2. Governments do not give a damn about people like me.	6.2	1.2
3. I would like to make sufficient money to be comfortable in life.	6.0	1.4
4. I look upon this squat as my home.	5.7	2.0
5. I definitely intend to keep out of hostels.	5.6	1.9
6. I really care about getting a good job.	5.6	1.9
7. I would like to own my own home.	5.6	1.7
8. Continuing on in my last place became impossible.	5.5	1.7
9. I regard people here with me as my family.	5.3	2.12
10. Finding people with whom I can get on with is the most important thing in deciding where I live.	4.7	2.0
11. I will squat for as short a time as possible.	4.7	2.3
12. I intend to stay in London wherever I live.	4.5	1.9
13. Most jobs open to me are boring and have no future.	4.5	2.1
14. For most people living on the street there is no other practical choice.	4.2	1.8
15. I will never end up sleeping rough on the street.	3.4	2.0
16. The only way I can get money to survive is by begging.	3.3	2.2
17. For me squatting is a political statement.	3.2	2.1
18. I have no skills to offer a future employer.	3.1	2.4
19. Being out of work does not matter to me.	2.6	1.8
20. Getting on with other people is quite difficult for me.	2.5	1.9

7 = very strongly agree, 6 = strongly agree, 5 = agree, 4 = neither agree nor disagree, 3 = disagree, 2 = strongly disagree, 1 = very strongly disagree

extent that the only way they could get money to survive was by begging although the statement drew most of the two extreme responses, 19 (46%) responding with 4 or 9. This may reflect extremes in hostility and acceptance for the activity. Yet studying this group a surprising finding was discovered.

Only a minority (25%) were pessimistic about their life chances. It is surprising in view of the general perception by homelessness workers, that beggars are the most desperate and helpless, but, as we will see in Chapter 10, the picture of that scene is far from simple and clear cut.

The responses regarding the way they saw the squat as their home and the other squatters as their family give rise to some problems. Although only three basic rules were set by the community, no violence, no alcohol and no drugs, the leadership was seen by some of the younger squatters as authoritarian. Later the squatters were asked to contribute £5 per week for food and this brought about some opposition with accusations of fraud. Just after the survey there was a steady trickle of squatters from the hospital squat, some voluntarily but others who were evicted. Now those who had once praised the squat blamed the leadership and other cliques for making it into 'a dump' yet these same people before had, in interviews, stressed that not only did they look upon the squat as their home, but also the other squatters as their family.

This is not to deny the validity of their reply but it does caution against interpreting the responses in too conventional a manner. Their emotional attachment to the place may have been increased by the sense of standing out against a hostile world, which in turn may have been strengthened by the security measures taken to exclude unwanted guests. The inner door was locked while gates had been placed outside. At first squatters took it in turns to sit as doormen but later visitors had to ring a bell to gain entrance. The security measures were probably justified but nevertheless they probably generated some feeling of being under seige, hence the strong attachment to the squat while people were there is entirely understandable. Sometimes comments on the questionnaire gave a clue as to why the squatters looked, at least temporally, upon the old hospital as a home and the fellow residents as their family.

> Put it this way, I was raped and abused by my parents when I was a young child and grew up in too many children' homes, so thank God for this place. I NOW HAVE A <u>FAMILY</u> WHO REALLY CARE FOR ME. Thanks for taking the bother to ask.
>
> (Female aged 23). (Comment on questionnaire, capitals and underline on original).

> I was on the street for 4 months , I glad to be in here so I can bring my life together.
>
> (Male 30). (Comment on questionnaire).

> This is the first family and home I've ever know. I have never known my parents, only children homes and foster parents.
>
> (Male 17) (Comment on questionnaire).

Others stressed the utility of the place.

> I came to be here because of lack of housing all I want is a place of my own and a decent job.
>
> (Male 22)

In conversation, other squatters stressed the deficiencies of their past life which may have influenced them in seeing the hospital in traditional terms of home and family, while at the same time giving evidence of mixed feelings.

> This place is OK, it's a home and that's more than I've had in the past. Pushed around from children' home to children' home. And the other people are my family. But what I want out of life is a good job, a good home and being able to give my family the things I never had.
>
> (Female 19).

> I would be really homeless if it wasn't for this place. But I want my own home because I am pregnant and I hope to bring the child up in a safe and secure environment.
>
> (Female 17).

> I want a home and a family. Male 19 who saw the hospital squat as his 'home' and the others as his 'family'.

What is being suggested here is the ambiguity of the term home. Home can mean various things to the individual at different times. The attachment to the place does not rule out the recognition that this is a temporary stage which probably fails to meet all of the requirements of a home. This applies also to the family, the other squatters were their family but in a different sense to the traditional idea of the family. A parallel can be seen in the way that 'family' is also used within the church, the church is the 'family of God' but belonging to that family in no way goes against belonging to the traditional family.

Despite their strong feeling that the government did not care there was little sense of political cohesion and certainly no strong attachment to alternative political parties was ever suggested. Item 2, 'For me squatting is a political statement' drew mainly a negative response although there was a core group for whom the political aspect of squatting was important. Southwark council in one sense recognised this for they tried to destroy the squatters' group arguing that destroying that would be to destroy the heart of squatting but the squatting group, in turn, took the council to court, won its case resulting in Southwark having to commence proceedings all over again and giving the group time to plan for its future. It became a registered charity.

Money, food and assistance was received from various agencies including the local council and the local trades union council. The local church was very supportive but a few of the other religious people who brought food and clothing appeared to want to play a too active part in the running of the squat, a desire which was both resented and opposed by almost every one of the occupants.

The researcher made several visits to the squat and recorded the deterioration over time. A number of events took place which vividly illustrated the tensions that were being experienced within the squat. Challenges to the leadership occurred sometimes, coming from younger people or others of a similar age to the present leadership. The first person who acted in a leadership capacity experienced a fall from the roof in mysterious circumstances, the explanations ranging from him falling when stripping lead off the roof, to being chased with hatchets by a group who wanted to take the squat over. A fire destroyed the top floor of the hospital and again various explanations were given ranging from deliberate arson to a drunken accident. The wiring in the hospital and other saleable items were stripped and sold by a group of squatters while one'leadership group' housed themselves in a building to the rear of the main hospital building which was kept warm, well furnished, in stark comparison to others who had to make do with the old wards where rain came through the lead stripped roof. Even at this level of society differences emerge based upon status, power and authority.

People continued to move away although at first their places were usually taken by other people. Hostility, complaints and criticisms were usually expressed and although there was no way to determine the truth of what was said their perception inevitably affected how other people saw the squat. There were statements that it had become a place where heavy dealing in drugs took place, complaints made by both people who had moved out and by one religious worker although no evidence of heavy dealing was witnessed, although there was a degree of social drug taking, and it hardly provided a safe and anonymous environment for that activity.

Numbers in the squat varied and it was difficult to determine the exact numbers in the squat at any one time. Estimates ranged from 50 to 250.

This could be due to the way people used the squat, some of the squatters staying there for the occasional night, staying in other places on other nights. Three rent boys made it their base who by the nature of their occupation were unlikely to be there on all nights. There was perhaps a tendency to exaggerate the numbers since if it could appear that the squat was keeping that many people from the street the more credibility it would have. Certainly on the visits that the researcher made the higher number appeared doubtful, and in all probability, at the height of its success numbers were in the low to middle 100s.

Other strong rumours asserted that grants had been paid over to the squat which brought about accusations of fraud with certain people being identified as guilty. Whether the accusations were well founded or not they can be seen both as demonstrating the deterioration of the cohesion of the squat and contributing towards that deterioration.

Environmental evaluation in the final study

There was a far stronger emphasis upon environmental evaluation in the final study. The purpose was to discover squatters' perception of the 'homelike' nature of their squat, what was important to them, their view of other residents and some notion of the state of their mental health. One section which was the Moos Evaluation Scale for Therapeutic environments (ref). Respondents were asked to respond to a series of items on a five point scale ranging from strongly agree to strongly disagree and items were recorded so that the higher score normally represented a more positive outlook and the scores on a number of items in the same domain were computed into one overall score or variable. For instance the two items which related to self esteem were made into one variable 'esteem' with the highest possible score being 10 and the lowest 2. In this way the squatters' mean score could be compared to the others. The domains were:

Evaluation of home items	=	Home
Mental stress items	=	Health
Self esteem	=	Esteem
Important to them	=	Aspire
Viewed other people	=	View

The possible scores for each computed item was:

Home	lowest =	7	highest	=	35
Esteem	lowest =	2	highest	=	10
Importance	lowest =	5	highest	=	25
View	lowest =	6	highest	=	30

However the Health Score remains in its original scoring since it can be used in comparison with others studies quite separate from this one. The lowest score (0) represents the highest possible score for mental stress while the highest (36) suggests a high degree of emotional disturbance. Some reservations have to be expressed regarding the validity of the mental stress scores. Being homeless inevitably results in a degree of emotional stress and anxiety so because of their situation homeless people are less likely to come out of it as well as people who live stable and settled lives. The best way to use the rating is to accept this but to point out that it measures mental stress and not mental illness. Anybody is likely to vary from day to day depending upon circumstances.

A mean score for all of the responses by the squatters was then worked out and compared to the remainder of the main sample.

Table 8.24: Compute scores

Computed Item	Mean for Squatters	SD for Squatters	Overall Mean All (531)	Overall SD All (531)
HOME	26.07	5.71	23.02	6.38
ESTEEM	8.37	1.65	6.78	2.19
HEALTH *	9.42	7.12	13.62	7.81
IMPORTANCE	22.75	2.15	21.06	4.21
VIEW	22.09	3.31	18.08	4.16

* NB. Low health score represents high level of mental stress.

Except with regard to what was important to them, the other differences were significant to <0.0005 level. Table 8.24 suggests that squatters view their squat in more positive homelike terms than the remainder of the sample, have a higher self esteem than the remainder, better mental health and view their fellow residents in a far more positive light.

The exception can be understood by the fact that there was a universal acceptance by almost the whole of the overall sample of what was important to them. In other words, the great majority of respondents felt the same things were important to them in places where they stayed.

The research was carried out at a time when many squatters were under threat of eviction and in a number of cases the squatter intimated that the threat was causing concern while other squatters responded to the threat in more assertive manner saying that they welcomed the challenge. Two quotes illustrate the opposing reaction.

> A lot of the strain at the moment is due to the local authority taking me to court in defiance of previous undertakings for possession of this flat.
>
> (Male 30 to 39 final study).

> The council is trying to get me out of my home which I have occupied for over a year, but all it does is to make me more determined to fight them. Since I got the notice to quit I have become very active in the centre advising other squatters of their rights.
>
> (Male 20 to 29:final study).

The two contrasting reactions to the same threat illustrates the importance of considering together both psychological and sociological factors in any understanding of squatting. As it happened the latter won his court case and the former, although losing his case, moved into another squat very soon afterwards.

The question arises as to why squatters scored so high on the computed scores compared with the remainder of the sample. The responses from the hospital squat gives some clue to this although not the whole story. Firstly the squatters perceived themselves as an in-group, hence others belonged to the out-group. Two ways by which in-groups differentiated themselves from out-groups are deprecating the out-group or by emphasising the benefits and virtues of their own group even if those virtues are those also valued by the out-group. In a paradoxical manner, differentiation is carried out by identification with common values. This is not a deliberate or conscious process, the in-group genuinely see themselves as superior - and may well be - to the out-group and neither does it assume that what they are saying about their home is untrue. What it does mean is that their situation within society - an in-group opposed to an out-group - inevitably affects how they perceive their environment. There was one other spin off from this identity process. In all studies there was a great reluctance to call themselves homeless; 'My home is my squat' or similar words was heard several times. Home to them was the place in which they found themselves.

> I am proud of my squat and do not regard myself as homeless. Homelessness could disappear if everyone occupied empty property. (Female aged 19 to 29: Final study).

Secondly the squatters operated within a cultural context and over the decade of the 1980's more than usual stress was laid upon the qualities of independence, self help, standing on one's own feet and lack of reliance upon state constructed solutions. This is not a new ideological culture but merely a re-emphasising of values that has always existed. The squatters were their problems of accommodation. Similar to the hospital group, hostels were seen as unable to provide the independence they required. In hostels they were told what to do, their lives were organised around rules. But that is not to say that the squatters were 'ruleless', their lives were ordered by self imposed rules which were based upon the need to live together. At the same time the squatters had a positive response to the item 'I can do what I want here'. If there were rules they were of their own making and did not interfere with their ability to do what they want.

Thirdly squatting can be seen in a historical context. There is a long tradition of squatting not only in this country but in other countries. Whilst the evidence is only anecdotal, some squatters said that there were contacts in other countries if they wished to travel abroad and be put up in other squats. Some squatters, especially those who were most active in the movement, were well aware of the history of squatting and its successes particularly in the formation of the co-operative housing movement, although not all approved of its latest developments. Hence they are part of an in-group which has its roots in history and tradition both of which adds to their sense of identity. 'I am a squatter' becomes not only descriptive but ascriptive.

Finally the squatters, because of the nature of their situation, were able to express their identity within their environment. Even in the most relaxed hostels there are certain limitations regarding the way in which residents can express their identity in their room or other part of the building, but in squats there is only the limitation of pressure from other residents. Mention has already been made of squatters decorating their squats often in very individualistic styles, hence imposing their own identity upon the place. Their attachment to the place was partly, if not mainly, brought about by how much they could create their own personal space in the manner of their own choosing. The ability to make this environment, as well as the fact that they have solved, for the time being at any rate, their problem of homelessness, results in pride in their place. The item 'Generally people here are very proud of this place' brought a higher level of agreement from squatters than the overall sample,3.64 compared to 3.03.

Many squatters' homes were well furnished and decorated, each room being decorated differently from the rest perhaps reflecting the different personalities. For example, while there might be a common room, or rooms, which everyone was entitled to use for social purposes, often including the kitchen, an individual squatter would have his/her own favourite records in their own room. It is proposed that a commonsense understanding of home would suggest that the more a person is able to utilise a property for his/her own ends and to decorate it and furnish it in a desired manner so the more s/he is likely to look upon it as a home. A person unable to furnish the property or to impart his/her own personality onto it through decorating, or being able to enjoy a particular type of music is, in all probability less likely to look upon a place as home. Ownership of property may be seen as an extension of the self, hence unable to enjoy one's own things entails being unable to enjoy part of one's own life experience. Squatters attached great importance to being able to decorate one's own place, the mean response being 4.18 compared to an overall mean of 3.75 and was in the top quartile. Unfortunately there was no way of determining whether those squatters whose homes were well furnished and equipped scored higher than those whose squat contained the bare minimum.

There is also a reciprocal process. In turn the physical environment becomes a part of the identity and losing the squat is like losing part of oneself as well as the ability to control one's own life. Making the squat a home is the process. The end result is the fusion of place and person.

The environment also consists of other people and squatters are, in this respect, similar to those on the street. They can choose the people with whom they are going to live, as the women did in the women only squats, and once again this is seen by comparison of responses to two items by the squatters and overall sample.

	Squatting mean	Overall mean
There is group spirit here.	3.37	2.82
People here help each other.	3.68	3.01

Whilst the differences are not all that high, they do support the hypothesis that the ability to express one's identity within a place and the ability to choose with whom you are going to live are two attributes which make squatting a preferred option for some young people. Together with the compute score they suggest the importance of those qualities in any assessment of home.

What happens to squatters unable to squat

In the overall study there was a group of people, totalling 46,who stated that the last place they had stayed was a squat. Twenty four of these had moved into their present squats while 23 had moved to other places 22 of whom went to various hostels. The two groups, therefore, can be compared to each other to determine any change in mental health, esteem, view of other residents and their perception of the homelike nature of their present place. Table 8.25 shows the results.

Table 8.25: Compute scores for ex-squatters

Computed Item	Mean for those now in another squat	SD	Mean for those now in hostel	SD
HOME	26.87	5.13	23.33	6.75 *
ESTEEM	9.09	1.19	6.09	1.78 ***
HEALTH *	7.74	4.59	16.30	7.18 ***
IMPORTANCE	23.17	1.95	21.32	3.36 *
VIEW	24.19	3.39	18.09	4.92 ***

* significance = <0.05
*** significance = <0.0005

What is interesting is that in all cases those who have moved to places other than squats are markedly lower on the compute scores. They see their place as far less homelike, have a lower view of other residents, a lower self esteem and also a lower level of mental health. Even on the importance scale, those who moved into hostels, considered the various items less important. Whilst a possible interpretation is that the move to a particular type of alternative accommodation brought about the lowering of the scores there are two other possible explanations. It is possible that there was a lowering of psychological well being prior to the move to hostels, that is the move to the hostels was a consequence of that personal change. The other possibility is that they had only been in a very temporary and low level squat. The last can probably be ruled out since comparing the length of time the two sub-groups had stayed in their last place there was very little difference as Table 8.26 shows. Generally, the better squats in terms of furnishings and utilities were associated with the longer stays.

This leaves two possible explanations. There are two small pieces of evidence that suggest the move to the hostel was a possible reason for the lowering of personal outlook. First there are the stated views of squatters regarding hostels as well as the high response to the item 'I definitely intend to keep out of hostels' in the hospital study. Secondly, although the numbers are too small to draw any definite conclusion, the general pattern that emerged was that it was the younger people (aged under 29) who showed the greatest lowering of self esteem, possessed a lower view of other people, and tended to deteriorate more in mental health. However no comparisons were significant to $p<0.05$ and there were also exceptions with older people showing the same pattern as the younger ones. But the general view was that most hostility towards hostels was shown by the younger people.

Table 8.26: Comparison of length of stay in last place

Time spent in last place	Squatting group. Number	Hostel group. Number
Less than 1 month	5 (21%)	5 (22%)
1 to 3 months	4 (17%)	5 (22%)
4 to 6 months	3 (12%)	4 (18%)
7 months to 1 year	6 (25%)	6 (25%)
Over 1 year	6 (25%)	3 (13%)
Total	24 (100%)	23 (100%)

N = 47

Therefore although one must be careful from drawing too definite a conclusion the evidence does support the possibility that squatting is seen as a better alternative than hostels by many. It is not only the loss of what squatters saw as freedom in the hostel but also development of one's personality within an environment that encouraged development within the squat.

That is not to say that all squatters developed as well as they could have done, or that none were unable to develop within a hostel environment. As we have seen, some squatters for whatever reason may give up the fight and some live in the most deplorable conditions and have no pride in trying to improve their place. Squatters themselves recognise this referring to such people as 'dossers'. What might be considered is that some people are unable, without losing some of their competence to develop, to exist within a communal setting, while others will be put off by residents for whom the hostel may be the only alternative.

In a later chapter further comparisons are made between the squatters and other groups within the overall sample. Readers may notice that the chapter gives a different number of squatters to that given in this sample. The reason for this is that the overall sample population contained a group of people who lived in short life properties and since there was no way that group could be included in hostels or any other group they were included with the squatters. Although, of course, there are differences between the two sub-groups the similarities support combining them when comparing people to streets, hotels, and hostels.

Conclusion

Whilst squatters can be seen by other people as a group with a strong ideological commitment that goes against some of the basic values regarding property that prevails in this society, only a minority were so ideologically committed. A core of squatters saw squatting as both an ideological and a necessary act but most saw it as necessary. The last group could also be divided into those who saw squatting as desirable and those who saw it as a desperate measure to escape the street.

Squatting, if a measure of security is provided, provided an environment in which the squatter was able to express his/her identity within the squat which in turn became part of the self. Both psychological and more general sociological processes affect the way the squatter made use of the environment. While it would be an overstatement to say that all saw themselves as part of a cohesive in-group that identity could be called upon whenever necessary.

The detailed examination of a few squats, in the pilot research, notably the study of an old hospital being turned into a squat, has served to illustrate the dynamic and idiosyncratic processes that characterise each place used as a squat. Perhaps because of the individualistic orientation that permeates squatting, each setting used takes on very distinct characteristics. The quasi-legal or illegal nature of these settings put them under pressure from various internal and external forces. These pressures will produce continuous changes. Clearly, many squatters thrived on the challenges these changes pose, but for others it caused real, deep distress. The tragedy of empty houses being unoccupied is not reduced by illegal squatting, although that may temporarily alleviate the plight of some homeless people.

9 Homeless People Living in Hotels in London

Introduction

This chapter examines the numbers and distribution of homeless people living in hotels in London and presents the characteristics and views of a small sample. The data is drawn from four pieces of fieldwork carried out during the course of the Surrey University study: a telephone survey of 465 hotels in London, a follow-up survey of 171 hotels in four boroughs; a pilot survey in Pimlico and finally from the wider questionnaire survey which included a small sample of hotel residents. Reference is also made to some of the literature on hotel homelessness, outlining the main themes and noting how the surveys referred to here relate to existing research.

Background

Hotel homelessness has attracted increasing research attention over the last five years. Before then people living in hotels were examined as part of studies of homeless people rather than as a specific group (see Randall, G. et al 1982; and Drake, O'Brien and Biebuyck, 1981). Even at that time Randall and his colleagues noted the poor conditions prevalent in hotels and the fact that homeless people in hotels were less likely to be satisfied with their accommodation than those in other types of temporary accommodation.

There are four main themes in the literature. Perhaps the most prevalent theme is the poor conditions in hotels and their effects on residents' health, the damage done to the health and education of the children, and the morale and well-being of the families who endure poor conditions for several months or even years before being rehoused (see Randall et al 1982; Conway and Kemp 1986; the Bayswater Project 1987; Murie and Jeffers ed 1987; West London Homelessness Group 1987; Conway 1988; Thomas and Niner 1989).

The most influential study of the poor conditions existing in hotels and their effects on residents was Conway's for the London Food Commission, the Maternity Alliance, SHAC and Shelter (Conway 1988). The report documents the storing, cooking and preparing of food; safety; overcrowding of residents; length of stay; health and diet of mothers, pregnant women and children; access to health care; and environmental health action on standards in hotels for the homeless.

Interviews were carried out with 23 single parent and 34 two parent families living in hotels and with health professionals caring for them, health visitors, General Practitioners and Environmental Health Officers. In addition, health records for 41 families in London and Manchester were examined. The movement of the families was traced through the records from their early months in the hotels through subsequent moves. Many families proved untraceable, many had no health records at all. From an original 116 families only 41 had health records which could be examined.

The majority of the women were of European ethnic origin. Asians were the largest non-European group. Eighty eight per cent of the Tower Hamlets sample were Asian in origin, 12% of the Hackney sample and 7% of the Manchester sample.

Eight women were pregnant at the time of the survey, five were having problems with the pregnancy - high blood pressure, weight loss, and three were assessed as having poor diet. Health visitors were concerned about the health of pregnant women in the hotels 'because of their generally poor nutrition and poor standards of health, homeless women are more inclined to post partum haemorrhages and severe anaemia'. (Conway 1988 p. 53). Women who were homeless during pregnancy had significantly higher recorded problems in pregnancy and labour than those who became homeless after birth (Conway 1988 p.55).

Nineteen children in the survey had been born in hotels. Twenty two mothers had brought a newborn baby back to a hotel and mentioned problems such as cockroaches, dirt, unhygienic conditions such that the baby could not be left to crawl, lack of heating, lack of space, and lack of cooking facilities. Babies born to hotel women tended to have a low birth weight. Hotel babies tended to suffer frequently from a range of illnesses and to be slow in their growth and development. They tended to have limited access to health facilities such as immunisations. They tended to suffer frequent accidents from burns, falls and so on. The lack of play space meant that babies tended to spend much of their time in the bedroom.

The costs of housing homeless people in hotels is the second most prevalent theme in the literature (see Conway and Kemp 1986; GLC 1986; and Walker 1987). Walker (1987) assessed the total and comparative public sector costs of keeping households in hotels, compared to equivalent costs incurred in building or rehabilitating publicly rented housing, or acquiring private dwellings for them. The total annual costs of keeping 4,000 households in hotels amounted to between £30 million and £38 million. It cost an estimated £11,600 a year to keep a three person family in hotels, compared to £7,700 as the first year costs of new build council housing.

The changes in benefit regulations and the way these have affected homeless households access to hotels is another theme in the literature. It was the subject of a study by the consortium of agencies dealing with hotels and Board and Lodging issues (BLIP).

BLIP (1986) carried out a telephone survey of prices in 710 London hotels in Winter 1985. The report gives the name, address and telephone number of each hotel, identifies its local DHSS office, gives the price per week of a single, shared and double room, indicates whether the hotel took claimants, whether it had vacancies at the time of the survey, how many rooms there were in the hotel, and how many sharers there were to a room.

The report monitors the effect of the DHSS 1985 board and lodging reforms on the availability of B&B accommodation to single claimants in London. The reforms made several changes in board and lodging payments and their delivery. Before the reforms each of the 50 London local DHSS offices set their own board and lodging limits for their own area, afterwards the limits were set centrally. After the reforms the limit became £70 a week full board rather than £110.

The DHSS assumed that hotels would drop their prices to within the new limits. But far from reducing their rents hoteliers increased them by 15% - 20%. Only 60 hotels charged below the rate for a single room, and only 44 below that for a double. Moreover only 382 hotels said they would let to claimants.

This was the first full survey of London's hotels and remains an important reference point for research in this field. BLIP carried out a further survey in September 1988 to discover what changes had occurred in hotels since their first survey.

The BLIP surveys covered hotels taking households placed by local authorities as well as those taking non-priority homeless and those who were not referred by local authorities. The London Research Centre Board and Lodging Information Exchange (BABIE) has been running quarterly surveys, from Spring 1988, asking local authorities how many households they place in which hotels, and how they have graded these hotels in terms of their conditions. Four small reports have been produced documenting the findings of the 1988 surveys. They are available from BABIE. The reduction in hotel placements from 7,637 households in September 1988 to 6,759 in December is noted (BABIE December 1987), three quarters of the reduction being due to policies of three authorities which were the biggest users of hotels for homeless people, Hackney, Westminster, Kensington and Chelsea. Despite its efforts Westminster remains the biggest user.

The household structure of the homeless people in hotels is a theme of several studies, although it is less covered than the other themes mentioned (see West London Homelessness Group 1987; Thomas and Niner 1988). The fullest account is given in Thomas and Niner.

Their findings are referred to in the body of this report to be compared to the findings of the University of Surrey/Salvation Army survey (below).

The themes drawn from the literature here are, the poor conditions in the hotels, the cost of hotel provision compared to other types of temporary accommodation for homeless people, the changes in benefit regulations and the supply of hotel accommodation, and the structure of the hotel homeless. A further theme in the literature not dealt with here are the multiple policy related issues analysed in reports such as that by the Audit Commission (Audit Commission 1989), or the Institute of Housing (IOH 1988). These and several others merit separate discussion since they raise issues not directly covered by the field work reported here.

Surveys: The University of Surrey/Salvation Army surveys of hotels

For the University of Surrey/Salvation Army study of homeless people in London hotels, it was decided to concentrate on the areas where there had been least direct research. These were, the numbers and the household structure of the homeless people in hotels, including the single and childless not placed by local authorities; and the attitudes of hoteliers' to their work with homeless residents.

The approach was meshed as fully as possible with that adopted in the other fieldwork described in the present volume. In this chapter are presented the findings related to the numbers and structure of the hotel homeless, some of the problems the hoteliers said they had with providing for homeless residents; and some aspects of the hoteliers conditions of work. In addition the hoteliers' attitudes to homeless people, and to facilities provided in the hotels are discussed. The findings are compared to similar findings made in relation to hostel managers who were the subjects of one of the other surveys carried out during the course of this project.

Because of the sheer numbers of hotels and their dispersal throughout

London, it was decided to use a telephone survey to cover all hotels known to be taking homeless households. In four areas with high concentrations of hotels, those hotels from whom responses were not obtained in the telephone survey were visited in a follow-up survey. Resources were not available to contact all those hotels in the rest of London which did not respond to the questionnaire.

On 26th April 465 hotels were telephoned using 24 volunteers drawn from Salvation Army officers. Twelve telephone lines and space at their Euston offices were donated by Mercury. The telephonists used a questionnaire to ask hoteliers about the numbers of people and households in their hotels and the structure of the population, what difficulties they had with accommodating homeless households which did not arise with tourists, what their own hours of work were and how long they had held their post, and some questions were asked to establish their attitudes towards homeless people as well as their levels of satisfaction with the facilities provided in the hotel (see the questionnaire in the Appendix). The Salvation Army provided considerable help with organising this part of the work.

The sample of hotels was derived from two sources. The first was the BLIP survey list of hotels for the 1988 survey including 371 hotels. One hundred and seventy of these said they did not take homeless people, neither single claimants nor homeless families. One hundred and ninety six said they did. During the pilot survey in Pimlico all hotels listed in Pimlico by BLIP and LRC were visited. This was to assess whether it was possible to rely on the hoteliers' statements to the BLIP interviewer that they did not take homeless families. Their statements turned out to be not particularly reliable.

The second source was the list drawn up by the LRC BABIE surveys during 1988. There were 634 hotels on this list. The LRC asked all local authorities to provide information for February and May 1988 about the hotels they used to house homeless families, the borough where these hotels were situated and the numbers of households placed in them.

Of the 196 BLIP hotels saying they took homeless people, 90 were on the LRC lists and 106 were not. To establish the total number of hotels taking homeless people, therefore the 105 BLIP hotels which said they took homeless families were added to the 634 hotels on the LRC list. Unless the local authorities were sending outdated information to the LRC all the hotels on their lists were definitely taking homeless households placed by local authorities. This method yielded a total number of 739 hotels in London taking homeless people in the Autumn of 1988. The LRC did not give the telephone numbers of the hotels they listed. Telephone numbers were found for 359 of them (including the 90 on the BLIP lists). BLIP gave the numbers of 106 hotels on their lists. The final sample for the University of Surrey/Salvation Army telephone survey was 465 hotels.

Of the 465 hotels which the telephonists tried to contact, 114 said they took homeless people and answered the questions; a further nine said they took homeless people and said how many they took but gave no further information about them; 63 said they only took tourists. No information was obtained from the remaining 279, 60% of the sample. In some cases the managers refused to answer the questions, in some cases the manager was not available and staff were unwilling to answer the questions themselves; in others the telephone was repeatedly answered by children or by people who did not speak English; in other cases the number was unavailable or constantly engaged; in others the manager asked for the form to be sent so it could be answered at a more convenient time.

Because the response or failed contact rate was so high a follow-up survey was carried out in four of the areas where there are the highest concentration of hotels for homeless people. Those which had been interviewed over the telephone were omitted. A team of 44 volunteers, Salvation Army cadets, visited the hotels. The cadets were asked to visit 171 hotels in all, 27 in Earls Court, 88 in Bayswater, 30 in Finsbury Park, and 26 in Kings Cross. Forty five of the hotels contacted at the door said they took homeless people and gave the information requested; 19 said they only took tourists. The remaining 107, 62% of the sample, either would not or could not respond to the questionnaire, or the wrong address had been given and the hotel could not be found.

Through the telephone and the follow-up surveys full information was obtained from 159 hotels. Information on the total number of residents was obtained from a further nine hotels in the telephone count. This latter figure is used for estimating the total number of homeless people in hotels but is not included in the analysis. Since the information obtained from the two surveys was the same it is consolidated and presented as if it were one sample.

Table 9.1: Hotels contacted, by number of homeless residents accommodated, telephone and follow-up surveys

Number Accommodated	Hotels % (N=168)
0-19	43
20-39	30
40-59	12
60+	13
NS	2
Total	100

The largest proportion of hotels accommodated under 20 homeless residents. The number of homeless residents most often accommodated (mode) was nine. At the other end of the scale 13% of the hotels accommodated 60 or more homeless families, five of these accommodated 175 or more homeless residents, one as many as 402. It is possible that some of these were hotel complexes solely catering for homeless residents.

Results: The Hotel Homeless

The numbers of homeless people in London hotels

5,710 people were living in the 168 hotels who responded during the telephone survey and follow-up survey. This figure can be assumed to under represent the true numbers of homeless people in these hotels. Interviewers repeatedly recorded feeling that some hoteliers were understating the numbers of homeless people in their hotels, and that others were being untruthful when they said they had none. During the pilot study a receptionist in a Pimlico hotel ran down the road after the interviewers to tell them that her employer had misrepresented the case when he had claimed that he had no homeless residents, but she could not give any figures. Several hotels who are known as big providers for homeless people refused to respond, and several others could not be located neither during the telephone survey nor during the follow-up door-to-door survey in four boroughs.

It was estimated that the survey covered between 23% and 30% of the hotel homeless in London. It is not possible to be more precise since there is no figure for the total number of homeless residents in London hotels. The 30% estimate was reached in the following way. The most reliable figure for the homeless households, not people, in London hotels is that given by BABIE for those placed in hotels by local authorities in December 1988. They found 6,759 households so placed (BABIE December 1988 p.1). This does not include those not placed but who came to hotels by other routes, who were included in the University of Surrey/Salvation Army survey. These are more likely to be single people (Thomas and Niner, 1989). Nevertheless the BABIE figure is the best available. To estimate the number of people living in the 6,759 households one can multiple by 2.8. This figure is the average number of persons per household placed in hotels by local authorities, according to (Thomas and Niner 1989. Table 4.8 p. 50). This calculation yields 18,925 people placed in hotels in December 1988. There may have been a decline in hotel placements from December 1988 to April and May 1989. BABIE found the number of placements declined 11.5% from 7,637 households in September to 6,759 in December 1988. The 5,710 people counted in the University of Surrey/Salvation Army survey constituted 30% of 18,925.

The estimate of 23% was reached in a different way. The University of Surrey/Salvation Army survey covered 23% of the hotels in London taking homeless people and found 5,710 people in them. Directly extrapolating from that would mean that there were 24,826 homeless residents in all London hotels, 5,901 more than those estimated to be living in the households listed by BABIE, which excluded the self-referred.

Some confirmation is given to this latter estimate by the following analysis. Thomas and Niner surveyed 1,060 households in hotels nationally, of which 73% were placed by local authorities and 27% were not. If the total found by the University of Surrey/Salvation Army survey of 24,826 is taken as the total in hotels, the BABIE 18,925 figure for those placed by local authorities constitutes 76% of the total. This is close enough to the Thomas and Niner proportion to inspire some confidence.

The types of people in the hotels

Table 9.2 gives the household structure of a total of 4,953 individuals interviewed in the University of Surrey/Salvation Army survey and Table 9.3 the percentage of households. For the remaining 757, no information is available on their household characteristics. The majority of the hotel homeless, 75%, or 3,703 people, were living in 1,116 families. Of the families, just over half were two parent families, the remainder were one parent families. Single people formed 23% of the hotel residents, but half of the households living in hotels. Only 2%, 123 people, were living as childless couples. In all there were 1,250 childless people living in the hotels.

Table 9.2: Individual hotels residents, by household type

Family Type	Number Individuals	%
Two parent families	1889	38
One parent families	1814	37
Single people	1127	23
Childless couples	123	2
Total	4953	100%

In some cases the figures for the number of individuals rather than families were given under question 2 of the questionnaire. Estimates were made by dividing the figure by 3 for two parent families and by 2 for one parent families. The reverse procedure was followed when the figure for families was given under question 2 and no figure for individuals was given under question 1. Niner and Thomas (1989, Table 4.8 p.50) found the average number of people in bed and breakfast accommodation was 2.8. This included single people.

It is likely that the above estimates may slightly undervalue the number of people in families interviewed in the University of Surrey/Salvation Army survey.

Niner and Thomas (1989, p. 50) found a similar household structure although theirs was a national sample of households placed by local authorities in bed and breakfast hotels, and their base was 229 residents. Their sample as already noted, was skewed away from single people whom their own study shows to predominate among the self-referred. They found 41% two parent families (including some where the mother was pregnant with no children) compared to 38% in the University of Surrey/Salvation Army survey, 33% single parents compared to 37%, 19% single (including single and pregnant) compared to 23%, 4% childless couples compared to 2% and 2% other types of household. The two studies are close enough in their findings on the household structure to offer some confidence. The balance of single people to people with children in the two studies is predictable.

Table 9.3: Households in hotels by type of household

Household Type	Number Households	%
Two parent families	579	24
One parent families	557	23
Single people	1127	48
Childless couples	123	5
Total	2386	100%

In the pilot survey in Pimlico 412 residents were found in the hotels which responded to the questionnaire. Fifty six per cent of these residents were living in families. Just over a third of the homeless in the hotels - 147 people - were single.

A large minority of the hotel homeless - 31%, 1,576 individuals were children. Some hoteliers in the survey mentioned that children tended not to go to school but to be around during the day, running around the hotel, the fire escapes, and even running up and down the road. Some were also worried about the childrens' health. The difficulties in raising children in the hotels has been documented in other studies (see particularly Conway and Kemp (1986): Bed and Breakfast: Slum housing of the 1980's, SHAC; Conway ed. (1988): Prescription for Poor Health. The Crisis for Homeless

Families; and The Bayswater Homelessness Project (1987): Speaking for Ourselves. Facilities in B&B. The later of the two studies by Jean Conway was sponsored by the London Food Commission, the Maternity Alliance, SHAC and Shelter, bearing witness to the concern felt by a diverse range of agencies involved with the different aspects of deprivation experienced by families in hotels.

The hoteliers were asked a series of questions about their homeless residents, such as how many were working, or how many were ill. Since this information was given by few hoteliers and was based on their impressions only, it is not reliable. It is recorded here for completeness.

According to hoteliers' reports 310 or 6% of the homeless people living in hotels were working. It was not always clear to hoteliers whether residents were working or not. As one hotelier said:

> Some might work. They leave home early and come back late.

According to hoteliers' reports 66 residents were known to be ill and 31 disabled; 116 had problems with drinking and 43 with drugs. It was not possible to establish how many were from ethnic minorities. Other researchers have found that people from ethnic minorities are more likely than white European people to be placed in hotels (Thomas and Niner 1989. p.52). Thirty six per cent of those placed in hotels nationally were from ethnic minority groups compared to 22% placed in all types of temporary accommodation. The authors postulate that this might reflect the fact that bed and breakfast placements are more predominant in London and higher proportions of London's homeless are from ethnic minority groups.

The problems associated with taking homeless people compared to tourists

The hoteliers were asked whether they found there were particular problems in taking homeless people which they did not experience with tourists. Nearly a third of the hoteliers mentioned problems with receiving the rent. Hoteliers were asked if they had noticed any changes during the previous two weeks in the ability of homeless people to pay their rent. Changes in the Board and Lodging payments available to homeless people had been introduced in the two weeks before our full survey. Fifty nine per cent said they had noticed no difference because the council paid the rent. Fifteen per cent said it appeared to be more difficult to get the rent and 3% said it appeared easier.

During the pilot survey 12 out of the 26 hoteliers who answered the questions said there were problems associated with taking homeless people rather than tourists.

Nine hoteliers said they had difficulties getting rent for homeless residents. Some residents would leave without paying. Sometimes the local authority might owe several months rent on families for whom they were paying rent directly to the hotelier. Problems were mentioned with the payment by the DSS of rent in arrears, a system introduced in April 1988.

After problems obtaining rent, hoteliers cited nuisance as being caused particularly by homeless residents. Fourteen per cent in the full survey and six out of the 26 hoteliers in the pilot survey who answered the question said that homeless residents were more likely than tourists to cause a nuisance by drinking, fighting, swearing and so on. Small proportions in both surveys mentioned being troubled by the children of homeless families. They tended to be unhealthy, to miss school and play around the fire escapes and the streets. Similar proportions in both surveys mentioned that some residents needed special help. They were ill or disabled. Small numbers also mentioned that it was difficult to clean the hotel because homeless residents tended to stay in all day. Several mentioned that having homeless people made the hotel unsuitable for tourists.

One hotelier in the pilot survey said that some homeless people booked a room and used it for only a few nights before going away. If the hotelier reports this to the local authority, the authority stops payment. If the family returns to the hotel, they may often be angry that they have lost their room. The hotelier expressed some annoyance toward homeless families for this behaviour.

The relationship with placing local authorities was obviously crucial to hoteliers. If there was trouble with a family the hotelier would need to refer to the authority. And, of course, a local authorities' performance in paying the rent was of crucial importance to hoteliers. Several mentioned that Tower Hamlets was a good authority and Lambeth and Newham were not.

The hotel market for homeless people

The hotel market for homeless people is subject to change and fluctuation which is certainly partly seasonal but is also a response to policies of central government and of the particular local authorities where the hotels are situated. The BLIP studies document the response of the hotels to the Board and Lodging reforms of 1985 and 1986. The main findings are documented above.

The second stage BLIP survey, the LRC survey and the pilot survey in Pimlico were all carried out during 1988 and yet there is some variation in the findings concerning the types of residents accepted by the hotels concerned. This variation might be due to error or to different versions of the facts being presented by hotel staff. Or it might reflect the rapidly changing hotel market, and its turbulence over the last four or five years; and that fewer hotels are now prepared to accept homeless people.

Comparing the LRC survey in February 1988 with the pilot survey in Pimlico reveals some variation in the type of clientele accepted by the hotels in the two surveys. In the pilot survey interviewers visited 12 hotels which were listed in the LRC survey as taking local authority referred homeless people. Twelve of these had homeless people in residence, 12 did not.

Comparing the BLIP survey in September 1988 with the pilot survey in Pimlico also shows great variation in the type of clientele accepted by the hotels. The hotels which did not reply in the pilot survey or which said they took no homeless people at all are omitted from the analysis. Replies were obtained from 12 of the hotels which said they took homeless families in the BLIP survey. Six of these had homeless families in residence at the time of the pilot survey, and six did not. Four hotels which in the BLIP survey said they did not take homeless families had families in residence at the time of the pilot survey. Seven of the hotels which said they took single claimants in the BLIP survey were visited in the pilot survey. Of these, six had single claimants in residence at the time of the pilot survey. Eleven of the hotels which said they did not take single claimants in the BLIP survey in fact had single claimants at the time of the pilot survey.

A more detailed picture of the hotels available to homeless people can be drawn from pilot survey interviewers' observations about the conditions and atmosphere in the hotels they visited. They recorded their observations on a checklist immediately after leaving the hotel concerned. The findings on this point are derived from the pilot survey. The interviewers tended to give less full information during the full survey than during the pilot survey.

There appeared to be three types of hotels in Pimlico. Those which took single people only, both workers and claimants; those which took homeless families only; and those which took a mixture of single workers and claimants, homeless families and claimants, and tourists. Some operated a different policy according to the season, taking homeless people during the low season and tourists in the Spring and Summer.

Ten hotels took singles only. This group was not likely to include the worst hotels and also the best, according to our counters' subjective opinion. Four of them were considered to be seedy. Only five of the whole sample of hotels were considered to be seedy, four of these were singles-only hotels and one was a homeless family-only hotel. Three of the singles-only hotels were considered to be in excellent condition, these were the hotels which specialised in taking workers; two were described as being in reasonable condition. The only problem that these hoteliers mentioned with taking homeless people was that there are problems with getting the rent.

Three of the singles-only hotels were lodging workers staying long-term only. They did not have any single unemployed people. Two of these hotels were considered to be in excellent condition. These were business hotels. One was considered to be seedy.

Four hotels took homeless families only. One of these was described as seedy, the rest as reasonable. All the hoteliers which mentioned children as being a problem fell into this group, four of them also mentioned drinking,
swearing and so on as being a problem. Of the remaining mixed hotels, four were almost entirely occupied by single people.

The hotels' practice in selecting and managing homeless residents

Even when hotels said they did not take homeless families they appeared to do so when it suited them. Some hoteliers said they assessed whether a potential resident had the money and looked right. They might take homeless people in if they were satisfied they would be no trouble. Some hotels taking homeless people did so seasonally. In the Summer they would take less homeless people in order to take more tourists. For these hoteliers, the homeless residents provided what one called his 'bread and butter', his basic reliable income. However some hotels took homeless people as their main residents all year round.

Many hotels took commuters, mentioning the North, Brighton and Birmingham as the places where these residents commuted from. During the pilot survey two hoteliers claimed that they were being 'harassed' (their words) by the Environmental Health Officer (EHO) to force them to refuse other boroughs' nominations. One quoted an EHO as saying 'I'll be on to you until you stop taking homeless people.' These claims cannot, of course, be confirmed or refuted by the surveys carried out during this study. They were, however, made by several hoteliers in the full survey, too. Westminster already places few of its own homeless households within the borough.

The council has a policy to reduce the numbers they place in Westminster's bed and breakfast hotels, and to increase the proportion of out-of-borough placements (BABIE 1988 p. 1).

Replying to the interviewers, 64% of the hoteliers in the full survey said they intended to carry on taking homeless residents 14% said they intended to cease taking them and 23% did not know what they intended to do or gave unclear answers to the question.

The conditions of work of hotel staff

Hotel staff, as is generally well-known, tend to work very long hours. Twenty five per cent of those interviewed in the main survey said they were on call or actually working 24 hours a day; a further 26% said their hours were undefined. Some of these would be family members working in a family concern. Thirteen per cent worked for between 10 to 18 hours a shift. Only 36% worked up to nine hours a day.

Forty six per cent (46%) of those interviewed in the full survey had worked in their current job for over two years, 11% for over a year up to and including two years and 30% had worked in a job for up to and including a year.

Seventy six per cent (76%) said their job was to manage the hotel. In fact, interviewers had asked to speak to the manager. Eighty two per cent (82%) considered their job was to offer a good service to residents. But although so many were managers, only 37% said their job was to collect the rent. This may reflect the fact that many of the hotels were part of chains of hotels catering for homeless people where a central office dealt with the administration.

Views of hotel staff

At first glance, there are some similarities between hotels and hostels as homeless settings. However the differences in organisation and staff are striking. This was clear from the onset of the research. It was always much easier to obtain information about the hostels and from the hostels than was the case for hotels. The attitudes of both groups also showed clear differences. During the telephone survey and follow-up survey several questions were put to staff of both hotels and hostels and they were asked to agree or disagree with them.

As similar questions were put to hotel staff, it is possible to compare some aspects of hostels and hotels. There were slight differences between hostels and hotels in the wording of two of the questions which are marked with *. The wording shown here was used for hotels and in brackets for hostels. On average 10% of responses were missing.

More hotel staff agreed that their hotels were well designed for cleaning and supervision (83%) than did hostel staff (72%).

Fewer hotel staff agreed that their hotel had enough space to satisfy residents' needs (45%) than did hostel staff (58%). In fact over a third of hotel staff did not give a response to this statement.

There would seem to be more to the different responses to the two types of Q.6 than wording, as a larger percentage of hotel staff agreed that homeless people in their hotel were in some way to 'blame' for their situation whereas only 5% of hostel staff would seem to be stating the same thing.

Table 9.4: A comparison of views of hotel and hostel staff

Question	Hotels % Agreement (% Disag.)	Hostels % Agreement
Q.1 This hotel/hostel is well designed for cleaning and supervision.	83% (6% Dis)	72%
Q.2 This hotel/hotel is a friendly place to work.	59% (25% Dis)	77% (22% Dis)
Q.3 Residents have enough space and privacy to meet everyday needs. * (excluding privacy)	45% (39% Dis)	58% (39% Dis)
Q.4 This hotel/hostel is a sociable place where residents can get to know one another.	75% (10% Dis)	93% (4%)
Q.5 Homeless people are just normal people who have hit on hard times.	67% (15% Dis)	71% (20% Dis)
Q.6 People in this hotel are homeless because they haven't made an effort to find a place of their own.*	18% (49% Dis)	--
Q.6 (Hostels) Homeless people could find themselves somewhere to live if they wanted to.	--	5% (88% Dis)

Table 9.5: Correlations of hotel and hostel staff responses

	Hostel	Hotel
Q2. Friendly Place to Work) Q4. Sociable For Residents)	.80	-.47
Q1. Well Designed for Cleaning) Q4. Sociable For Residents)	-1.00	.06

The correlations presented in Table 9.5 suggest that for hostel staff the benefits for residents are positive experiences whereas they are not for hotel staff. For hostel staff, having a sociable place for residents and being a friendly place to work are highly positively correlated (and therefore the opposite is true that if the hostel was not considered to be a sociable place for residents it wasn't a happy place to work for staff). For hotel staff the reverse is the case as the two aspects of hotel experience were negatively correlated so that hotel staff did not find residents' social life contributing to their idea of a friendly place to work.

Questionnaire survey

Background

The hotel sample in the questionnaire survey was the smallest due to methodological difficulties described. Despite the size of the sample (N=15) the findings are presented here in brief if only to demonstrate the contrast to the other settings.

The hotel sample were the youngest in the survey with 74% aged 29 or less and 6% over the age of 50. Seventy three per cent (73%) were also women which again is the highest across the settings. It would seem that at least in terms of the survey itself, the hotel resident emerges as a very different type of person out-of-home.

Although there were slightly more married or cohabiting people in the sample (19%) than other settings, there was still a majority of single people (67%). In terms of employment status, the hotel sample were for the majority, unemployed (92%). Unlike the other settings, there were no people working in the hotel sample and the lowest percentage carrying out voluntary work (7%). This sample had the lowest number of educated people as well with 62% stating they had no educational qualifications.

In terms of where people were born, there were fewer people born in England in this sample (53%). The remainder were born in Scotland and Wales (26%), Europe or Other (14%) and Ireland (7%). The lowest percentage of white Europeans were in this sample (73%) with 20% black or Asian.

This sample had stayed the least time in their setting with 74% having stayed there for six months or less.

Day centres were the least used by this setting with 80% stating they never used them. This suggests perhaps, that there is lack of centres that are appropriate to the needs of the hotel homeless.

Psychological aspects

The figures on mental stress suggest that on average hotel residents have the highest level with 30% higher than the lowest of the settings, squats.

There were lower levels of self esteem in the hotel sample than in any other with only 31% considering they make a contribution and 38% agreeing they were not a failure. Only 27% felt part of a community living in the hotel which is the lowest across the settings.

Residential history

The highest percentage across the settings (40%) had come straight from a house or flat to the hotel. Nearly half (47%) had stayed in their earlier home for longer than one year which is one of the highest among the samples. Furthermore the highest percentage of this sample had left home later (47% left between the ages of 19 and 25) and had lived in fewer places (86% lived in 10 or less places).

The last place which most of this sample considered home was described as a specific place (50%) with a further 40% referring to a house or flat or family home. Having left there, a third went to a hotel and 27% went to a house or flat. Only 7% went to another homeless setting, a hostel. For 85% of the sample this happened less than two years ago. Thus in many ways this sample would seem to be the most stable and distinct as it does not seem to spill over into other settings, except hostels to a small extent.

The highest percentage of any setting is on a housing waiting list in this sample (93%) which indicates that this setting is distinct also because it is the only 'official' temporary accommodation provided by local authorities.

Evaluation

The hotel residents evaluated their hotel relatively highly with only squatters giving a higher evaluation on average. For those in hotels the items which people evaluated highly were feeling 'safe', 'getting a good night's sleep' and 'I can do what I want here'. However as only 27% 'feel part of a community living there', the psychological and even symbolic aspects of home would seem to be missing from hotel living. In other words, although hotels are safe places to get some sleep and with a certain amount of freedom, they are not social or comfortable places and are not liked as temporary accommodation. In this sense from these findings, it may be that on average hostels are more hearthful places than hotels, although one would except otherwise.

In terms of stating what aspects were important to them, the hotel sample were second highest on average overall, in that most considered all of the aspects to be important, the least being 'to live in London'. The item which all of the hotel sample considered to be important was 'having a room of my own'. Whereas this item would be considered in terms of sharing with other people out-of-home for the other settings, in this setting it would seem to refer to having a room away from their children.

The hotel sample would seem to explain things in terms of luck but more in terms of their lack of skills, their inability to settle down at that time and the actions of others. Only 40% agreed that they were just 'unlucky in finding somewhere to live'; 87% agreed they were 'not too lazy to look for somewhere to live' and 79% agreed that 'if they could settle down they would get a job'. Fifty three per cent (53%) agreed that the 'shortage of housing prevented them from finding somewhere to live'.

Conclusion

This chapter outlines the projects findings on the numbers and types of people in hotels for homeless people in London. There are probably more than 18,925 people, possibly as many as 24,826 homeless people in hotels. Having covered 23% of the hotels in London the project's findings are the best available on the numbers and structure of the hotel homeless in London. Nevertheless, they are presented cautiously since the subject defies a watertight analysis.

The majority of hotel homeless are living in families, almost as many in single parent as in two parent families. Almost a third of the hotel homeless were children, for whom hotel living has been shown to be unsatisfactory. Hoteliers themselves referred to being concerned about the childrens' health and schooling. Hoteliers most often cited problems receiving rent when accommodating homeless people. They sometimes mentioned that the problems arose because of administrative difficulties within the placing authorities.

The fluctuating hotel market for homeless people was a reality for the survey as well as for homeless people. Thirteen per cent of the hotels originally contacted no longer accepted homeless people. A number of those listed by interviewers as being unlocatable or unobtainable could have closed down.

The sample of hotel residents would seem to be very different from the other settings. They are mostly young unemployed women on a housing waiting list. They do not go to day centres. They would seem to be suffering high levels of mental stress and have low self esteem. Physically they are perhaps better off in housing terms than some of those in the other settings, but they do not feel part of a community and most of them do not like staying there or find it comfortable or sociable. It seems that hotel living may be the loneliest setting in which to find oneself.

Taking the administrative and psychological aspects of hotel living together it is clear that the equivalent of the population of a small town is living a confused, uncaring existence scattered throughout London's hotels. The reluctance of much of hotel management to participate in surveys accords with the similar disinterest that many of the hotel residents themselves feel. In effect these hotels are local authority housing estates scattered across many small crowded streets throughout London. But there appears to be very little of the control or accountability and virtually none of the community that a local authority estate at its worst would take for granted. The irony, that it is probably cheaper to build new local authority homes than keep people in poor quality hotels, indicates that this is an area where government policy could be productively developed.

10 Begging

Introduction

Over the last few years the media and campaigning organisations have commented upon the perceived growth in begging and in particular, aggressive begging in central London. Yet despite the many confident assertions by newspapers and television no research has been carried out into the phenomenon. This chapter provides an account of a small exploratory observational study. In particular the relationship of begging to homelessness is explored.

The result is a descriptive analysis of present day begging which, while not claiming to be based upon a representative sample of beggars in London, suggests that existing accounts may conceal important issues. The chapter looks at the backgrounds of some of the beggars and their stated reasons for begging, the phenomenon of 'aggravated begging' (that is begging which was little short of 'demanding with menace') and the media portrayal of begging. It is suggested that this portrayal may have contributed to the growth of the activity as well as exaggerating it. The chapter concludes with some analysis of the research and speculation as to the underlying causes of the perceived increase.

Method

The fieldwork was carried out in the winter of 1989/90. Over that period the researcher spent various days in central London either as part of his normal occupation or for the purpose of carrying out the study. Time was spent observing beggars at work or talking to them informally. The project was divided into two stages: observation and interviews.

Observation

The first stage consisting of straightforward observation when the following was recorded.

1. Gender.
2. Perceived age.
3. Where the activity took place.
4. Type of begging.
5. Number of people passing by.
6. Who it was who gave to the beggar.
6. Whether the police were seen to be involved.
7. Whether the beggar was aggressive either verbally or physically.
8. Whether passers by showed any aggression.
9. Whether watchouts were employed.
10. Whether dogs were present.

The difficulty in devising a suitable sampling frame and achieving a random sample led to this informal and casual approach. The begging population is fluid and changeable and there is no one place which every beggar visits. A person may be a beggar one day and take the following day off or work at a casual job. It could be argued that rigour in sampling and method is more suited to a stable, settled population than it is to the moving and changing population of the street.

Casual observation and interviews took place over a wide area of central London ranging from the Oval to Highbury and Islington Station. However the great majority of systematic observations (95%) were carried out in an area around Waterloo Station and the Festival Hall, Hungerford Bridge and the Embankment Tube Station, and the Strand and West End. All interviews with beggars were from these spots.

Towards the end of the first stage any opportunity was taken to ask simple questions such as age, where he or she was from and where they stayed. If the conversation became prolonged the researcher noted down interesting areas meriting further examination.

This led into the second stage where informal and unstructured interviews - often little more than relaxed conversations - were used. Questions centred around the beggars' life history, attitudes and reasons for begging. A rolling programme of questioning operated. Formal interviewing techniques were not used nor was the interview recorded at the time but as soon as possible afterwards. Wherever possible indirect questions were used. For instance in the two months before Christmas a stock question was 'Are you going home for Christmas?' and answers to this question gave some clue as to the beggar's relationship with the family, or indeed whether he or she had a family. Sometimes in ordinary conversation a person would give a number of details. One 19 year old male said,

> As soon as I was sixteen I .... well got away from home. Bloody glad to see the back of them all, the old man, ... social workers and teachers. And Wolverhampton didn't hold much for me so I soon scarpered from there.

Such a statement gives a wealth of information and it was all unwittingly confirmed by a third party. The method used resulted in a greater amount of detailed information being obtained from the last 20 or so people interviewed.

As to the question of validity, the researcher, like any other, had to use his judgement when there was no way of verifying a story. In some cases it was decided that the element of uncertainty was so strong that it was better that much of the historical background was omitted from the final analysis.

Description of beggars

The majority of beggars were male, young - in their late teens or early to middle twenties and white. Only one member of an ethnic minority was observed although some time after the research was completed the researcher noted a small increase in young black people amongst begging groups. In calculating the age, the age stated by the informant always took precedence over the perceived age by the researcher but if there was no opportunity to ascertain the age the perceived age remained.

Table 10.1: Gender of sample

Gender	Number	%
Male	89	78%
Female	25	22%
Total	114	100%

Contrary to the statements of representatives of many homeless organisations 16 and 17 year olds, who have been most seriously affected by changes in legislation, form only a small minority of the sample and the figures probably understate the number of older beggars since in the second stage of the research there was a deliberate concentration upon the younger element. (This is also supported by the press statement given out by the National Association of Probation Officers on the 14th May 1990 which gave the breakdown of ages as follows; under 21 187, 22 -30 203, 30+ 508).

Table 10.2: Age

Age	Number	%
16-17	15	13%
18-19	37	33%
20-22	29	25%
23-26	12	11%
27-29	6	5%
30+	15	13%
Total	114	100%

Most beggars were clean (81%) and tidy (59%) and only 10 beggars showed any obvious signs of physical disability. In three cases the researcher had cause to suspect that the injury was feigned. Two beggars used crutches while begging but were observed a few hours later walking without them while in the other instance a beggar who had his arm in a sling showed no obvious difficulty in using the arm whenever required. On the other hand two beggars who showed no obvious signs of physical disability had suffered severe industrial injuries making it impossible for them to obtain the heavy work they were used to. An article in the Daily Telegraph (Monday June 18th 1990). commented on a supposed difference between people in the Bullring, a large area underneath roads and roundabouts just outside of Waterloo station, and those in the Strand arguing that the latter make efforts to live normal lives by showering each day, eating properly and drinking in moderation. There is certainly truth in the distinction for those in the Strand see themselves as apart from, and superior to, the more long stay people in the former situation and there is probably less drinking, but eating properly and regular showering are common to all groups.

Just under a third of the beggars - mostly the older ones - openly drank while begging, the general opinion being that any signs of drinking deterred people from giving money. However many more both drank and/or used illicit drugs when not begging, about half a dozen of the beggars informing the researcher that they begged just enough to buy drink or 'gear' (usually cannabis) together with a bit of food. Cannabis, amphetamines, (speed) ecstasy (a designer drug but more often a mixture of LSD and amphetamines) and LSD were the most popular drugs with a high concentration upon the first named. A few beggars took part in minor street dealing usually with other beggars as customers or with people living in the same conditions as themselves. As far as could be known not one person who regularly used heroin was found. All of the beggars who spoke about the subject said that they had started on drugs before they had entered their present stage of life and there was little evidence to support the theory that they drifted into drugs because of their present life style.

Beggars took advantage of the food and clothing handouts, the former supplementing the food they purchased and it was not unusual for a beggar to leave his/her pitch when news of a handout was broadcast.

Whenever possible beggars were asked where they stayed at night but the following figures may not reflect the exact situation since in three cases, where the response from the beggar, was 'the street' other beggars said 'he was just playing a bloody game' or 'he was a weekend beggar' and could go back home. The critics were subsequently found to be correct. Some of those who lived in squats belonged to one big squat at Belgravia hostel in South London but generally people moved from place to place either because of new friendships or because they had been evicted from squats or hostels.

Table 10.3: Where beggars lived

Place	Number	%
Street	23	31%
Hostel	10	13%
Squat	28	38%
Flat/House	13	18%
Total	74	100%

Strategies of Begging

Begging is not a haphazard activity without forethought or plan and beggars adopted various strategies which could be divided into a number of types.

Table 10.4: Types of begging strategies

Types of Begging	Number	%
Mute Sitting	9	8%
Vocal Sitting	49	43%
Standing	15	13%
Accosting	26	23%
Aggravated	15	13%
Total	114	100%

The four types are mostly self explanatory the most common form being the person who sat down and verbally asked for alms. The 'mutes' tended to look down at the ground and have a hangdog expression on their faces. However, they generally displayed a piece of cardboard which stated 'Homeless and Hungry, please help.' Those who stood would stand to one side allowing a free passage while the 'accosters' actively approached the pedestrian but still allowed them free passage. The aggravated beggars not only accosted but made the pedestrian move to one side of the beggar. Another type which the researcher saw when he lived on the street but which failed to turn up over the period of the research is the story teller although one was observed after the research. An African approached several people over a number of days saying that he had lost his return plane ticket to Lagos as well as the key to the left luggage locker and asked people if they could let him have £12 for the fare to Gatwick where he would be able to sort things out. The story teller tells a story usually centring upon lost railway tickets or having lost the fare back home and very often there is an entertainment value in the telling of the story which helps a successful beg.

Strategies could be adopted to fit the physical situation. In one instance a beggar who regularly sat on Hungerford pedestrian bridge, over the Thames, verbally asking passers by for money, was seen on other occasions at Waterloo Station with another beggar both facing in different directions, not only in order to accost people coming from different directions, but also to watch out for the police. Sometimes a team of two beggars would sit on either side of the walkway so that they could beg from people walking in opposite directions.

Time was another factor which was taken into consideration, most beggars only staying on one particular spot for one or two hours. The length of time a beggar stayed at one spot would be determined by a number of factors including, weather, other beggars, the amount of money obtained and the proximity of the police.

Dogs played an important role, beggars asserting that dogs encouraged people to give money. A 17 year old girl said that one woman every day brought a plate of food for the dog and a sandwich for her. 'Saves me money on buying dog food' was her pragmatic comment. Three beggars said that 'punters' had said to them, 'the money's for the dog not for you.' In two cases beggars had previously taken puppies with them and had sold them to passers by and one,a female beggar commented, 'The bloody bitch is expecting again anyway.' A dog might encourage passers by to stop in order to pat it on the head to initiate a conversation which was more likely to result in a successful beg.

The importance of demeanour and attitude towards passers by was well known. Three beggars remarked that it was important to smile at people and to remain cheerful, 'They're more likely to drop if you're not a wimp' one said. This contrasted with a small minority who adopted a whining and moaning voice to ask for money. One person had tried both methods and said that he now took half as much again if he smiled and made some jokes. However, the majority of beggars appeared to adopt a neutral non-threatening tone of voice when they asked for money. Most stressed the importance of thanking people when they gave while a few made a habit of thanking even those who politely refused.

The police are significant in the world of begging and even the suggestion that they are nearby is enough to persuade some beggars to leave their pitch. Being 'busted' or 'lifted' by the police was seen as an occupational hazard and little evidence emerged suggesting undue hostility towards the police although some individual policemen were considered worse than others. Two beggars remarked that making the police out to be 'bastards' who were always 'harassing' them was a useful ploy to tell 'social workers'. The term 'social worker' as used on the street may differ from usual usage. It may be a generic description applying to all of the workers who come into contact with people living on the street. One hostel worker was told by a resident when he denied being a social worker that as far as he - the resident was concerned, 'you all are social workers' while another resident told the hostel worker that he had to remember that he was 'on the other side of the line.' 'They moan to "the pigs" and say that we're forced to beg and there's less chance of them (the police) getting on our backs'. At the same time it was not unknown for a policeman to make a beggar turn out his/her pockets and take the money after warning them about their future behaviour.

Nearly all beggars, especially the younger ones, took some precautions against being caught by the police. While some wore placards to announce that they were both 'homeless and hungry' others argued that it was unwise to do so. 'The pigs can spot you a mile off' and 'You can't say you weren't begging in court if you've got this bloody great piece of card around your neck.' After one 'purge' by the police the researcher noted an absence of cards as he walked from Waterloo Station to the West End. Two beggars remarked that they preferred to stand or accost because they were better able to keep a lookout for police and there was more chance of them acting as if they were just part of the normal pedestrian traffic. It was noticed that after arrests of beggars at good begging sites, the sites appeared to remain unoccupied for the remainder of the day but one beggar, while agreeing that successful police activity deterred others from making use of the sites, argued that they were safer since it was unlikely that the police would return. He made a practice whenever possible, of occupying the site as soon as an arrest had been made.

People begging in the Strand rarely used placards, instead they sat in small groups in the doorways of shops and one of the number would ask passers by for money. The object was to make it appear that begging was not taking place and the person carrying out the begging activity might stand on the pavement detached from the group, who would sit in a shop doorway, while two others might each stand 20 yards on either side to watchout for the police.

Half of the beggars observed appeared to have watchouts and, similar to those on the Strand, on some pitches two watchouts operated looking out for police coming from different directions. Various signals were employed for indicating danger one being a watchout walking quickly past the beggar but saying nothing whereupon the beggar would cease his/her activity and walk away. Only in three instances were verbal warnings given. Some people, while objecting to begging themselves, nevertheless were willing to act as a watchout for a beggar including the researcher who acted as a watchout on four occasions during the period of research. On explaining to the beggar what he was doing he was asked if he would 'mind watching out for the pigs.'

The organisation of begging has been a subject of comment in the press. In conversations with police and workers in the homeless field allegations were made that there was a 'Mr Big' who was organising the begging, or that older beggars were organising younger people in groups allowing them to beg on certain spots in return for a 'cut' of the takings leading onto suggestions that protection rackets operated. There was also discussion concerning older beggars teaching the younger people to beg.

Taking the last point first, there is a danger of attributing a formality and organisation to an activity that is spontaneous and springs from normal social interaction. A person setting out on begging may learn to beg by merely watching friends or other beggars and so acquiring begging skills without in any way being formally taught while even the giving of hints on begging may mean something quite different to the participants than 'teaching.' There is both teaching and learning within normal social situations yet to describe a process as teaching can sometimes give a misleading impression. Certainly there was informal teaching. Hints were given to newcomers if they were part of a friendship group but what generally was taking place was ordinary socialisation with all beggars taking an active part in the process. Two people made comments which suggested that a particular beggar had been a role model for them but they were exceptions.

Organisation of groups may also operate at such an informal level that applying the term 'organisation' gives an incorrect impression. In a case that concerned an alleged murder one person was described as the 'leader of the gang' (Evening Standard 21st May). The term 'gang' was used by different people in conversation with the researcher and the terms may have been deliberately used in order to reinforce any perceived criminal connotations of the activity that neither the organisation nor the activity merits. Despite being attentive to the possibility of organisation, where older men used the younger people to beg on their behalf in a formal and organised manner, there was very little sign of such organisation. Certainly there were small groups, sometimes of people who came from similar areas or who had formed friendships in London, who worked together in a loose knit group. The young beggar who occasionally earned £60 a day once complained that his two mates had gone off drinking leaving him to both beg and act as watchout and on two occasions a beggar looked around for someone to watch out for him and persuaded people who did not form part of his normal friendship group. One or two girls might attach themselves to a particular man but whether the attachment was primarily for safety or sexual purposes was impossible to determine.

Although there were sometimes arguments about the use of pitches and even less often a degree of everyday threat there was, in fact, little real violence and the activity was mostly marked by a mutual understanding and an implicit acceptance of internal rules. Another factor which decreased the chances of violence was that few beggars wanted to beg for more than two hours and for some the time was even less. This meant that pitches would be shared out, not on a formal basis, but as a consequence of the normal patterns of begging. With two exceptions, in every case of changing over that was observed the change over was conducted in an amicable manner and the two exceptions did not result in physical aggression.

Neither does the activity lend itself to organisation on a large scale. Begging is spread over a wide area and if someone tried to assert too much authority then escape would be comparatively simple. The younger person simply moves to another area. There is also a dislike of one person 'pushing his weight about' although this is not to say that one person may not be dominant in a group, but this would be no different from what takes place in any friendship group. It must be emphasised that only one area of London was observed. During the period of research there were several accounts of begging activities in other parts of London, for instance, there was one station where there were women with young children begging while Kings Road appeared to be the field where punks begged. Afro Caribbeans were known to beg around Brixton station.

As for protection rackets their existence is notoriously difficult to disprove but once again they fit well with the traditional imposition of criminality upon poverty. A term used by two voluntary workers was 'beggar barons'. In a few instances beggars begged on behalf of someone else, in one case a beggar who had previously occupied a very good pitch went away for a short time allowing another beggar to take his place in return for a percentage of the takings. Whether this could be called a protection racket depends upon the perspective of the person explaining it. There are two interpretations, protection or an ordinary business transaction set within an ordinary socialisation process, the latter being more likely the understanding of the participants. The emphasis upon protection rackets could have been used as another myth to heighten the law and order aspect of begging while once again the beggars could be portrayed as victims not only of economic and political policies but of older men, instead of active players in a situation. The story of Oliver Twist and Fagin that dealt with the corruption of innocent youths by the criminal classes has its modern counterparts. The young are seen as innocents caught in a trap and corrupted by older people in a criminal milieu.Beggars, themselves, also were able to make use of what most people wanted to believe in order to increase sympathy.

While it is possible that there were a very small number of minor protection 'rackets' it is repeated that the begging culture does not lend itself to large scale criminal organisation and what were seen as 'protection rackets' could have been arrangements of mutual benefit to both sides, or the protection may have been required not to combat hostility from other beggars but from outsiders.

Aggressive begging and reactions

From anecdotal evidence and the accounts in newspapers the alleged growth of 'aggressive' or 'aggravated' begging was a matter of concern. In discussing aggravated begging care must be taken to realise that the same action may be interpreted in far different ways by different people since no single action is perceived in one manner therefore any aggressive begging whether verbal, physical, or merely intimidating through looks was carefully noted in the study. Verbal and physical aggression is fairly easy to recognise but threats can be suggested through body signals, tone of voice, eye contact and movement, and though the aggressive intention may have been lacking on the part of the beggar, it was decided to try to look at the situation from the point of view of the ordinary pedestrian. Although this proved difficult it was felt that some success was achieved. One criterion was whether the beggar blocked the passage of the passer by so that he or she had to move one side. Using this very wide definition of aggression it was found that in only 15 instances could the begging in some way be considered as threatening or aggressive. In none of these cases did physical violence occur and in only three cases was there verbal aggression. In contrast to this on 28 occasions passers by either verbally abused the beggar (25 times) or aimed a kick at him (3 times). Two beggars in the study were beaten up by young men.

Likewise verbal aggression by passers by may be countered by insolence and abuse from the beggar and the latter is far less likely to consider it necessary to bring the matter to the attention of the police or the media while the passer by may decide that it is aggressive. The passer by, who expects a submissive reaction from a beggar is offended that he or she does not conform to those expectations.

Pedestrians may be intimidated by the assertiveness of a beggar especially if there is a strong attempt to maintain eye contact and interpret it as aggressive. Several beggars were aware of the importance of making eye contact with the passer by one saying that providing he could hold the attention of a punter for ten seconds he was reasonably certain of making a successful beg. 'I look them straight in the eyes and they have to break.' (Male 18) Another said, 'If you can get them to look at you long enough they usually break.'(Male 20) A girl said that a smile at 'a guy' was far better than any threat. 'They can't resist it.' It was also recognised that a potential punter who deliberately avoided eye contact was signalling a definite negative message but this was not always acted upon. A beggar might raise his voice in order to catch the attention of the punter.

Most beggars argued that violence was counter productive. 'It's more likely to wake up the pigs.' (Male 21) 'You'll get far more by being nice than trying to scare the punters.' (Male 17) 'You can get away with plain begging but force is something different.' (Male 18) However one group boasted of how they had forced a young male to turn out his pockets when he refused to give any money and again how they had turned another man upside down so that all his change dropped out of the pocket. There was no way of determining whether the stories were genuine or bravado but even the repeating of such stories act as myths which help to create an aggressive climate.

Who gave to beggars and how often

What of the people who gave? Was there any particular pattern? Some beggars said that they always knew who was likely to give and ignored those who did not look like giving. Three made a moral issue of deciding whether to ask a person or not. 'I won't beg from old people or those who don't look as if they have much money.'(Male 18) 'I go for the yuppies, they're fair game, but I wont go for the old people.' (Female 17) 'If someone looks hard up I wont ask them.' (Male 20) It was felt that women were better givers than men especially younger women.

Results suggest that women were more likely to give (333 women:198 men) but this need not necessarily mean that women are more generous. Although unlikely, it is possible that more women passed by the beggars at these times but there appears to be no particular reason why more women than men should be about in central London. Certainly there was a general feeling that younger women were 'the best touch'. Also people were more likely to give if they were on their own and this applied to both men and women. The researcher subjectively divided givers into young, middle aged and elderly, and although it was felt that it was unsafe to use this division in the analysis, the results did conform to the general view that young people were more likely to give than older people.

Table 10.5: Who gave to beggars

	Women	Men	Total	%
Alone	194	102	296	56%
In company	139	96	235	44%
Total	333	198	531	
%	63%	37%		100%

It was disputed who made better beggars, men or women but some argued that this depended upon the gender of the passer by. Two girls argued that they stood more chance of making a successful beg from men while men were more likely to be successful with women passers by. However this was unable to be confirmed.

In some instances the researcher observed the begging activity for the whole of a half hour period and no successful beg was made but on other occasions ten successful begs were made in less than half an hour. The shortest period was 11 minutes and there appeared to be no general pattern regarding the frequency of success. Overall, one successful beg was made for every 40 people who passed although this too varied greatly, in one case 86 people passed by with 10 successful begs being made while at the opposite extreme 486 people passed by, none of them giving at all.

Only seven people who gave during the study were spoken to but sometimes the researcher was able to overhear conversations as they passed him by. Of the seven, four people explained that they gave because they felt sorry for the beggar believing that they should not be homeless in such an affluent country as England. Another male was more pragmatic arguing that it was better for them to beg than to earn money through crime or prostitution. One person remarked that it was difficult to know whether the beggar was genuine or not. This was a topic that was raised constantly with the researcher by colleagues and friends, all saying that they never knew who was genuine or who was not and wanted to know if he could help them but there was no way of knowing. There were expressions of anger at the government for creating such a situation or remorse at the 'plight' of the beggar. Some hostile conversations included comments such as 'getting off their asses' 'getting a job' or 'should be locked away'.

Some times people would stop to talk to the beggar to ask them how they had reached this position and although this wasted valuable begging time the opportunity was used to reinforce sympathy. One 21 year old solemnly explained to a woman that he had to beg because the government had stopped giving income support to 16 and 17 year olds, the same beggar featuring prominently in a newspaper article a few days later. But beggars sometimes did not reveal certain details that may have evoked strong sympathy, one boy saying that he was not going to tell strangers that his father had buggered him, while a girl kept back details of being drawn into prostitution before she reached the age of 14. At other times details were omitted for strategic purposes. A 17 year old boy would not give the real reason why he had left home which was that he was gay and came from a fundamentalist Christian background.

A few beggars became so used to being asked to tell their story that hearing them gave the impression of a well rehearsed acting part. Although occasionally a different story was heard from the same beggar most kept mainly to the same story. An identity was constructed, based around certain key points, so as to encourage the giver to show pity and participate in a successful beg. In a rough analysis of 12 accounts told to passer byes the following points were referred to more than 4 times;

conflict at home (7)
inability to return home (10)
catch 22, no home no job, no job no home (6)
hunger (9)
in care (5)
inability to obtain income support or social security (5)
trying to obtain work (5)
desperately wanting somewhere to live (8)

Despite the excellent telling of a story, in some cases there was no material reason at all for the person to beg although as will be seen later, whether a person is judged to have reason or not depends very much upon the ideology of the person making the judgement.

Background and history of beggars

Finding out where they were from posed some difficulty. Many had lived in different towns either because of family movement, they had moved while in local authority care or they had lived an itinerant life style for some time. It was decided to ask the simple question, 'Where are you from?' or 'where do you come from?'

Beggars' perception of where they were from was considered more important than place of birth, where parents live and often from this question further information might be gained. 'I was born in Coventry, brought up in Liverpool and sent to a kids home in Essex. Work that one out.' In the event he decided that he came from Coventry because he supported its football team. Some beggars had moved from one place to another during their childhood. The biggest group consisted of those who came from London and the South East and it was from this group that the small group of beggars who were obviously exploiting begging for no good reason came. Those from the Midlands included one group of four from the same town. Contrary to the view sometimes expressed there were few beggars from Scotland and Ireland although more of the older beggars came from the latter country. They were drinking beggars with which the study was not concerned.

Table 10.6 : Origin of beggars

Place	Number	%
Greater London	10	18%
South East England	15	27%
South West England	1	2%
Wales	2	3%
Midlands	10	18%
North West	4	7%
North East	6	11%
Scotland	5	9%
Ireland	3	5%
Total	56	100%

Table 10.7 : Time spent in London

Time	Number	%
Under 1 week	2	4%
1 week to 1 month	11	21%
2 to 3 months	22	42%
4 to 6 months	7	14%
7 to 12 months	1	2%
Over 1 year	9	17%
Total	52	100%

The time spent in London in Table 10.7 refers to the present visit but excludes those who said that they were from London. It was rare for London to be their first port of call. From conversations with ten people only two came to London immediately after leaving home while in the other cases people moved in with friends in their own home area, moved to a bigger town or city nearby or went to a different part of the country. Other information that supports the view that people move about the country is that 13 young people had been on the convoy. What was meant by the convoy was sometimes difficult to determine but a common feature was that they moved about the country in groups which included families. The importance of the convoy as part of a sub-group's culture was supported by information from three other people who lived on the street in London. One remarked about a person who had been involved in a violent incident, 'He's so brain damaged that he was thrown out of the convoy because of fights. And you've got to be pretty violent to be kicked out of the convoy.' (Male 18) He too had been on the convoy two years previously. The second when talking about the whereabouts of her brother remarked casually, 'Perhaps he's back with the convoy.' (Female 17) The third spoke about some of the good times he had when he was there and said that he would be going to Glastonbury with them this year.

Since the data was collected in winter what is particularly interesting about the figures in Table 10.7 is that few appear to have been in London for the summer months, a fact supported by the above statements. The last comment gives a clue to how some had spent the summer. Going to festivals played a large part in their lives. It is possible that for a group London was seen as the place to stay between the end of the festival season and Christmas. News about the festivals was either found out from magazines or often by word of mouth.

Several places where they had previously stayed were mentioned including Amsterdam, Paris, Cologne, Birmingham, Glasgow, Liverpool, Blackpool, Brighton, Margate, Plymouth, Winchester Eastbourne. London was not universally popular. 'London's a shitty place to be in at any time but at least there's the handouts.' (Male 20) 'Roll on the summer, then I'm away from this shithole.' (Male 21) The evidence throws considerable doubt upon such 'explanations' as, 'They come to London thinking the streets are paved with gold' and 'they are attracted by the bright lights.' For a majority of the beggars London appeared to be one place amongst many which were used and according to some, one that they would prefer not to use.

Some beggars said that they had been on the road for a number of years. Of those who said that they had left home at 13 or 14 years of age two were now aged 17, one 18, one 19 and the other 23. Some care must be taken over statements regarding the age when they left home since a few may believe that giving such an early age confers a degree of kudos. Care was taken to ensure that as much information as possible was obtained either through asking similar questions more than once or through corroboration of the story. In two instances the stories were rejected since on different occasions the stories were completely different.

Table 10.8: Age beggar left home or local authority care

Age	13	14	15	16	17	18	19	Total
Number	2	5	7	13	9	11	1	48
%	4%	10%	15%	27%	19%	23%	2%	100%

Peoples' work experience supports the view that they moved about the country. Of 46 people 12 had been on either YOP or YTS schemes and 29 had worked. Beggars sometimes engaged in work in the period of study, the jobs being similar to those in Table 10.9 although one beggar sometimes obtained work as a computer operator. Such work was obtained either through agencies or, mainly, informal contacts. Attitudes to the YTS were almost universally hostile. Few of them had bothered to complete the scheme and bitterness was expressed at what they saw as exploitation and the type of work they were expected to do. 'They said it was a training scheme but for seven months all I did was to sweep the floor. I wouldn't have minded that so much if I could have seen something at the end of it but whenever I asked about training they said they had nothing suitable.' (Male 18) 'When you see your mates used and then chucked out at the end you don't see no reason to go on.' (Male 17) 'They said I could learn about computing but the nearest I go to them was watching this bird work on them.' (Male 17) 'I went to work for this bloody small shop and was expected to do everything. One morning the manager came in, chucked his fag on the floor and told me to pick it up. I told him to fuck off and he told me to do the same. So I did.' (female 17) 'Bloody YTS, it's just exploitation.' (male 17)

Table 10.9: Work experience

(N=29)

Type of work	Number
Street market	10
Kitchen portering	14
Fruit picking	11
Labouring	9
Seaside	13
Fairground	4
Festivals	5
Other jobs	5

Evidence existed for other kinds of money making activity. The majority were hostile to the idea of prostitution denying that they had been involved in the activity at all, but 10 said that they had (eight males, two females). The discrepancy in numbers may be due to the fact that different life styles operate for male and female prostitution, the latter being more organised and settled, while sexual activity in male prostitution may be more intermittent and possibly less planned. Females 'on the game' also may be more likely to find a pimp with whom they can share the accommodation whereas pimping is not so evident in the rent boy world (there are signs that male prostitution is becoming increasingly organised). Whether a person had been engaged in prostitution or not appeared not to affect other beggars' attitudes towards them. While not personally liking the activity one beggar remarked when discussing a rent boy, 'If you've got to live you've got to find some way of making bread.' Two of the males included denied that they had been involved in prostitution although they said that they had lived with a man for a year or more for the purposes of sex and neither saw this as prostitution. All but two denied that they were homosexual.

Prostitution was seen instrumentally and not as the satisfaction of any sexual desires. Three had been abused as children.

Petty thieving was not unusual although to say it was common is perhaps an overstatement. A cardinal rule was that 'you do not steal from your own kind' and punishment would be meted out to a person caught stealing from another beggar. This attitude was identical to the rules of the street. Six people (4 males, 2 females) other than those who are presented in Table 10.11 admitted to stealing, breaking and entering or robbery. Shop lifting in the West End was sometimes regarded as too risky but the risk was not only from the security guards and the police. Organised shop lifters might take objection to a group becoming too successful (one beggar was badly beaten up by a group of shop lifters for being too effective on what they considered to be their patch).

Some comments suggested that expectations held by teachers, social workers, careers advisers had been low and also supported their views about YTS. 'When I told the careers officer what I wanted to do he just laughed and told me I hadn't a dog's chance in hell.' (Male 17) 'Because I didn't talk posh and came from a childrens home the teachers didn't want to know me'. (Male 18) 'They put me in right at the bottom even though I had done well at my first school.' (Female 18) 'The social workers said that I was being unrealistic when I said that I wanted to be a stage designer. Said it would be better if I set my sights lower.' (Male 18) 'The last thing the social workers seemed to care about was education. I wanted to get on but was told there were more important things to get sorted out first.' (Female 17) 'This teacher called me out and told me he didn't expect much from me seeing where I came from.' (Male 17)

For some young people this was a chosen way of life saying that they enjoyed being able to move about the country working at casual jobs especially in the summer, but most realised that this style of life could not go on for ever. In any case any judgement regarding choice must be made in the context of the option open to them for it is quite understandable that such a way of life may be preferable, at least temporarily, to other options. Possibly there was little difference between the low level YTS schemes open to them and the seasonal jobs which they took, except that the latter were better paid and their element of choice was enlarged.

Information about their home life was patchy and varied, some preferring not to talk about it, others were very open about their families. Just as some people exaggerate the poor conditions at home for their own purposes, so some people may not wish to advertise a failure at home. An assertion that the family home was 'OK' may hide a reality that the young person has no wish to share with strangers however well meaning. The assumption that it is 'therapeutic' for the young person to share his or her private life is unlikely to be a value that springs from the culture the young people have known in the past.

Six beggars appeared to be weekend beggars and were no longer there during the week. This group tended to come to the West End at the weekends, beg enough money to do whatever they wanted to do and dissapear at the end of the weekend. Regular beggars looked upon this group with a mixture of scorn and hostility and fights did break out between members of the two groups. Their attitude to begging was that it was a 'bit of a laugh' and 'a game' and it seemed that they were playing at being homeless.

At the other extreme five, according to their stories, could not under any circumstances have returned to their natural home either because of sexual or physical abuse. One beggar did return home for a brief period when he heard that his father had been hitting his mother but came back to London soon afterwards. Other beggars seemed to know which stories to believe and in three cases that said that some young people were talking 'a load of shit'. Sexual abuse had taken place in three cases (2 girls, 1 boy) and physical abuse together with drunken behaviour in the other two. Of those who had been in care at least three had no knowledge of their natural family at all and another four had been taken from their natural family for reasons which made it unlikely that they would want to return.

In the majority of cases it was difficult to judge to what extent the person was able to return home, such judgement in any case depending upon the values of the person making the judgement. Physically they were able to do so and would face no danger of abuse, sexual or physical. What held them back were the conditions at home, the state of one or more parents, or the lack of work in their home area. The young man whose parents were fundamentalist Christians was gay and outwardly had every opportunity to go back home but once back home he would have been pressurised to receive counselling so that his gayness could be 'cured'. In fact he and his friend, a 19 year old male begged enough to pay the deposit and rent for a flat in advance and moved in together. At the time of writing they are still together. Another boy had watched his father, whom he had idolised from an early age, deteriorate from the time he was made redundant. They lived in a town where skilled manual work was held in great esteem but his father found that his skills were no longer required. In the boy's words, 'I watched my old man become a zombie.' A 17 year girl was unable to get on with her mother's new husband and the mother began to automatically take her husband's side against her. The pressure became too much for the girl and after several bitter arguments she left the home. For others the opportunities for work appeared far more favourable in London than in their home towns. Most came from manual working class backgrounds usually those with greater economic and social deprivation resources and only two of the young people could be classed as 'middle class drop outs.' Just under half of those interviewed had experienced local authority care.

Table 10.10: Beggars who have been in care

In Care	Not In Care	Total
24 (47%)	27 (53%)	51 (100%)

In most cases their experiences of care were described in a hostile and negative manner and their experiences of their natural home only slightly less so. For those who had been in care the chances of returning home were far less than those who had not experienced care. Three could not recall anything about their natural home, they had been brought up in foster or childrens' homes from a very young age. Two people said that they did not want to talk about care, they just wanted to forget and other comments portrayed a disturbing picture. 'My step father screwed me physically, then I was put in care and the social workers screwed me mentally.' (female 17). 'My real home wasn't much but foster homes were a damn sight worse.' (male 18). 'I was pushed from place to place just like a bit of paper.' (male 17). 'When I wanted to speak to my social worker she always had some sort of excuse.' (female 16) 'You're not a social worker are you because if you are you can .... off. I've had enough of those in care.' (male 18)

Three young people (1 male, 2 females) said they had been sexually abused by 'social workers' two of whom, plus two others, said that workers had been physically violent towards them. But these were extremes, the picture painted was one of the system's indifference and the general feeling that they had been ill served by being placed in care. Most had been in a number of foster and childrens' homes. In the study only two people had been with the same foster family for the whole of their time in care. A common accusation against foster parents was that they were too stuck up and in two cases there were complaints that attempts had been made by evangelical Christians to impose their own form of Christianity on the young people. Four people remarked that their foster parents no longer wanted to know them now that there was no chance of them being paid.

There are some interesting differences between those who have been in local authority care and those who have not. Of the 10 people who had left home before the age of sixteen, 7 had been in local authority care. Out of 22 people only 7 drew income support compared with 10 out of 14 who had not been in care. Of those who had been on the convoy 11 of the 13 had been in care compared to 7 out of 20 who had not. Only four had been on a YTS or YOPs course whereas four times that number had been on such courses who had not experienced care. More had left home, whether it was foster home or children home before they were 16 and all who had done so had been to other parts of the country. Some had managed to avoid being caught for as long as four years. They had worked at various jobs such as fruit picking, seaside work or on travelling fairs or at other times had found themselves somebody to live with.

Of more concern was the fact that only one of the people who had been involved in prostitution had not been in local authority care. Two remarks suggest that even before they abscond some are aware of the possibilities of surviving in this fashion. 'When I thought about scarpering somebody said with my good looks I could always find a queer to look after me.' (Male 18). 'When my mate got caught he told us how he had stayed with this geezer for four months. Stupid sod he was onto a good thing and he mucked it up.' (Male 17). Three spoke about male prostitution in a very pragmatic manner arguing that it gave them a chance of earning money and having a good time.

Attitudes of beggars

Aspirations of beggars appeared to be no different from many other young people. 'When I settle down I want a job with a good future. One that pays plenty of money and lets me buy the things I want to for my family.' (Male 18). 'God what wouldn't I do to be able to buy a Porsche.' (Male 18). 'We moan about the yuppies but we'd be in their place if we had a chance.' (Male 19). 'This life is a shit really and I'd get out quick if I really thought that a job would lead somewhere.' (Male 16). 'I want to get married, have a nice house and have some children.' (Female 18). 'I'd want to get on and get a really good job but am not sure how.' (Female 17).

Political attitudes were often revealed when discussing income support but such attitudes generally bore little relation to those of the mainstream political parties, the best way to describe the overall attitude being 'militant apathy'. Out of 42 people who gave information about income support, 25 were drawing state benefit although in some cases the amount had been decreased because of failure to find work or for some other reason. Of those who did not draw any state benefit a number did not do so by choice. 'OK so Maggie doesn't like us drawing the dole. ...., I'll beg instead.' (Male 17). 'Begging for an hour a day is better than queuing up at some shitty hole.' (Male 20). 'If I'm treated like shit I'll behave like shit.' (Female 18). 'My old man worked his fucking guts out for most of his life then when the factory went bust no one wanted to know him. I'm not going to be like him.' (Male 18). Although Margaret Thatcher was very often a target for abuse this did not translate into positive support for the alternative, it being seen as no better than the one in existence. In fact she was praised for her honesty which was contrasted against the dishonesty of the other parties. 'Kinnock's worse he pretends to be on our side but he'll look after his own.' 'I'll never .... vote, why go to the trouble?' If there was any positive political feeling it was focused on such issues as the poll tax, lack of income support and the economic effects on their home towns and lack of jobs. Some of the beggars took part in the 1990 poll tax riots and expressed great pride when they described their own actions in violence. Although sometimes such descriptions may have been illusory they still showed that they identified with the violence and destruction of the riots. Surprisingly housing was hardly ever mentioned on its own. There was very little explicit or overt racism with only two people (1 male 1 female) expressing any kind of support for the National Front.

Either breaking the law or living in an environment where law breaking is common is obviously more likely to increase the chances of contacts with the police. The first part of the study was concerned to find out the number of times that police appeared on the scene and started off badly in that the first beggar to be observed was arrested after ten minutes. On another occasion two beggars were arrested but a plain clothes policeman merely took the money that was in his pocket and let him off. But on the majority of occasions when the police appeared on the scene the beggar had disappeared. Beggars were asked if they had been involved in criminal activity. Of the 38 people who gave any information, 24 had been involved with the police for various offenses with some as many as five times.

Table 10.11: Known charges

Nature of offence	Number
Begging	13
Affray	3
Theft	7
Assault	3
Breaking and entering	2
Armed robbery	1

However, the above figures must be taken only as indicative. In the Kate Adie radio programme one of the participants remarked on how degrading and embarrassing it must be to beg and that in doing so self respect and pride is lost. Is this how the beggars see it? Few beggars I spoke to enjoyed the activity. Those who said they enjoyed it were not genuine homeless people, but most saw it as a necessary means either for survival or getting out of the situation. Yet despite their dislike of it they were able to distance themselves mentally from the activity, it being common to see beggars approach their pitches laughing and joking but on sitting down assume the 'appropriate' role. As discussed earlier not all assumed a pitiful and pleading manner but there were limits to the extent that cheerfulness was manifested in the actual begging. Smiles, when seen, were mixed with a degree of solemnity, the beggars trying to obtain the right mix to bring the desired results. It was similar when they ceased begging. On putting a few yards between themselves and their previous pitch they would start talking and laughing together as if nothing had interrupted them. It was as if they had been playing a part in a stage play.

A number of people were asked how they felt when they were begging. There were several answers. 'I try not to think of it. Just think of the girl.' (Male 18). 'I make up stories about some of the people that pass by, rotten stories for them that piss me off, good ones for those that drop.' (Male 16). 'Think about the good times I've had.' (Female 17). 'I just leave myself behind.' (Male 20). 'Doesn't bother me at all. So what?' (Male 19). 'Doesn't worry me. It's just life.' (Female 19). 'It's not me who begs. It's someone else.' (Male 18). 'It's something I have to do, I try not to think about it.' 'I dream of what I might be if I wasn't me.' (Female 15).

For many of them, a clear division of roles and identity existed between their ordinary lives and the begging activity. There is a public self and a private self, the public I and the private me which enables them to separate their work from their ordinary lives. In many cases they assume a different role so enabling themselves to distance themselves from what is seen by the outsider as a degrading activity. One beggar added, 'It gets easier as you do it more often. You never like it but you learn to switch on and off into the begging mode. It's just not you who is begging. It's somebody else.' (Male 18) Five people were asked if they knew the other characters and whether they liked them. Two of them replied in the negative but the other three said. 'Yea, bloody great guy. Damn good beggar.' 'Yea, he's a real laugh.' 'Great mate of mine. Keeps me in dope.' Although said in jest it does reinforce the distinction that is made between the two lives.

Certainly, even though they disliked the activity, many did not admit to seeing begging as a degrading and lowering activity but argued that it was necessary in the circumstances or better than drawing the dole. When approaching agencies or when being approached by reporters they instrumentally stressed the popular perception of the activity in order to confirm other peoples' beliefs that they were the helpless and downtrodden young person. They were able to quickly adapt to different roles as and when the necessity arose.

Interpretation

Towards the end of the research period the researcher looked out for the beggars whom he had interviewed and observed. There appeared to be as nearly as many beggars and the regular spots were still occupied but by new faces. A few old faces were recognised but usually they were by the older drinkers. The question was, where had they gone?

It is suggested that the information that had been gathered, including beggars' remarks about the sort of work they had experienced, gives the clue. Some had gone to the parts of the country where such work is available. For those London was only one stop, whether of many or of few it is impossible to stay. Questions to the remaining people who were known gave additional information. Others had returned home, some had found homes and jobs, or perhaps squats and jobs and one had gone to prison. Begging in London was not an activity that was ever seen as an occupation that they would partake of forever but as an interlude that led from and into other periods of life.

Just as there are opposing ideological understandings of the beggars' life style so there can be opposing sociological / psychological understandings. Beggars can be seen as drifters devoid of goals and values who occupy a deviant sub-culture which may be defined within several different frameworks of reference; the political, social, medical, moral/religious. Whatever the ideological reference of the person or organisation making the judgement, whether right, left or centre, caring or harsh, deviancy may be attributed to the begging sub-culture. What may differ is whether one attributes the deviancy to individual or economic/political failings, but they still inevitably affect the individual so making him or her appear in some way faulty. Sometimes a degree of permanency is attributed to the life style of the participants unless a rescue operation - moral, religious, social or medical - is mounted to extract the individual from a 'Fagin' sub-culture.

On the other hand those who occupy the begging sub-culture can be interpreted as taking part in a deliberate life style with goals and values in many cases no different from people who would be considered as 'normal.' Behaviour has to be adjusted to fit the sub-culture where survival is a primary aim and when the choices made have to take into account what is appropriate to that sub-culture at a particular moment in time. More importantly, choices may be limited to only a few strategies open to them, given the nature of their previous life. They respond within their limitations in order to attempt to carry out the rescue operation themselves.

Such an interpretation requires certain qualifications right at the beginning. Firstly, it is a high risk strategy. The person comes into touch with a street culture that may draw him or her into its grip as well as with other sub-cultures such as prostitution or crime. The sub-culture is on the margins of society; its participants are seen as neither fully in society nor out of society. Secondly the sub-culture includes people at either ends of a spectrum, those who do require some kind of rescue operation and those who will use the strategies open to them to the best advantage. Thirdly, it is definitely not asserted that this style of life is either desirable or should exist. It does exist but the style of life that a person is drawn into or chooses to operate rarely has either completely negative or positive consequences. Finally, in no way is it asserted that people necessarily 'choose' this life style; such a statement being meaningless unless one examines the options open to them.

It is the second perspective, together with the qualifications, that forms the basis of the analysis of begging and beggars. Two groups stand out; the first consists of those unable to return home whether because of the conditions or because they simply had no home, and secondly those whose conditions at home while not so bad as to make it impossible for the young person to return makes returning an unsatisfactory solution at that particular time. Included in the first group were those who had experienced local authority care, or had left their home some years previously, loosing all contact with natural parents. Even had they not been in care or had it been possible for them to return home, after such a long period of absence a great deal of support and assistance would be required to overcome the trauma of both parents and the young person.

If they had run away from home the length of time away suggests that running away was not merely a symbolic act that might be carried out by many young people. How many children have marched determinedly to the gate only to look up at the overcast sky and promptly march back in again.

The young people we are discussing are unlike that; they ran away and, it is suggested, they ran away for a reason. They took a deliberate decision in order to achieve a particular end or to avoid a particular situation. The young people who contributed to the research were not usually aimless drifters without goals or reason, their behaviour and goals may have been different from what society would wish but they still possessed goals. Neither did their behaviour lack reason and probably neither did their running away. A worker at a hostel for young people leaving care remarked that there are occasions when young people between the ages of 13 and 15 go to the social services to demand that they are taken into care. They have had enough of being physically or sexually abused at home. An alternative is to run away. That is not to say that every one who runs away has been sexually or physically abused, the reasons may have been far more mundane. Possibly the parents were forcing expectations upon the child that were inappropriate or perhaps some sort of bond snapped and the child just wanted to get away for good. An article in the Sunday Express highlighted runaway children (Sunday Express, June 24th 1990, 'THE LOST GENERATION'). The emphasis was upon bringing them back home not to determine why they ran away in the first place. The children were seen as foolish taking a rash and unthought out action not, as some of them might have been, people who were taking one solution to meet a problem they were unable to overcome in any other way.

The young man who said that as soon as he was 16 he 'got way from home' saw the street as a better option, not as the ideal option and certainly not the option he would have chosen had there been better ones, but as a better alternative to staying at home. The circumstances are such that it is impossible to say that he did not choose wisely.

The young people in the sample who had experienced local authority care were in a particularly difficult situation. They had been taken away from their natural homes for various reasons, sexual and physical abuse, the inadequacy of parents, a troublesome young person whom the parents found impossible to control or the death of a parent, and in some cases the break had become permanent. A few had never seen their natural parents while for others the separation had been one of many years. Even had there been the inclination to return on the part of the young person there is certainly no guarantee that the parents would reciprocate that desire.

They had been given less opportunity to develop relationships with peers and adults in a conventional environment than other young people who had enjoyed a normal upbringing. In some cases the needs of education (and thus their future) had taken second or even third place. They had become part, an almost inanimate part, of a process within a bureaucratic and - to them - controlling organisation; instead of a home there was a placement. Several had made it apparent that they felt stigmatised not only because of what they experienced but because of their status of having been in care. There were two possibilities open to them, either see the period of care out to the bitter end or escape from it as soon as possible but even were they to take the former course there was no guarantee that they would be able to obtain suitable accommodation or to be able to cope with it. The local authority's legal responsibility ends when the period of care expires. Neither, it has to be said, could it be certain that they would have been prepared for the adult world.

Arriving in London or other cities they may hesitate to approach the agencies that can assist them for, despite protestations, workers in the field of homelessness are often seen as part of the same system that the young people have come to loathe. Once more they have to enter the world of 'care' even though this care is said to be different from what they have experienced. For young people there may be no differentiation, both 'care' in the social services and 'care' in the hostels may perceive the history of the 'client' in a different manner to the young person. In order to co-operate, the 'client' has to accept the interpretation of the worker. There is a natural reluctance to go into a hostel on the part of many young people but for young people who have been in care a hostel may appear too much like a children's home.

Whatever the tabloids say there are those young people who cannot return home but all the help that is offered by government and charities is through agencies - whether voluntary or statutory - which belong to the domain of their past. The result is that they challenge the widely held assumption that people should be grateful for the sort of help offered them by well meaning people by their rejection of what is on offer.

The second group consists of those young people who have problems at home with which they were unable to cope. Three cases have been cited. It is simple to assert that they should return home and face up to their problems but that leaves aside questions that the person making the judgement usually does not have the competence to answer. How could the young gay lad face up to the problem of having fundamentalist Christian parents who saw his natural sexual orientation as a sin that had to be exorcised? How could the young man face the loss of a father he had once worshipped yet continue to see the person in the flesh each day? How could the girl have stood the loss of her mother's loyalty? There is a danger of forcing people back into a home in order to solve an immediate problem only to store up greater problems in the future.

Response

What are the answers? To the specific activity of begging there may be no answer since begging has been with us for a long time and the only change might be that it has become more prominent and overt. To a certain extent begging itself must remain a law and order issue. Answers, if there are any, to begging by certain groups of people may lie elsewhere than in the activity itself. These people need to find other situations in which they feel they are of value. Indeed, most would take a reasonable job if it were on offer.

The view that there is something intrinsically good in absolutely every young person staying at home should be challenged. That is not to say that young people should be encouraged to leave home in every case but to recognise that leaving home is a natural step.

11 A Comparison Across Settings

Previous chapters have focused on the people who were staying in different settings of the street, hostels, hotels and squats. This chapter begins with an overview of these differences and discusses in broad terms their significance. Firstly, there are differences in terms of the background and residential history of these sub-groups of homeless people.

Background

Tables 11.1 to 11.17 illustrate the biographical information for each setting and for the whole sample of 531 people.

Age

Table 11.1 shows that those in hotels had the most older people staying there with no one over 60 found in any other setting. Those staying in squats were a much younger group with 73% under 29 years. Those staying on the street had the lowest number of young people across the settings. This is important in the light of the continuing concern with young street homeless people, even if this sample is largely from day centres.

Table 11.1 Age across settings

	ALL %	HOSTELS %	STREET %	SQUATS %	HOTELS %
Under 18	7	5	4	25	7
19-29	39	38	29	48	67
30-39	18	16	38	25	7
40-49	14	15	22	2	13
50-59	8	10	7	-	6
60-69	9	11	-	-	-
70+	5	5	-	-	-

Gender

Table 11.2 shows that those in hotels were mostly women - three times more than men. No other setting had this high a proportion of women. This is not surprising given the role of bed and breakfasts in the provision of temporary accommodation to single parents and families and the shortage of hostel provision for women. There were slightly more men than women on the street than any other setting (89% male).

Table 11.2: Gender across settings

	ALL %	HOSTELS %	STREET %	SQUATS %	HOTELS %
Male	81	83	89	75	27
Female	19	17	11	25	73

Family status

There were more single people in squats than in any other setting (75%). Sixty seven per cent (67%) of those staying in hotels were single, with 20% married or cohabiting. The highest divorce rate was in the street sample (20%) with a further 9% separated. More of those on the street had suffered marital breakups than any other setting (29%), with fewer of the squatters having the least (10%). See Table 11.3.

Table 11.3 Family status across settings

	ALL %	HOSTELS %	STREET %	SQUATS %	HOTELS %
Single	71	72	62	75	67
Widowed	3	4	-	-	-
Married/ Cohabiting	8	7	9	15	19
Divorced	13	13	20	6	7
Separated	5	4	9	4	7

Employment status

Table 11.4 shows that more of the hotel residents were unemployed than in the other settings (92%). This is most likely to be due to mothers with young children and little if any child care facilities. A higher percentage of people were working in squats than in any other setting (53%), as compared with hostels (28%), the street (35%) and hotels (0%). Surprising here is the percentage of the street sample working in some form, given the extremely difficult circumstances of keeping down a job while sleeping rough. This adds further weight to the removal of the stereotype of 'dosser' from those homeless on the streets.

Table 11.4: Employment status across settings

	ALL %	HOSTELS %	STREET %	SQUATS %	HOTELS %
Full-time	13	12	4	29	-
Part-time	6	5	2	16	-
Retired	10	12	-	-	8
Casual	8	7	27	2	-
Unemployed	47	45	53	43	92
Self-employed	2	2	2	8	-
Government scheme	1	1	-	-	-
Ill	13	16	12	2	-

This is supported by the finding that 20% of those on the street sample did voluntary work, as compared with 17% of hostel residents and 7% of those staying in hotels. A high 37% of the squatting sample carried out voluntary work as shown by Table 11.5.

Table 11.5: Voluntary work across settings

	ALL %	HOSTELS %	STREET %	SQUATS %	HOTELS %
Yes	19	17	20	37	7
No	81	83	80	63	93

Education

In terms of educational qualifications, those staying in squats were educated in general with 19% having degrees and only 21% with no educational qualifications at all. See Table 11.6. The highest percentage with no qualifications were those staying in hotels (62%), followed by those staying on the street (45%).

Table 11.6: Education across settings

	ALL %	HOSTELS %	STREET %	SQUATS %	HOTELS %
Degree	6	4	7	19	8
Profession	5	5	2	12	-
A - Level	8	7	2	17	8
CSE/GCSE	24	24	28	29	7
Other	11	13	7	-	15
None	40	41	45	21	62
School Cert	6	6	9	2	-

Table 11.7 shows that more of those on the street had trade qualifications than any other group (36%), with the least (19%) in squats.

Table 11.7: Trade qualifications across settings

	ALL %	HOSTELS %	STREET %	SQUATS %	HOTELS %
Yes	30	30	36	19	29
No	70	70	64	81	71

Place of birth and ethnicity

Table 11.8 shows quite clearly that more of those on the street were born in England than any other group. This group had no-one from outside the British Isles and Ireland. There were people from Ireland staying in hostels (13%) and in squats (12%) than on the street (2%).

Table 11.8: Country of birth across settings

	ALL %	HOSTELS %	STREET %	SQUATS %	HOTELS %
England	62	61	74	70	53
Scotland	9	8	21	6	13
Wales	2	2	-	-	13
Ireland	12	13	3	12	7
Europe	2	1	-	4	7
N.Ireland	2	3	2	-	-
Other	11	12	-	8	7

Table 4.10 shows there were very few black people in the street or squatters sample, (0%) and (4%) respectively. Thirteen per cent (13%) of those staying in hotels and hostels were black in both hotels and hostels, and a further 7% and 2% Asians. Eighty eight per cent (88%) of those staying in squats and 85% of those staying on the steets were white European and a further 2% and 10% were white from outside of Europe.

Table 11.9: Ethnicity across settings

	ALL %	HOSTEL S %	STREET %	SQUATS %	HOTELS %
White Europeans	77	75	85	88	73
Asian	2	2	-	4	7
Black	11	13	-	4	13
White (outside Europe)	8	8	10	2	7
Other	2	2	5	2	-

Length of Stay

More people on the street had been staying longer than a year (41%). This suggests that generally this group is the longest homeless group. This is surprising given the image of hostels as having those who have made it their home and have been there a long time. Table 11.10 shows the different lengths of stay. More squatters had been staying in the squat for less than a month than any other setting (24%). Twenty eight per cent (28%) of those staying in hostels, 41% of those on the street and 35% of those in squats had been there longer than one year.

Table 11.10: Length of stay across settings

	ALL %	HOSTELS %	STREET %	SQUATS %	HOTELS %
Less than 1 month	21	22	18	24	-
1 - 3 months	19	21	14	12	27
4 - 6 months	15	15	9	8	47
7 months - 1 year	15	14	18	21	26
More than 1 year	30	28	41	35	-

Day Centres

The group that used day centres the most were those staying on the street (45% use them every day). Most of the others never used day centres (80% of hotel residents, 67% of squatters and 63% of hostel residents). See Table 11.11.

Table 11.11: Use of day centres across settings

	ALL %	HOSTELS %	STREET %	SQUATS %	HOTELS %
Once a day	12	9	45	8	-
Once a week	17	15	33	19	7
Once a month	7	8	8	4	6
Twice a year	4	5	6	2	7
Never	60	63	8	67	80

Summary

Overall there were some clear differences between the settings and the characteristics of the people staying on the street, in squats, hostels and hotels. There were more older residents in hostels and more younger people in squats. This is a simple finding which has consequences for the care and provision for these sub-groups.

More women were found in hotels than any other setting.

Those on the street had been the longest homeless with 41% having been without a home for over one year.

In terms of family status, there were 10% fewer single people on the street, many had been married. This suggests that family breakups were more a feature of street homeless life than other settings. This might suggest more single people found themselves in hostels. This could be due to allocation procedures or due to characteristics of the hostel population. In terms of ethnic background, there were more English people in the street sample and there were few black people in squats or on the street.

There was higher unemployment in hotels, and more people were working on the street (35%). Thirty seven per cent (37%) of squatters do voluntary work. This is not an idle population. Squatters also tended to be more educated than those in the other samples, with 19% having degrees. Those on the street had more trade qualifications.

Residential history

Last place before this one

People were asked where they had been staying before the place they were in at the time of interviews. Of those in squats, 46% came from squats. Similarly, of those on the street, 30% came from the street and 19% of hostel residents came from a hostel. This is not a simple relationship however as 30% of the street sample also came from a house or flat. What the figures do suggest however, is that people tended not to come from hostels to squats (4%), or from the street to hotels (7%), but rather from a house or flat primarily (see Table 11.12).

Table 11.12: Last place before this one across settings

	ALL %	HOSTELS %	STREET %	SQUATS %	HOTELS %
House/Flat	31	27	30	14	40
Hostel	17	19	11	4	7
Street	10	9	30	6	7
Squat	8	4	-	46	-
Other	34	41	29	30	46

Length of stay there

Those staying on the street and in hotels spent the longest on average in their last place (both 47% longer than one year). Table 11.13 shows that more squatters spent a shorter time in their last place (15% there longer than one year). This may reflect the nature of squats which is that there is rarely an opportunity to stay a long time in one squat, but that people move from squat to squat.

Table 11.13: Length of stay there across settings

	ALL %	HOSTELS %	STREET %	SQUATS %	HOTELS %
Less than 1 month	13	14	19	12	18
1 - 3 months	18	17	13	25	13
4 - 6 months	13	13	7	19	20
7 months - 1 year	14	12	14	29	2
More than 1 year	42	44	47	15	47

Age left home

Those on the street tended to move from home at an earlier age than those from any other setting (43% had left home by age 15). Only 21% of hostel residents had left home by this age. Fourteen per cent (14%) of hostel residents did not leave home until aged 26 or over. This link between sleeping rough and leaving home at a young age may be important. See Table 11.14.

Table 11.14: Age left home across settings

	ALL %	HOSTELS %	STREET %	SQUATS %	HOTELS %
Less than 10	5	5	9	6	-
11 - 15	18	16	34	12	27
16 - 18	41	41	32	51	26
19 - 25	24	24	14	27	47
26 - 30	5	6	4	2	-
31 +	7	8	7	2	-

Number of places have lived in

Generally more of the hotel sample lived in less than 10 places than any other group (86%) with the hostel and squat samples following behind (65% and 67% respectively). More of the street sample lived in over 11 places than any other group (43%). This suggests that those in hostels, hotels and squats were less transient than those on the street.

Table 11.15: Number of places have lived in across settings

	ALL %	HOSTELS %	STREET %	SQUATS %	HOTEL %
1 - 5	40	43	27	28	29
6 - 10	25	22	30	39	57
11 - 20	19	18	27	22	7
21 - 30	5	5	-	4	-
31 - 40	1	1	3	-	-
41 +	1	-	3	2	-
Too many	9	10	10	4	7
Don't know	-	1	-	1	-

Last place called home

Most revealing in the comparison across settings for this item is that 24% of the street sample said they had never had a home. In contrast 40% of the squatting sample felt that where they were was their home. In this way it could be said that 40% of squatters in general do not consider themselves to be without a home. For the hostel sample, 26% considered their family home their last home while 50% of the hotel sample referred to a particular place. See Table 11.16.

Table 11.16: Last place called home across settings

	ALL %	HOSTELS %	STREET %	SQUATS %	HOTELS %
House/Flat	13	13	18	5	20
Hostel	4	6	3	-	-
Family house	24	26	12	21	20
A place	23	22	21	19	50
None	10	9	24	7	10
Marital	3	3	9	-	-
Not moved	10	7	3	40	-
Other	13	14	10	8	

Where after that

For the hostel residents, 37% went to a hostel after they left their last home, while 33% of hotel residents went to a hotel and 22% of the street sample went to the street. Approximately a quarter of all the groups went to a house or flat. This is distinct from staying with friends which was the highest for the hotel sample (33%) See Table 11.17.

Table 11.17: Where after that across settings

	ALL %	HOSTELS %	STREET %	SQUATS %	HOTELS %
House/Flat	18	16	28	27	27
Hostel	32	37	14	7	7
Street	7	7	22	-	-
Squat	5	3	6	37	-
Friends	6	5	3	7	20
Hotel	6	5	8	3	33
Other	26	27	19	19	13

The length of the homeless varied across the groups as 46% of the squatters left their last home less than 6 months before and 63% of the street sample left over 3 years before. This again supports the contention that the street homeless group were the longest homeless group of all four settings. See Table 11.18.

Table 11.18: How long ago across settings

	ALL %	HOSTELS %	STREET %	SQUATS %	HOTELS %
Less than 6 months	32	32	17	46	39
7 - 12 months	15	15	7	21	23
13 months - 2 years	16	15	13	4	23
3 - 5 years	14	12	35	21	-
6 - 10 years	11	13	18	4	15
11 - 20 years	8	8	10	4	-
21 years +	4	5	-	-	-

Present and prior area

More of those staying in squats were staying in Inner London than any other group (92%) with only 64% of those staying on the street staying. Approximately a third of the hotel and street sample were staying in Outer London.

Table 11.19: Area now across settings

	ALL %	HOSTELS %	STREET %	SQUATS %	HOTELS %
Inner London	85	86	64	92	71
Outer London	15	14	33	8	29

The area most people came from directly before this one was Inner London. Although this does not suggest that this proportion were born there as other findings suggest that a large percentage were not from London.

Table 11.20: Prior area across settings

	ALL %	HOSTELS %	STREET %	SQUATS %	HOTELS %
Inner London	52	51	34	63	64
Outer London	18	17	17	21	29
Other England	23	23	40	14	7
Wales	1	1	-	-	-
Scotland	1	1	6	2	-
Ireland	3	3	-	-	-
Europe	-	1	-	-	-
Other	2	3	3	-	-

Housing list

In comparing those on a housing waiting list across settings it seems that only the majority of those in hotels were on one. Seventy seven per cent (77%) of those staying on the street sample were not on one while about half of squatters and hostel residents are not. Thus comparatively, more people were on housing waiting lists in hostels than in the other homeless settings. This reflects the fact that those in hotels were placed by the local authority and were automatically put on the list for re-housing. It also reflects the practical impossibility of entering into semi-permanent accommodation from the street. Table 11.21 illustrates this finding.

Table 11.21: Housing list across settings

	ALL %	HOSTELS %	STREET %	SQUATS %	HOTELS %
Yes	33	32	23	37	93
No	57	56	77	55	7
Don't know	10	12	-	8	-

Summary

There seem to be identifiable patterns of residential history for each of the settings in terms of the 'last place they were in before this one' and in terms of 'where they went after they left their last home'. Hostel residents tended to have stayed in hostels, those in hotels in hotels, those on the street on the street and so on. This is not surprising but nonetheless important to illustrate. Furthermore, people from hostels or hotels, tend not to have come from squats or the street. There may, therefore, be different homeless routes for sub-groups of people. Those who find themselves in squats tend not, from this study, to have stayed in hostels and vice versa.

Squatters spent less time in their last place than any other setting.

More people on the street left home at a young age and have lived in more places.

Nearly a quarter of the street sample had never had a home, as compared with only 7% of the squatting sample.

Those staying in squats were on the whole more recently homeless than other people. Those staying on the street for the longest time were homeless.

More of those in squats were based in Inner London than any other group. In terms of prior area, 40% of the street sample lived in some other part of England whereas only 7% of hotel residents did.

The highest percentage of people not on a housing waiting list were to be found on the street with the lowest in hotels.

Health across setting

Taking a standard measurement of mental stress levels, and comparing the scores across the settings there was a wide variation of scores for different groups. As discussed previously the maximum score is 36 and minimum 0. The higher the score the more mental stress in the sample. Table 11.22 presents the mean scores and standard deviations for people in each setting. The setting which showed least signs of mental stress was squatting with hotels being the highest. This pattern supports other findings presented in this book which serve to illustrate the squatters were a reasonably contented and stable group while hotel residents had low self esteem and high mental stress levels.

Table 11.22: Health scores across settings

Setting	Mean	SD
Squats	21.84	6.69
Hostels	25.68	7.61
Street	27.22	8.55
Hotels	29.47	8.37
All	25.52	7.74

Range 0(low) to 36(high)

Evaluation

How people evaluated where they were staying has been explored in detail with regard to each setting in the previous chapters and again further on in this section as comparisons across the settings reveal interesting distinctive features of the four faces.

Table 11.23 presents the means and standard deviations of the home-evaluation score across settings. The *lower* the score the more highly evaluated the setting overall. This score is made up of the average response to the Meaning of Home Questionnaire (described in the Appendix).

Table 11.23: Home evaluation scores across settings (1=Strongly agree; 2=Agree; 3=Neither; 4=Disagree; 5=Strongly Disagree)

Setting	Mean	SD
Squats	15.96	5.50
Hotels	17.31	5.22
Hostels	19.04	6.37
Street	21.63	6.27
All	18.86	6.36

Squats were more highly evaluated in general across the settings and the street the least. This supports the hearthlessness idea in which hotels and squats would be more hearthful than hostels and the street. For squatters the items evaluated positively by more residents, although they were all positively evaluated, were being able to 'do what I want' and being 'the only way I can afford to live'. The highest for those in hostels, were 'getting a good night's sleep' and being 'the only way I can afford to live'. For those on the street, there were only two items which were positively evaluated by the majority and these were 'afford' and 'do what I want'. For those in hotels it was feeling 'safe', 'sleep' and 'do what I want'.

There were differences across settings which is demonstrated by Table 11.24 in which the home evaluation items are presented across the settings.

Table 11.24: Percentage agreement with evaluation items across settings

STATEMENTS	ALL %	HOSTELS %	STREET %	SQUATS %	HOTELS %
'Social life'	45	44	36	65	40
'Do what I want'	43	37	59	75	53
'Comfortable'	56	59	28	58	47
'Sleep'	60	61	36	63	73
'Only way I can afford to live'	63	61	65	79	47
'Like it here'	50	51	22	67	40
'Safe'	58	59	40	64	62

Self esteem and view of others

Those in squats had the highest levels of self esteem and those in hotels had the lowest. This suggests that those staying in squats had positive images of themselves and those in hotels had more negative images.

Table 11.25: Percentage agreement with self esteem and view of others across settings

STATEMENTS	ALL %	HOSTELS %	STREET %	SQUATS %	HOTEL S %
Make Contribution	45	43	38	70	31
Not a Failure	60	59	50	83	38
People here are Like Me	43	40	60	56	20
Community	43	44	36	53	27

Expectations

People were asked to consider different aspects of life and indicate how important they were to them. The importance of aspects of home varied slightly from setting to setting, as most people tended to consider all the items important. Table 11.26 presents the mean scores for the importance score across settings, and Table 11.27, the percentage importance for each item. The lower the score the more important aspects were overall.

Table 11.26: Importance of home scores across settings

Setting	Mean	SD
Squats	9.88	2.66
Hotels	9.92	3.30
Street	10.56	4.65
Hostels	11.16	4.83
All	10.91	4.58

This table illustrates the differences generally between settings in which more squatters considered more aspects of home important and fewer hostel residents did. There was less variation among the squatters than among the hostel sample.

Table 11.27: Percentage agreement with importance of aspects of home

	ALL %	HOSTELS %	STREET %	SQUATS %	HOTELS %
Decorate	64	61	68	77	80
Quiet	75	77	77	52	73
Own Place	80	79	87	77	93
Friends	71	68	65	94	73
Cheap	76	79	79	87	67
Kitchen	82	78	89	96	85
Own Room	89	87	96	96	100
London	56	58	38	54	62

Explaining their situation

People were asked to consider some statements which might or might not have described how they see the world. They could consider their lack of housing in personal terms, in terms of chance or outside influences.
Table 11.28 illustrates some of the locus of control items across the settings.

Table 11.28: Locus of control items across settings

STATEMENTS	ALL %	HOSTELS %	STREET %	SQUATS %	HOTELS %
'Unlucky finding somewhere to live'	47	46	65	38	40
'Not too lazy to find somewhere to live'	76	76	54	80	87
'Shortage of housing-live'	49	47	50	64	53
'Would work if offered a job'	73	73	80	62	67
'No luck getting a job'	46	44	71	38	43
'Lack of skills -no job'	45	46	56	32	57
'If settled down would get a job'	69	69	55	54	79

These items address the different ways that people attribute causation of their actions. For each of the settings there were characteristic themes which underpin their rationale. For those on the street, their actions related to finding somewhere to live and a job were explained in terms of luck, primarily and a lack of skills. But for those in hostels, the emphasis was on getting settled and being offered a job. For squatters, the emphasis was on a shortage of housing (more socio-political) and not being 'too lazy to find somewhere to live'. For those in hotels, more emphasis was placed on getting settled, 'not too lazy to find somewhere' and that they have a lack of skills. Over the whole sample, more people thought they were 'not too lazy to find somewhere to live', 'would work if offered a job' and 'if they were settled they would get a job'.

Summary

The background health figures indicate that squatters were suffering less from mental stress than people from other settings, with the hotel sample suffering most. Again in terms of evaluation, squatters emerged as the most satisfied with their setting and those on the street the least satisfied. Hostel residents were 'less able to do what they want' than in any other setting.

In terms of self esteem, squatters again had higher self esteem and a sense of community. For both those on the street and those in squats, the majority felt the others there are just like them, but those in hotels and in hostels agreed less. Those in hotels had the lowest self esteem and lowest sense of community.

For the importance of home items, people in squats considered more things important than other settings. Fewer of those in hostels considered fewer items important. Overall though, most people considered these items to be important, there was not much variation.

Overview

The previous chapters have described the experience of aspects of homelessness in London. They have painted an overall picture about the range and variety of people who find themselves in a homeless situation.

Broadly from the 531 people interviewed, the homeless population was mostly young men with the majority under the age of 40 who were active. Many of the people interviewed were doing work of some kind (a third) and voluntary work and only about half were unemployed. This picture directly challenges the image of homelessness which places the inactive older man at the core.

However it is perhaps of greater value to examine the differences across the settings. Strong contrasts emerged between those in squats and in hostels; those in hotels and on the street. There are pathways which do not seem to be crossed. Hostel residents tended to have stayed at other hostels, those in hotels in other hotels, those on the street on other parts of the street and so on. This is not surprising but nonetheless important to illustrate. Furthermore, people from hostels or hotels, tended not to have come from squats or the street.

Hostels had older men in them on average, whereas hotels have young women. Hostel residents were less able to do what they want than in any other setting. Those on the street were the longest out-of-home with 41% of the sample without a home for over one year and with more of them married or separated than in other settings. More people on the street left home at a young age and have lived in more places. Nearly a quarter of the street sample had never had a home, as compared with only 7% of the squatting sample. More people were working on the street (35%). This is not an idle population.

Thirty seven per cent (37%) of squatters did voluntary work. Squatters also tended to be more educated than those in the other samples, with 19% having degrees. The squatting sample was generally more recently homeless than the other samples with those on the street being the longest homeless. In terms of self esteem, squatters again had higher self esteem and a sense of community, and lowest levels of mental stress. For both those on the street and those in squats, the majority felt the others there are just like them, but those in hotels and in hostels agree less. In terms of evaluation, squatters emerged as the most satisfied with their setting and those on the street the least satisfied.

Those in hotels had the lowest self esteem and lowest sense of community. There was higher unemployment in hotels, and the highest levels of mental stress. However the highest percentage of those on a housing waiting list were to be found in the hotel sample.

This comparison presents a strong set of images about life in each of these settings. It would be difficult not to select the squat as the preferred setting if one had to choose. Squatters seem to be recently homeless, working and reasonably satisfied with their setting. Furthermore life on the street may have its advantages in terms of a sense of freedom and independence but it surely is the hardest way of life, especially if people are holding down jobs with no roof over their head. Presenting the settings as they are experienced in this way offers insight into the strengths of a particular setting as well as the obvious weaknesses. By breaking homelessness down in this way, it is hoped that it will be easier to build solutions. There is a need to devise different solutions for people in each of the settings that respects their experiences and perspectives and does not seek to undermine them.

12 Routes to a Home

A Network of routes

Most people who find themselves homeless do so for a limited period of time. A crisis in their domestic or financial circumstances forces them out of a place were they have some form of tenure onto the streets, in search of a bed and roof. In a city of the size and maturity of London, as of a small town like Guildford, there is a limited network of options available for the homeless person to choose between. It must be emphasised that the great majority of these options are very uninviting and are likely to pull the person down into a further stage of despair. They are likely to make it more difficult for the person to find a productive way of life than before they became homeless. The determination of most people who find themselves in this destructive cycle, and the broadly civilised society that still makes up modern Britain, is illustrated by the number of people who manage, eventually, to climb out of this impasse.

The various studies reported in this volume also tell us a simple story about the sort of people who find themselves in these parlous situations. They are mainly drawn from those members of our society who have been denied a conventional, supportive home life from their earliest years. They do not choose to go onto the streets or to knock on hostel doors, to traipse around seedy hotels to find a roof for themselves and their children, or to eke out a semi-secret existence in a vacant building. They are forced to choose from these options by the fact that their current situation is intolerable or no longer available.

Our results show that although the crisis that makes people homeless may be sudden there are often aspects of their earlier lives that would indicate homelessness as a possible outcome. Is it the nature of the people themselves that produces the eventual crisis or the circumstances of their lives?

All our studies, whether of beggars, of people in squats or people sleeping on the streets have found no distinct psychological factors that mark out the subjects of our research from the population at large. Indeed, the only distinct group in our studies who were difficult to interview or who were reticent to fill in questionnaires, were the managers of hotels that took homeless people. The squatters, beggars and other groups who we might have expected to be so disturbed or socially inadequate that they could not participate in our studies turned out often to be not only articulate, but often witty and extremely aware of the nature of their situation. We did find that many of them knew the role expected of them and were ready to embrace it for their own purposes, just as an obedient civil servant will take on a role at work that they do not necessarily maintain at home. What we did not find was great evidence of psychosis, alcoholism or extreme anti-social behaviour. Even such subtle indexes as general health and self-esteem were not dramatically different from what would be expected of a similarly low income population that was housed.

Of course, as in the population at large there were many disturbed people. The comparisons are difficult to make, but it is to be expected that those who are particularly vulnerable are likely to be over represented in the homeless population. It is nonetheless important to emphasise that there is no evidence that psychological vulnerability is either the dominant cause of homelessness or typical of the homeless population we have studied.

Another important point of emphasis is that if a vulnerable person is homeless then it is even more difficult for them to cope than when they had a home. It is therefore very appropriate to be concerned about mental patients and alcoholics, ex-prisoners and single parent families, roaming the streets. However, it is the fact that these people need help to find their way back into an acceptable way of life that needs to be considered and that help is more difficult to achieve if they are homeless, rather than focusing on the fact of their being without a bed and a roof. Finding a home is one step back towards a productive, satisfying life. It is not a definition of happiness.

The essence of our findings may be summarised in the aphorism, that runs the risk of being too glib, that British society is a caring society, but it does not care enough. Any one who has experience of third world shanty towns or of the treatment of dispossessed peasants in India or South America will be overawed by the range of support facilities that are available to the destitute in a small home counties town like Guildford. They will be even more impressed by the network of resources that are available in a major city like London. The comparison with the rest of Europe, especially Southern Europe, also shows that the impact of Victorian philanthropists and the creators of the British Welfare State have left us with an infrastructure of support for those in need which is still fundamentally sound. The problems come firstly from the erosion of this support system, aggravated by the increasing pressures it is under, and secondly from the lack of monitoring of its quality and effectiveness.

This lack of quality control starts when children are separated from their families, or when disadvantaged families are not helped to relate effectively to their own children. Over and over again, throughout our studies, the destruction of interpersonal support that takes place within settings that are supposed to be of benefit to the children, have been described. Step parents, foster parents and those who run children's homes come in for criticism frequently. Of course, the great majority of people who find themselves in these, often difficult, conditions of child care are extremely helpful, but enough are not to set in motion the cycles that lead to the crises that brought people into our sample.

Once people, young or old, have the need to draw upon community support, in hostels, bed and breakfast hotels or even the nether world of squats, they are further vulnerable to abuse and exploitation. Our studies indicate that the most destitute area is, possibly surprisingly, in the many hotels scattered through London that provide for people sent there by local authorities. Hostels are more open to assessment and are usually part of some larger organisation that can impose standards. Although our studies did indicate that at least a third of the hostels in London could greatly improve the quality of what they have on offer within the resources available.

Compromise perspective

This book is only a beginning. It presents the outline of a composite perspective on homelessness and the findings of research guided by that perspective. Homelessness is studied here as a multivariate problem with a complex interaction of personal, social, cultural processes, none of which can be excluded in any attempt to understand the phenomenon. Although exploratory and not conclusive, this approach will have to be the way forward if this complex problem is to be analysed by social scientists. Perhaps the emerging 'field' of homelessness could benefit from this genesis and become more integrative and less divisive in its perspectives and approaches. The extremes have been set over the last 20 years in terms of how homelessness is studied, from the individual and her characteristics to society and its influence. It is time now for compromise and a perspective which seeks to avoid simplistic analyses and instead focuses on the complex issues involved.

The American literature presents a bleaker picture to the one presented here, however the themes which emerge are the same and the approaches taken by those trying to understand are similar. It seems that although many research findings in the USA and in Britain indicate that homeless people are as heterogeneous as the general population, it needs to be stated again and again. It is important to ask why this is. It seems that part of the problem is the media's response to homelessness and the desire to present simple analyses and solutions. However this is influenced by the work of social scientists who are studying the problem and the dissenting views and paucity of sensitive analyses may also be at fault.

The methodological emphasis of the socio-psychological perspective, demonstrated throughout the book, is firstly on observation and secondly recording experience. In terms of exploring life on the street, the starting point was observing where people were sleeping and in what numbers. The main conclusion from this observational study was that there is structure to the way the street is used. People tend to use different areas for sleeping and for socialising, and most people tend to sleep rough in groups. This finding that the street has meaning and structure is one which supports the approach that in order to understand a particular environment it is vital to see how it is used.

Following on from observation, the next approach is to ask people for their views and evaluations and in this way tap their experience. This is perhaps best demonstrated by the study of hostels in which residents indicated that there are distinct types of hostel with different styles and atmosphere. These types are equally liked by different sets of residents and together provide a typology of hostels which seem to work. By starting at the level of experience, the value of the results and recommendations increases. The birth of a new perspective carries with it a research agenda. Research is needed which would explore smaller sub-groups of people out-of-home, their experiences and perspectives, in settings, age groups, regions and gender. Longitudinal studies are needed which examine the gateways people enter and the decisions people have to make on reaching them. The relationship between poverty and homelessness and the distinction between them need to be examined in Britain (cf Rossi 1991 in the United States). A further area which requires examination is the personal contacts and networks of friends and families which would seem to enable some people to avoid homelessness, which has parallels to the German studies of 'resilience' and a lack of which can contribute to someone becoming out-of-home. Furthermore the meaning of home and hearth has to be fully examined in relation to people with and without homes.

The characteristics and qualities of each of the settings in which people out-of-home can be found presented in the previous chapters paints a distinctive picture of their differences and similarities. There are few commonalities across settings. People with no homes may experience such varied experiences as living independently in a squat to living in an institutionalised hostel with little independence. Once this is acknowledged it must result in the examination of these settings in detail and an understanding of homelessness not simply as an experience shared by one heterogeneous section of society, but rather as a range of people with varied views and experiences who all find themselves in a particular homeless setting.

It would seem for example, that squatters are mostly an educated group with high self esteem, who are working and reasonably satisfied with their squats. If squatting were legalised, would these people still be considered as homeless people? And if not, what are the assumptions that go with that label which when removed, leaves little to bind people other than the type of house or flat or area they live in? In other words they would be members of this society and subject to all mechanisms for classification which makes up the way we look at the world. The findings of the research presented here have indicated that it is possible to look at people out-of-home as one large group and to discuss their demographics and views. However it has been demonstrated that of more use in terms of understanding and aiding people out-of-home is to start to examine people in these varied settings and work from there. By beginning with the setting, the phenomenon of homelessness is explored from the perspective of those people who experience it. Someone in a hostel experiences 'living in a hostel' as much as, if not more than, 'being homeless'.

The categorising of people is necessary in order to make the world more familiar and in order to explain and understand different phenomena. However it is a process which comes with a certain amount of danger, in that those who categorise may lose sight of other patterns or links or explanatory frameworks in their sticking to the boundaries of definition. It is recognised that this is as likely to occur when placing the focus on settings, as many people flow from setting to setting and are not 'bounded in'.

The faces presented have identifiable qualities. The street is the most extreme setting in terms of exposure, lack of any form of shelter and the physical experience. However in other terms the characteristics and views of those who are on the street suggest that they have personal aspects of home which they carry with them:their self esteem, independence and sense of personal control. For those in hotels, this is lacking. There may be more than one continuum of homelessness. There is the spectrum or continuum of homelessness which focuses on the physical characteristics of homelessness which at one extreme is to be without a roof and at the other to have a house of one's own.

The other continuum may be a quality of life: 'hearthlessness'. For those in hotels, there may be better physical characteristics to their setting than those on the street, but they do not have as much independence, self esteem, and a sense of control. These are aspects of home which are not physical, but are rather social, personal and symbolic. In other words, the general consideration of being homeless as a physical experience is undermined by the existence of an additional range of experiences which are to do with being *out-of-home*. Thus for some people in settings such as squats and the street, lower on the physical continuum than the others, their experiences may be hearthful: the psychological, social and symbolical constituents of home.

In the attempt to help some people in physically extreme settings, the hearthful aspects of a person's experience has been destroyed. Those who have to enter a strict hostel may not wish to lose the sense of independence and control they have on the street or in a squat.

There is a need to accept the ways in which street homeless people compensate for the loss of a physical structure by the creation of a social and personal one. As Rivlin argues with reference to the New York situation, 'we need to recognise the efforts of homeless persons, themselves, to provide needed resources...Rarely are the homeless given the help that might lead to permanent housing improvements in places where they are squatting on lots or where they have built make-shift housing' (Rivlin 1990). Helping homeless people should not be at the expense of what they have, but should complement what they have. Independence and control are the central aspects in the evaluation of a temporary life on the street, for example, which is ordered and structured by activities. These should not be taken away in any attempt to provide them with shelter, which would seem often to be the case.

Although all are still homeless settings, each has a taste of homeful aspects at its core. The independence and control are at the core of street living; safety, security, sleeping well and independence would seem to be central to hotel living;and sleep, comfort and affordability are central to hostel living while for squats all aspects are present. This characterisation is useful as it presents the settings as they are experienced and contributes to our understanding of home in general. In non-homeless settings, there will be even greater variation and typologies of home aspects and many different cores. It could not be suggested that there is one type of home for all people. Homeless people have views, experiences, evaluations and choices, albeit constrained. These psychological and social aspects of being out-of-home are the starting point of any exploration which seeks to understand and explain.

A system of support

In considering the support systems which any civilized city should have in place to help those who face the crises of being without a home the first step is to recognise that the variety of homeless people have to be offered a variety of accommodation which is aimed to meet their differing requirements. But this mixture of support needs to provide a co-ordinated network.

The development of an integrated system is technically possible in terms of the availability of new technology to aid its monitoring. It is also possible due to the current interest being shown by the Government in new developments. By identifying particular types of facility, those currently providing help could move their existing range of provision in definite directions either as new facilities or developing the old ones. The outline of such a system was implicit in earlier pages. It now needs to be more explicit.

The development of hostels as a type of provision for homeless people was in its infancy in 1888 with the establishing of a cheap food depot and shelter for men by the Salvation Army in London. They began to convert old warehouses and storehouses in to shelters in order to 'contain' homeless men. This type of hostel provides an example of a very basic model of therapeutic care, in which residents are kept off the streets in very basic
conditions. The hostels provided shelter but no privacy and no individual space.

Hostel provision today in London has moved on from this extremely basic cot provision. However, there are still echoes of this former model in some of the facilities. An integrated system of care has been developed by many providers in the last few years. This system is designed to help people move from crisis through to permanent residence. The difficulty is that there is inadequate provision to cater for demand from homeless people.

The notion of a process through which people flow is not new. The development of such a process was discussed by Madeline Drake in 1988 who argued 'A three stage process should exist which allows people to move away from emergency accommodation, through supported or half-way housing to more permanent types of accommodation.' However the models have been developed into which people can come in at one point and one through to another. People can then move on to more permanent accommodation. However, demand for such provision outstrips supply.

Piecemeal development by disparate agencies leaves holes in the net of support and does not facilitate the provision of help that is most appropriate for each individual. An example would be Shelter Nightline, a telephone helpline for street homeless people which provides information on vacancies and places homeless people in emergency bedspaces. A system of a variety of facilities integrated by an information system and by a central administrative body would be of great advantage. It could serve all organisations in London linked, say, by a computer information system listing details and day-to-day vacancies, monitoring how long people have been in a specific place and what services or help has been made available to them.

Figure 12.1: Model of provision network

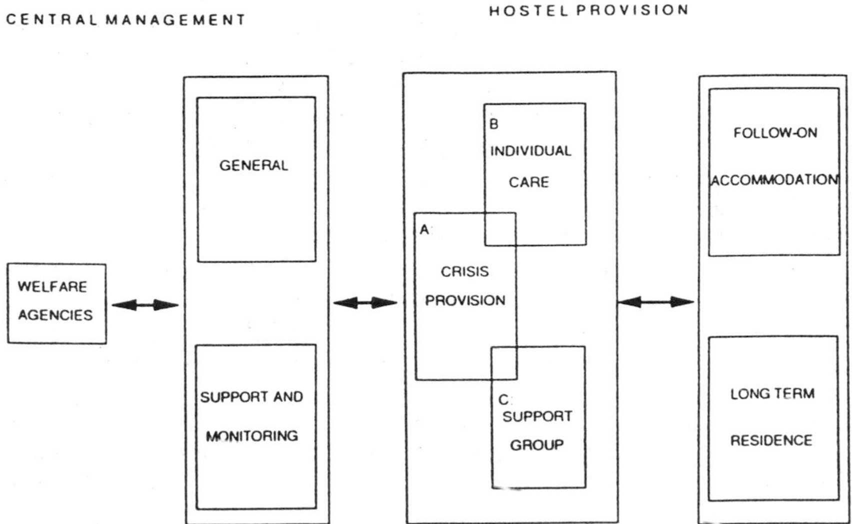

Networks would recognise the three areas of support that are necessary:

a) crisis provision,
b) individually oriented care and
c) group support facilities.

People are encouraged to move from type A into either type B or type C, but it would also be essential to have integrated lines to follow on accommodation and long-term residents as indicated in Figure 12.1.

Central management and effective interaction with the many related welfare agencies is not yet fully developed across all provisions. Nor does the system exist to monitor support being given to people. Its sights would be set *beyond* the provision of a roof to the provision of a hearth as its major task would be to move people through from crisis to settlement.

Conclusions

In this book we have discussed the variety and distribution of homeless people in London. It became clear that there are many more homeless people in hostels than on the streets. The Salvation Army has traditionally catered for single homeless people who by and large are not provided for by Government legislation. There is no reason why this targeting of types of people and types of provision should not continue. However if it is to be successful it should reflect the variety and diversity of people who are homeless. This can be done by developing an integrated system of facilities which provide for clearly identified groups of people.

Our research has served to reiterate previous findings that the homeless population is a heterogeneous one (Drake et al 1981). Drake has argued that 'the homeless are a heterogeneous federation of different types of people, some simply needing accommodation, some needing social or even medical support' (Drake 1988). She found in 1981, that the majority simply needed housing which was sensitively managed and flexibility allocated, but an important minority needed more than that (Drake 1981).

Our research has attempted to focus on this hetergenous group. There are several obvious characteristics to group people together, such as age, employment status, current length of stay.

The survey of hostel residents revealed that homeless people vary on many levels. Earlier work also demonstrated that there are different groups of people within hostel accommodation who have different aspirations and evaluate their hostel in different ways. These groups have different priorities and see the hostels in different ways. There may be many more such groups in hostels in London, and each will have different requirements.

In summary then, there is a wide range of people in hostels and in other homeless settings who differ from each other in many ways and require different programmes and varied forms of accommodation. These differences must be reflected in the range and scope of the facilities provided.

Bibliography and References

Archard, P. (1979) *Vagrancy Alcoholism and Social Control*, MacMillan Press Ltd.:London.

Audit Commission (1989) *Housing the Homeless: The local authority role.* HMSO.

Bailey, R. *(1973) The Squatters: Penguin.*

Bailey, R. 'Squatting, Trespass and the Law Commission Report'. *DIB.*

Balfe, R. and Merriton J. (1975) 'Squatters'. DIB (5258).

Banks,M., Clegg, C., Jackson,R., Kemp, N., Stafford, M. and Wall, T.(1980) 'The use of the GHQ as an indication of mental health in occupational studies', *Journal of Occupational Psychology*, 1980, 53, 187.

Beacock, N.J. (1973) 'Social Needs of the Single Homeless'in '*Soc. Services Q*. Jul-Sept, 47(1) 15-18.

Bethoud and Casey (1989): *The Costs of Care in Hostels.* Policy Studies Institute. London.

Boleat (1989) *Housing in Britain.* The Building Societies Association.

Booth,W. (1970) *In Darkest England and The Way Out*, Charles Knight and Co, (Reprint of the Original Salvation Army Ed. 1890).

Brandon,D., Wells,K., Francis,C., Ramsay,E., (1980) *The Survivors: A study of homeless young newcomers to London and the responses made to them.* Routledge and Kegan Paul Ltd.:London.

Brittain, V. (1975) 'Squatters' Rights and Wrongs'. *Illus London News* Aug, 263(6925) pp41-43.

Canter, D., Drake, M., Moore, J., Stockley, D. Ball, J. (1989) 'The Faces of Homelessness', Interim Report to the Salvation Army, University of Surrey.

Canter,D.V. (1977) *The Psychology of Place*. London: Architectural Press.

Canter,D.V and Canter,S.(1979) 'Building For Therapy', in Canter,D. and Canter,S. (1979) *Designing For Therapeutic Environments: A Review of Research*, Chichester:Wiley.

Canter,D.V.,(ed) (1985) *Facet Theory: Approaches to Social Research*. New York, London: Springer-Verlag.

Cara (1988) *Irish Homelessness-The Hidden Dimension: A Strategy for Change*, Cara Irish Homeless Project.

Cardiff Housing Action. Before you open your big mouth - a report on squatting. *CHA*, Jan. 1976.

Caton, C.L. (1990) *Homeless in America*, Oxford:Oxford University Press.

Central Statistical Office, *Social Trends No. 13 (1983), No 17 (1887) and No 19 (1989). HMSO.*

Centrepoint Soho (1986) 'Building on Experience': Annual Report.

Chalk,J.,Twigger,C.,Andrews,R.(1989) 'A Study in Behavioural Mapping', Presented at the Postgraduate Conference, Portsmouth Polytechnic.

Commission for Racial Equality (CRE) (1989). *Race, Immigration and Housing. A Guide.*

Commission for Racial Equality (CRE) (198Housing and Ethnic Minorities. Statistical Information.

Commission for Racial Equality (CRE) (1989b). *Homelessness and Discrimination*. Report of an Investigation into the London Borough of Tower Hamlets.

Community Action and the Police. *Community Action* Aug/Sep 1974, (15) pp11-26.

Conspiring to Squat (1975). *Criminal Law Review*. June, pp342-51.

Criminal Law Bill (1976). *HMSO*: London.

Crossley,B. and Denmark,J.(1969) 'Community Care: a study of the psychiatric morbidity of a Salvation Army hostel', *British Journal of Sociology*, Dec. 1969.

Cutting, M. (1974) *Housing Rights Handbook (333.32).* Shelter.

Daly, M. (1993) 'Abandoned': A Profile of Europe's Homeless People. FEANTSA.

Dashwood, A. Davies, B.J. and Trice, J.E. (1975). 'Squatting and the Criminal Law - A General View'. *Criminal Law Review*, June, pp317-37.

Davies, K. (1975) 'Squatters and the Law' (9673) *Estates Gaz* 23 Aug., 235(5743) 549, 551, 553.

Department of the Environment (DOE) (1989) *The Government's Review of the Homelessness Legislation.* HMSO.

DOE (1988-) *Local Authorities Action Under the Homelessness Provision of the 1985 Housing Act:England.* Quarterly Returns.

DOE (1988) *Housing and Construction Statistics 1977 - 1987.*

DOE (1985) *Housing Act (Part III).*

DOE (1983) *A Home of Their Own: A Survey of Rehoused Hostel Residents.* DOE: London.

DOE (1977) *Housing (Homeless Persons) Act.*

DOE (1974) *Housing Act.*

DOE (1974) *Circular 18/74.*

DOE (1972) *Local Government Act.*

DOE (1957) *Housing Act.*

DHSS (1980) *Management and Objectives of Four Day Centres,* HMSO.

DHSS (1968) *Health Services and Public Health Act.*

DHSS (1966) *Social Security Act.*

DHSS (1959) *Health Act.*

DHSS (1945) *The Children Act.*

Drake, M., Neilson, E., Garside S. (1987) *Managing Hostels: A Report for Discussion.* National Federation of Housing and Social Policy Research Unit.

Drake, M. and Middleton, (1985) *Policy and Provision for the Homeless in the Voluntary and Housing Association Sectors in London.* A Report for the GLC Homelessness Enquiry. Unpublished.

Drake, M.,O'Brien, M.,Biebuyck, T. (1981) *Single and Homeless.* DOE: London.

Drake, M. and Biebuych, T. (1977) *Policy and Provision for the Single Homeless.* Personal social Services Council. London.

Drake, M. (1989) *Fifteen years of Homelessness in the UK.* In Housing Studies. Volume 4 No. 2.

Drake, M. (1989b) *Breakfast Crime.* In New Statesman. 3 Nov. p20.

Drake, M. (1989c) *An Act of Mercy.* In New Statesman. 3 Nov. p23

Drake, M. (1986) *Hostels in London.* London: Housing and Policy Research Unit.

Eardley, (1989) *Move-on housing. The permanent housing needs of residents of hostels and special needs housing projects in London.* Single Homeless in London and NFHA.

Edwards, G., Hawker, A., Williamson, V., and Hensman, C., 'London's Skid Row', *The Lancet*, January 1966.

Evans and Duncan (1988) *Responding to Homelessness: Local Authority Policy and Practice.* HMSO.

Festinger, L (1954) *Theory of Cognitive Dissonance*, Stanford University Press.

Friedman, D. and Pawson, H. (1989) *One in Every Hundred. A Study of Households Accepted as Homeless in London.* London Housing Unit.

Garside, P., Grimshaw, R. and Ward, F. (1990). *No Place Like Home: The Hostels Experience. DOE, HMSO.*

Geddes, D. (1976) 'Should squatting be a criminal act?' *The Times* 28 Jan, p14.

Geddes, D. (1976) 'Squatting in Britain'. *DIB* (Times Europa, 3 Feb. p121).

Gimson, M. Win, C.L and Wates, N. (1976) 'Squatting the Fourth arm of housing. Archit. Design Apr. 46(4) 24-214.

Ginsberg, G. M. P. (1975) 'Squatters and the law'. *DIB* (3618) (Sunday Telegraph 3 Aug. p18).

GLC (1981) *Hostels for the Single Homeless in London.*

Goffman,E.(1961) *Asylums: Essays on the Social Situation of Mental Patients and Other Inmates*, Penguin.

Goldberg, D.(1978) *Manual of the GHQ*. Windsor:National Foundation for Educational Research.

Greve, J., (1964) 'London's Homeless', Occasional Papers on Social Administration No.1 The Social Administration Research Trust.

Greve,J. and Currie,E.(1990) *Homelessness in Britain*, Joseph Rowntree Trust.

Greve,J.(1985) 'Investigation into Homelessness in London', University of Leeds.

Gunzburg,H. and Gunzburg,A. (1979) 'Normal Environment with a Plus For Mentally Retarded Children' in Canter,D.V and Canter,S. *Designing For Therapeutic Environments: A Review of Research.* Chichester: Wiley.

Hamilton, A. (1976) 'Inspection of London squats'. *DIB.*

Hamilton, A. (1976) 'London squats'. *DIB* (1708).

Hamilton, A. (1976) 'Tour of London squats in Rust Square, Camberwell'. *DIB.*

Harmer, M. (1975) 'No Place Like Home'. *New Statesman.* 21 Feb, p239-40.

Herzberg, (1987) 'No Fixed Abode', *British Journal of Psychiatry*, 150, p621- 627.

Hillman, J. (1975) 'Squat's My Line'. *The Guardian. 21 Jan, p13.*

Hodge, H. (1973) 'The Occupying Power'. *New Statesman* 15 June, p868.

Home Office (1971) *Criminal Justice Act.*

Home Sweet Home, if you've got one (1975). *Time Out*, 2 Jan, (251/252) pp11-13.

Homelessness (1976). *DIB* (5793).

Hughes-Onslow, J. 'Counter Squatting'. *Spectator* 21 Feb, 236(7704) 13-14.

Humphry, D. & Hughes, W. (1975) 'Squatting'. *DIB* (Sunday Times, 20 July, p4).

Humphry, D. & Hughes, W. (1975) 'Who are Britain's Squatters?' Sunday Times, 20 Jul, p4.

Insurance and Squatters (1975) *Estates Gaz,* 22 Nov, 236(5736) 576-577.

Institute of Housing (1992) A Handbook for Local Authority. London.

Ittelson, R. (1974) *An Introduction to Environmental Psychology,* Holt:Rinehard and Winston.

Kennedy,S.(1985) *But Where Can I go?: Homeless Women in Dublin*, Focus Point.

Kensington and Chelsea Race and Housing Action Group (1989). *Behind the Facade. Migrant Workers and the Private Rented Sector in Kensington and Chelsea.*
King,C.(1988) 'Psychological Analysis of a Long Stay Psychogeriatric Ward', Unpublished MSc Environmental Psychology, University of Surrey.
King,R., Raynes,N., and Tizard,J.(1971) *Patterns of Residential Care: Sociological Studies in Institutions for Handicapped children.* London: Routledge, Kegan and Paul.
Kinghan, M. (1974) 'Squatting in London'. *New Society*, 2 May, 28(604), pp254-5.
Kingham, M. (1974) 'Society at Work; Squatting in London'. *New Society* 2 May, 28, pp254-5.
Kingham, M. (1974). 'Tenant self-management - the experience of family squatting associations (7242). *Housing Review*, Jul/Aug 1974, 23(4), pp97-99.
Kroll,J.(1986) 'A Survey of Homeless Adults in Urban Emergency Shelters', *Hospital and Community Psychology*, Vol.37, No.3, March 1986.
LABOS (1990) *Project pour la réalisation d'un sustème d'information européan sur les sans abris,* available from FEANSTA. Brussels.
Legal Action Group (1975) 'Law in the housing crisis' (P19654). *Lag*, Sep.
Less Welcome Guests (1975). *The Economist* 25 Jan, 254, p24-25.
Lingoes,J.,(1973) *The Guttman-Lingoes Non-Metric Program Series.* Michigan:Mathesis Press.
Lodge Patch, P., (1978) 'Homeless Men- A London Survey' *Royal Society of Medecine* 63, pp441-5.
London Housing Unit (LHU) (1988) 'Bed and Breakfast hotel prices cut'. Joint action success of London Councils in London Housing News No. 10 February.
London Research Centre (LRC) (1989) *The London Housing Survey. 1986 - 7. Full Report of Results.*
LRC (1989) Private Sector Leasing in London. Forthcoming.
London Resource Centre (1988) 'Access to Housing in London:A Report based on the results of the London Housing Survey 1986-87'. LRC:London.
McBrien, J.P. (1975) 'The home owner's rights in meeting an invasion by squatters (9941). *Building Soc. Gaz. Oct , 57(1294) pp954-6.*
Maitland, R. (1975) 'Squatting and the Criminal Law - Old crimes with a new image'. *Criminal Law Review, June pp337-42.*
Mayo, M. (1974) *Community development and urban deprivation.* Bedford Sq. Press.
Mazis,S. and Canter,D. (1979) 'Physical Conditions and Management p practices for mentally retarded children', in Canter,D. and Canter,S. (ed) *Designing For Therapeutic Environments: A Review of Research,* Chichester:Wiley.

Mind (1983) *Common Concern, Mind's Manifesto for a new Mental Health Service.*

Moore, D., Simpson, A.W. and Smith R., (1968) *Homeless Men in East London*, mimeo East End Mission:London.

Moore,J.,(1989) Developing an Architectural Test: A Study of Four Salvation Army Hostels, Unpublished MSc (Environmental Psychology), University of Surrey.

Moore,J. and Canter,D. (1991a) 'Home and Homelessness' a paper presented at Housing and Design Education Conference organised by the International Association for People and their Physical Surroundings, Southbank Polytechnic, London July 10-15 1991.

Moore,J. and Canter,D. (1991b) 'Home on the Street:An Exploration of Street Homelessness in London', Paper presented at the MAB-UNESCO Symposium on 'Perception and Evaluation of the Quality of the Urban Environment:Toward Integrated Approaches in the European Context', Rome, 28-30 November 1991.

Moore,J. and Canter,D.(1992) 'Varieties of Transitional Home Experience and Their Significance For Homeless People', ESRC End of Award Report Ref:R000 233029, Spring 1992.

Moos,R.(1974) *Community Oriented Programs Environment Scale Manual,* Consulting Psychologists Press, Palo Alto, Calif.

Moran,R.A.(1978) Environmental Psychological Input to the Design of a Day Centre: Development of a Place Brief, MSc in Environmental Psychology, University of Surrey.

Morris, R. (1973) 'Squatters' community'. *Observer*, 4 Mar, p32.

Morton, J. (1976) 'Who'll house the single?' *New society*, 25 Mar, 35, p664-665.

National Assistance Board (1966) *Homeless Single Persons,* HMSO:London.

National Council for Civil Liberties. (1976) 'Squatting trespass and civil liberties'. *NCCL*. Jan.

O'Connor, P., *Britain in the Sixties: Vagrancy*, Penguin: Harmondsworth.

Oakley, R.(1973) 'A Study of the Environmental Conditions for Housing Homeless men' unpublished.

Oakley,R.(1980) 'Profiles and Perspectives of Hostel Residents- an Exploratory Study of the Residents of the Salvation Army Mens Hostels in London and Their Perspective of these Hostels', Unpublished MSc Environmental Psychology, University of Surrey.

Office of Population Censuses and Surveys, *1991 Census:Preliminary Statistics*, HMSO, London.

On the Move (1975) *The Economist*, 27 Sep, 256, p36.

Orwell,G.(1933) *Down and Out in Paris and London,* London:Victor Gollancz Ltd.

Patch, Lodge (1971) 'Homeless Men in a London Survey', *Proceedings of the Royal Medical Society*, 63, pp437-41.

Peacock, A. (1972) 'Homelessness: some preferences and annotations'. *GLC Dept. of Planning and Transportation, Research Library, Research Bibliography* No 34, March.

Point Charities Group on Homelessness (1989) *Who says there's no housing problem? Facts and Figures on Housing and Homelessness.*

Pollard, J. (1973) 'Squatting in the City'. *Architectural Design,* 43(8) 504-6.

Proposal by Tower Hamlets to Lend a Group of Squatters £500,000 to buy and renovate a block of council flats. *DIB*, 1975(4813) (Times, 14 Oct., p3.)

Randall,G. (1988) *No Way Home*, Centrepoint, Soho.

Resource Information Service (1986) *First Come First Served: Young People and Equal Opportunities in Emergency Nightshelters.* R.I.S: London.

Resource Information Service (1988) *Women's Housing Handbook,* RIS. London.

Resource Information Service (1988-1992) *The London Hostels Directory*, R.I.S :London

Reynolds, M. 'Dealing with Squatters'. *Municipal Journal*, 9 Nov, 1671-2.

Rivlin,L. and Wolfe, M. (1979) 'Understanding and Evaluating Therapeutic Environments For Children', in Canter,D. and Canter,S. (1979) *Designing For Therapeutic Environments: A Review of Research*, Chichester:Wiley.

Rossi,P., Wright,J., Fisher,G., Willis,G.(1985) 'The Urban Homeless: Estimating Composition and Size', *Science*, Vol.12, March 13.

Rossi,P.H.(1989) *Down and Out in America*, London: The University of Chicago Press.

Salmon, E. (1976) 'A social experiment'. *New Society*, 10 Jun, 36(714), pp586-7.

Satchell,M. (1988) 'Health and Homelessness : a study of health problems in single homeless men'. MSc Polytechnic of the South Bank.

Shattock,L., (1988) 'Relating Therapeutic Models to Ward Design For Senile Demented Patients', MSc Environmental Psychology, University of Surrey.

Shelter (1976) 'Another empty house'. *Shelter.*

Sherman, A. (1975) 'Squatters and socialism-symbols of an age', *Local Government Review*, 15 Nov, 139(45) p763.

Sherman, A. (1975) 'Squatting and the response by the GLC'. *DIB* Local Government Review, 15 Nov, p763.

SHIL (1986) 'Single Homelessness in London'. GLC.

Single and Homeless in London Working Party (1986) *Hostels in London.*

Smith, J. (1973) 'Keeping roofs over troubled heads'. *Municipal Review* May, 44, pp136-7.

Snow, A. (1976) 'How the Law stands on squatting'. *Valuer*, Mar, 45, pp31-2.

Soho Project (1983) Annual Report: London.

Squatting and the Law (1975) *DIB*.
Squatting in London (1975). *DIB*.
Squatting trespass and civil liberties (1976). *National Council for Civil Liberties*, Jan.
Squatters at Elgin Avenue, Paddington (1975) *DIB*. (Time Out, 24 October, p.7)
Squatters under Fire (1975) *Community Action*. Aug/Sept, (21) pp29-30.
Teasdale, J. (1975) 'Rules are made to be broken - recent squatting decisions'. *New Law J*, 2 Oct, 125 (5719 pp949-52.
The Independent (1988) 'Do Tramps make their own luck'? Sat. 12 November.
The Independent (1987) 'Growing Plight of London's Destitutes' 20 March.
The National Forum (1989) *Housing Needs in the 1990's. An interim assessment.*
The Picadilly Advice Centre (1988) *The London Hostels Directory.*
The Times (1987) 'Down and Out of Sight' 14 January.
Thomas and Hedges (1986) *The 1985 Physical and Social Survey of Houses in Multiple Occupation in England and Wales.* DOE/HMSO.
Thomas, A and Niner, P. (1989) *Living in Temporary Accommodation: A Survey of Homeless People*. DOE, HMSO.
Thornton,R.(1990) *The New Homeless,* SHAC, Housing Aid Centre Publications.
Tidmarsh, D. (1978) *Camberwell Reception Centre* DHSS.
Tiplady, D. (1975) 'Housing Welfare Law'. *Oyez*, p162.
Toro,P., Trickett, E., Wall,D., Salem,D.(1991) *Homelessness in the United States:An Ecological Perspective*, American Psychologist, Vol.46, No.11, Nov. 1991
Towards Better Use of the housing Stock (1975) *Estates Gaz* 29 Nov, 236 (5757), pp631-2.
Tremlett,G.(1989) *Homeless But for St. Mungo's*, Unwin Hyman:London.
Trespass on Squatters' Rights (9455) (1975). *Time Out*, 25-31 July, (280) 5.
UJIMA Housing Association (1988) *Annual Report*.
Underwood, J. 'Squatters'. *Housing Monthly*, Jul 11(7) 18.
Walsh, L. (1976) 'GLC's policy towards squatters'. *DIB*. (Local Government Chron 6 Feb, pp132-3)
Ward, C. (1976) 'Housing - an anarchist approach'. *Freedom Press*, p.182.
Ward, R. (1975) 'Old squatting laws await reform'. *Estates Times*, 27 Jun (304) 4
Wates, N. (1976) *The Battle for Tolmers Square*. Routledge & Kegan Paul: London.
Wates, N. (1975) 'The Tolmer Village Squatters. *New Society*, 14 Aug, 33(671) pp364-66.
Watson and Austerberry (1983) *Women on the Margins. A Study of Single Women's Housing Problems*. Housing Research Group. City University

Watson, S. and Austerberry, H. (1986) *Housing and Homelessness,* Routledge and Kegan Paul plc. London.

Watts, M.A. (1971) 'The Caravan Sites Act 1968'. *Justice of the Peace and Local Govt. Review.* 5th June, 135(23), pp393-4.

Weller,B.G.A and Weller M.P.I. (1986) 'Health Care in a Destitute Population:Christmas 1985'. *Bulletin of the Royal College of Psychiatrists,* 10, pp233-35.

White, D. (1972) 'The New Settlers'. *New Statesman*, 18 Jul, pp75-6.

Whiteley,J.S.(1955) 'Down and Out in London: Mental Illness in the Lower Social Groups', *Lancet*, ii, 608-10

Wingfield Digby,P.(1976), *Hostels and Lodgings for Single People,* HMSO: London.

Wooley, T. (1975) 'History of squatting'. *D/B* (Architectual Design, Nov, v p700)

Women's National Commission (1983) 'Report on Homelessness Amongst Women', Cabinet Office.

Zander, M. (1975) 'Question of home areas'. *The Guardian*, 16 Jul, p13.

Yeung, Y.M. & Yeh, S.M.K. (1976). 'Time Budgets; extended methodology and application. *Envir. Plann. A*, 8(1), pp93-107.

Appendix: Methodology

Data Collection

The Salvation Army Research Project commenced in the Autumn of 1988 and was completed in October 1990. The overall aim of the research was to:

> 'generate the research basis from which co-operation on a strategic plan of the provisions necessary for the homeless in London, at present and in the foreseeable future, may be developed. From this general framework specific tactical objectives will be established that will enable the Salvation Army and other agencies to identify the particular provisions to which they should give priority'.

A secondary aim was to:

> 'bring together a comprehensive review of homelessness in London in a way that will encourage the responsible authorities to take effective action to ameliorate the situation'.

From the commencement of the project it was decided to limit the research to four 'sub-groups' of homeless people; people living on the street, hostel residents, residents of bed and breakfast hotels and squatters. It was pointed out by some groups working with homeless people that this omitted a major group, that of the hidden homeless, i.e. people sleeping on friends' and relatives floors or as second households. Although it was recognised that this was a major concern, it was decided that including this group would pose both methodological and practical difficulties and that more effective results would be achieved by concentrating on identifiable groups. As will be seen the difficulties that were encountered during the research justified that decision.

The research project was divided into four phases:

Phase One	This was sub-divided into two stages: the first stage consisting of the assembling of literature and material on homelessness and the pilot count culminating in the writing of a short interim report, and the second stage consisting of pilot field work, preparation for the final count, and writing of interim reports. This comprised the whole of the first year.

Phase Two	Four workshops with people from streets and hostels, continuing pilot work with squatters, hostel and bed and breakfast residents and design of main questionnaire. This phase lasted for four months.
Phase Three	Main data collection from people living on the streets, in hostels, in bed and breakfast hotels and in squats and writing of interim report and working papers. This took three months.
Phase Four	Analysis of data and writing of final report. This took the final five months.

Regular contact was maintained with the Salvation Army by two means;

i) The incorporation into the research team of a member of the Salvation Army, Mr Tom Littler;

ii) The forming of a research committee comprising of members of the Salvation Army and the research team which met regularly for discussion and review of the research.

PHASE ONE - THE FIRST STAGE

The first priority was to contact as many groups working with homeless people as possible in order to assemble existing literature both on homelessness in London and homelessness in general and to make use of organisations' personal experience and knowledge. In order to contact groups use was made of the following directories;

Hostel Directory published by the Resource Information Service,
Homeless Handbook published by Intercommunication Trust.

There were many organisations contacted either for assistance or information in this phase. The literature that was consulted is listed in the bibliography.

The main objective of the first phase was to form an overview of homelessness in London by plotting the pattern, distribution and volume of homeless people throughout London. Initially some concerns were raised by some organisations contacted that a psychological perspective was being adopted. However these were generally abated by both the multi-disciplinary nature of the team and the environmental psychological approach. The approach is concerned with the social and cultural context within which an individual is and therefore is more social than traditional psychology. The team consisted of environmental psychologists, a sociologist and a political scientist as well as the Salvation Army representative who possessed considerable experience in residential care and one member of the team who had considerable experience of sleeping rough on the street.

It was decided that the best method of determining the pattern and distribution of homelessness in London was to organise a physical count of street homeless people and to survey hostels and bed and breakfast hotels. This was not possible for squatting which posed even more difficulties owing to an understandable suspicion on the part of many squatters and the semi-unlawful nature of the activity.

To assist with the research and, in particular, the organisation of the count, a Working Party was formed consisting of representatives of different groups working with homeless people. Groups represented for most of all of the meeting that were held were;

The Simon Community
Thames Reach
St Mungos Housing Association
Resource Information Service
Church Housing
Salvation Army

Representatives of other groups attended one or more meetings at the commencement of the project but withdrew for various reasons. It was anticipated, justifiably, that the research in this stage of the project would be considerable assisted by the experience of such groups.

The Street Count

In order to see whether a count of people living rough on the street was feasible a pilot count was organised for the night of Tuesday 22nd November 1988. The particular date was chosen as providing a time of year when possible casual sleeping on the street, for example touring students, would be at a minimum and a time of the week when there would not be a lot of additional activity that might arbitrarily increase numbers on the street. It was also the night of the full moon so that the light would assist the people counting.

The pilot area was chosen upon after consultation with both the Salvation Army and other organisations. It was both a compact enough area and yet at the same time large enough and having sufficient facilities so as to be a useful preparation for the full count. The pilot area was defined as the area bounded by Oxford Street and the Thames ending at Blackfriars Bridge to the South and Park Lane and Vauxhall Bridge to the North (See Figure 3.1).

The area was divided into regions which were then further sub-divided into patches small enough for a team to cover in two hours. Each region had a leader as did each individual team which normally consisted of three people. Volunteers came from the Salvation Army, St. Mungo's, the Simon Community and Church Housing. In all there were 70 counters who commenced counting at mid-night and all had returned safely by 3 am. Each team was carrying a map of the area they covered, a torch, telephone numbers for any emergency and a flask of hot drink. Before going out counters were briefed on safety precautions and counting procedures. Use was made of the knowledge of the member of the research team who had experienced sleeping rough and of the Simon Community from their own survey of Camden.

Counters were requested to mark on their maps the location of any people who were found sleeping rough, the numbers and describe in as much detail as possible their gender, age, ethnicity and perceived general state of health and any particulars of the surroundings in which they were found. Counters were asked to explore car parks, hidden entrances etc. but not to put themselves at risk by, for example, entering derelict buildings.

In all 271 people were counted in the designated area and a further 261 were counted the other side of the Thames in the Waterloo area. The pilot count showed that it was possible to organise a street count on a future occasion.

Pilot count of hostel and night shelter residents

A total of 16 hostels were found to be in the pilot area. Contact was made with the manager of each hostel who was requested to complete a form providing information on the number of residents and empty beds in the hostel on the night of the count. In order to encourage co-operation, the minimum of information was requested. Response was extremely good with 14 out of 16 (87.5%) hostels co-operating.

Pilot count of Bed and Breakfast Hotels

The pilot count of residents in bed and breakfast hotels took place during the day of Wednesday 23rd November and since there were no hotels in the area for the street and hostel count, an adjacent area was chosen for hotels. Fifty-four hotels were identified via previous research as catering for homeless people in the Pimlico area. Volunteers were selected from the University of Surrey and the Salvation Army and were provided with questionnaires seeking a variety of information on the numbers of homeless people, their family and health status as well as the general state of the hotels. It was found that of the 54, only 26 were still taking homeless people.

Pilot count of police stations and hospitals

All hospitals and police stations were identified in the pilot area for the street and hostel count and were requested to provide details of all people who were registered as being of 'No Fixed Abode'. Phone calls were made on days subsequent to the 23rd November. Four out of the six police stations responded and some hospital information was obtained.

Pilot study for squats

It was decided that prior to any preliminary data collection contact had to be made with a number of squatting organisations and the Advisory Service for Squatters (ASS) in order to obtain their co-operation. Although some squatters were suspicious of the principle of research fearing that the object was to bring out findings that were hostile to squatting, co-operation was achieved by the researcher staying at squats over-night. The preliminary stage of analysis suggested the existence of a number of types of squatters with varying degrees of capability in managing their situation.

PHASE ONE : THE SECOND STAGE

From the experience of the first stage of phase one, a considerable body of knowledge of the possible difficulties was built up and the main objective was to organise the full count for some time in the spring of 1989. However, due to the difficulty of organising a complete London wide street count, and the number of people that would have to be involved in such an exercise, it was decided to limit the count to areas where people were known to be sleeping rough. This involved a great deal of preliminary work to identify such sites.

The Street Count

In every London borough a number of organisations and/or individuals were identified as either working with, or having knowledge of, homeless people sleeping rough. The organisations were selected from directories and ranged from voluntary organisations to local authorities and campaigning organisations to churches. Each organisation or individual was telephoned until contact was made. In some case over ten calls had to be made to an organisation before the appropriate individual was contacted. When communication was made they were asked whether any people slept rough in their borough and if the answer was in the affirmative details as to the actual location and numbers involved was gathered. Organisations' and individuals' knowledge of the situation existing in specific boroughs varied considerably. Sometimes one organisation asserted that no person slept rough in their area while another organisation asserted that there was a serious problem. At other times ignorance of the true situation was professed although the researcher might have been referred to another source which was thought to have more knowledge of the situation. Questioning was rigorous and even if all contacts denied that a problem in their borough existed, the denials in turn were counter-checked by contacting organisations not on the original list.

At the conclusion of the exercise, a total of 17 London boroughs were identified as having varying numbers of people sleeping rough. The groundwork that had been carried out enables confidence to be expressed, that while there may have been the occasional one or two people sleeping rough in each of the remaining boroughs, the areas containing the great majority of street homelessness were firmly identified.

In two boroughs previous attempts had been made to record the number of people sleeping rough and the experience of the organisers was drawn upon, while often the contacts produced more information and material on homelessness.

In parallel with the gathering of information attempts were made to recruit people for the count, the main work in this area being carried out by the Salvation Army. Co-ordinators were to oversee the survey in each borough. As a general rule people were allocated their own borough, but if people expressed an interest in the work and could not be utilised in their own borough, then they were placed somewhere else.

Both the police and hospital authorities were contacted and requested to co-operate with the count. Both the police and the medical authorities, particularly the British Transport Police who counted those found on railway stations, assisted the survey.

The street count took place on the night of Tuesday 25th April 1989. Already experience and knowledge suggested that some homeless people varied the sleeping habits according to weather and other circumstances, and the date was chosen in order that the subsequent outcome of the count would not be distorted by an influx of people arriving in London for the summer months, yet at the same time as being sufficiently distant from winter which, it was thought, might encourage people to find shelter. As it turned out 25th April turned out to be unusually cold, and it is possible that the cold weather encouraged some people to find shelter.

A total of three meetings were held at which each co-ordinator was briefed and given information as to how to go about the survey. Maps had been prepared for each area based upon the Geographers' Street Maps of London. Each borough had a base which was manned at all times and all checkers were instructed to report to the base for briefing. It was the responsibility of the co-ordinators to ensure that all checkers were properly briefed. They were issued with maps on which to mark the sites where homeless people slept, check sheets in order to not the gender, age, ethnicity, health, appearance and behaviour of each person sleeping rough, whether he or she was sleeping or awake, and the number in the group. Each checker was instructed that on no account should they go into derelict buildings or to endanger themselves in any way.

A total of two hours was allocated for the count and all checkers returned on time. The number physically observed as sleeping out was taken as the minimum sleeping rough. Despite the instruction to checkers not to endanger themselves in any way, that only 17 boroughs were surveyed and the cold weather, the thoroughness of both the count and the preparation enabled a figure of the number of people sleeping rough to be estimated. This was based upon the number physically observed, and was thought to be reasonably accurate.

Hostel count

The range of hostels in London is described in some detail in the London Hostels Directory and range from temporary short-term emergency accommodation to independent accommodation no different from flats or self contained bed sits. This raised the problem of whether all hostels should be included in the count since arguably people occupying the latter could be said not to be homeless. In addition it had been noted that several residents had lived in the same hostel for ten years or more and were said to regard it as their home. It was decided to include all hostels and residents on the following grounds;

a) exclusion of any hostels would, at this stage of the research and knowledge of the subject, have been arbitrary,
b) it was felt important to contact all hostels in order to gain an overall picture of the situation,
c) initial contact would encourage future co-operation,
d) even if individuals had resided at the same hostel for a considerable length of time they could still be technically homeless and form part of the 'reservoir' of people who could end up sleeping rough,
e) there was no independent evidence that they were satisfied with their situation.

It was therefore decided to carry out a postal survey on all hostels in London but due to the range of information in the London Hostels Directory it was decided that the survey would require on the following minimum information to be given;

i) the number of people sleeping in the hostel on the night Tuesday, 25th April,

ii) the number of empty beds,
iii) whether any beds were kept empty for specific reasons,
iv) whether empty beds were available for use,
v) whether the hostel was direct access or not.

The supplement the postal survey a telephone survey was also carried out on the 26th April in which 100 traditional, emergency and short stay hostels were phoned and asked to respond to the same questions on the postal survey. The total number of hostels contacted was 444 out of which 267 (61%) responded. In view of the response rate, it can be reasonably assumed that a representative sample of hostels was achieved.

Attitudinal Questionnaire

In addition to the information requested, the telephone survey included some statements put to managers in order to draw out attitudes to residents, similar questions being put to hotel staff. This was in order to compare some aspects of hostel life with that in hotels. The statements included four each of which focused on the social and physical aspects of hostel and hotel life for staff and for residents. Two further statements were included which draw out attitudes to homeless people in general.

In order to give a pattern to the statements a short mapping sentence was constructed. A mapping sentence is part of the facet theory approach which links statements or questions to specific facets of the domain to be researched. The mapping sentence used to construct the first four statements was;

The extent to which (x) agrees that		[social] [physical]		aspects of the
[hotel] [hostel]	help/hinder	[residents] [staff]	----->	agrees disagrees

where (x) is a member of staff of a London hostel/hotel.

The six statements put to managers were;

1. This hostel\hotel is well designed for cleaning and supervision.
2. This hostel\hotel is a friendly place to work.
3. Residents have enough space (and privacy) for their everyday needs.
4. This hostel\hotel is a sociable place were residents can get to know each other.
5. Homeless people are just normal people who have hit on hard

times.

6. Homeless people could find themselves somewhere to live if they wanted to/people in this hotel are homeless because they haven't made an effort to find a place of their own.

Staff were asked either to agree or disagree with the questions which many found a difficult task. Two possible reasons may account for this difficulty;

a) the questions were, in principle, difficult to answer either affirmatively or negatively,
b) there was difficulty in asking attitudinal questions over the telephone.

Because of the difficulty interviewers sometimes recorded questions or clarified them which may have led to a different response than would otherwise have occurred. However the questions were useful in indicating differing attitudes amongst hotel and hostel staff and were valuable in contributing to future research.

Hotel count

For the survey of hotels it was decided to concentrate on the areas where there had been least direct research. These were, the numbers and the household structure of homeless people in hotels, including single people and childless couples not placed by local authorities; and the attitudes of hoteliers to their work with homeless residents.

Because of the large number of hotels scattered throughout London it was decided to use a telephone survey to cover all hotels said to be taking homeless people.

On the 26th April, 465 hotels were surveyed by telephone using volunteers drawn from the Salvation Army. Twelve telephone lines and rooms were donated by Mercury communications. Interviewers used a questionnaire to ask hoteliers the homeless people in their hotels, the composition of households, what difficulties they experienced in accommodating homeless people, their own hours of work and how long they had held their post, and the same statements presented to hostel managers.

The sample of hotels was drawn from two sources. The first was the BLIP list of hotels for their 1988 survey consisting of 371 hotels and the second source was the London Research Centre during 1988 which listed 634 hotels. The latter list was compiled from local authorities' registers of hotels used for placing homeless families. Some overlap occurred between the two records but taking account of this, the final list from which the sample for the telephone survey was derived included 739 hotels (62.9%).

Of the 465 hotels the telephonists tried to contact, only 114 said that they took homeless people and answered the questions, a further nine said they took homeless people and gave the numbers they took but no further information and 63 said they took only tourists. No information was received from the remaining hotels (279 (60% of the sample)). In some cases the managers refused to answer the questions, in others the manager was not available and staff were unwilling to answer the question themselves, in other case the telephone was answered by children or people unable to speak English and in other cases either the number was unobtainable or no one responded to repeated attempts to contact the hotel. Owing to the high rate of refusals and failure to contact, a follow up survey was carried out. The follow-up survey was in four areas with a high concentration of hotels and Salvation Army cadets were used to visit hotels who had not responded to the telephone survey with visits. The cadets were asked to visit a total of 171 hotels in all;

27 in Earls Court,
88 in Bayswater,
30 in Finsbury Park,
26 in Kings Cross.

Only 45 said they took homeless people and gave the required information while 19 said that they took only tourists. In total 168 both took homeless people and gave all or part of the required information. This represented 36.12% of the survey list but only 23.13% of the list compiled from the two registers.

Two problems arising from the research were particularly highlighted;

a) unwillingness of managers to respond,
b) discovering that hotels no longer took homeless people.

These two problems were to continue throughout the research. Some doubt must be expressed whether a truly representative sample of hotels was achieved since those who were willing to co-operate may have been willing to do so because their standards were higher than those who refused. Despite this, however, much useful information was discovered.

Survey of squatters

As has been stated previously, carrying out research into squatting poses particular difficulties owing both to the nature of the subject and the difficulty of contacting squatters. By the nature of squatting, most squatters hesitate to advertise themselves and may well be suspicious of people representing official institutions, such as a university, who ask questions.

It was decided at first to work through squatting groups and to gain the trust of their workers, but this strategy in turn lends itself to the objection that it is probable that not all squatters go through the squatting groups. Therefore in addition to working through the groups every attempt was made to contact individual squatters.

Three groups were contacted;

> Squatters Network of Walworth,
> Brixton Squatters Aid,
> Advisory Service for Squatters.

As was expected there was understandable suspicion on the part of the workers in the organisations regarding the aims of the research and the political outlook of the researcher. In two cases the researcher had to attend meetings of squatters who were part of the group. He was quizzed on his views on squatting, the aim of the research and whether authorities would be able to make use of the information. There was also understandable concern about confidentiality and anonymity. On all counts the researcher was able to allay any anxieties but the preparatory work emphasised that conventional research would be particularly difficult. Finally one squatter group, in the London Borough of Lambeth was chosen as the base to contact squatters. A total of eight visits were made to the group. Each person who came to the group for advice was asked if he or she was squatting and if the reply was in the affirmative were further asked if they were willing to co-operate in the research. There was little hostility and only two people refused to complete the questionnaire.

Two main methods were utilised in this phase of research on squatting;

1. two questionnaires,
2. participant observation.

The first questionnaire was designed to;

a) describe the condition of the squat,
b) acquire basic information about individual squatters and some historical background leading to their present situation.

All respondents were asked to complete the individual section but only one person from each household was asked to complete the section on the description on the condition of the squat. In total 34 squatters completed the questionnaire and information was gained from 28 squatted properties.

For the first questionnaire respondents were requested to answer questions by placing the appropriate code against the question. This caused some difficulty and the method was discarded for the second questionnaire.

The researcher spent a total of four weeks living in squats. Conversation with squatters suggested further lines of enquiry and also revealed attitudes and perspectives which assisted further development of the research. In this stage their varying life styles were observed.

The second pilot study centred on a large squat in South London and based in a disused hospital. The hospital had been 'opened' by a group of people from local churches and given over to the homeless people. Estimates of the number of people at the squat varied widely ranging from 40 to over 200. An objection may be made that this was an atypical group of squatters, but this objection raises the question as to whether there is any 'typical' squatter. Also, from the researcher's experience of living on the street, it was known that several people in the squat had 'lived rough' for a number of years and therefore it was assumed that their movement into shelter was goal orientated and deliberate. Whether the squat contained 'typical' squatters or not, it was part of the squatting scene in that people whose only alternative was to sleep rough, had decided to squat.

In order for the research to take place the researcher had to attend a committee meeting. Leaders of the squatters had already emerged and the meeting was under the chairmanship of the 'leader' a man in his forties. He was fairly unenthusiastic about the research but was overruled by the predominately younger membership. The deciding factor in gaining their co-operation was the payment of £2 to each person who completed the questionnaire. While payment to respondents may be criticised, in this case it was felt justifiable in that it was the one way of continuing the research.

The questionnaire dispensed with the section dealing with the description of the squat but an attitudinal section consisting of 20 statements was included. This section contained statements referring to their attitude to the squat, to their perception of other squatters, to the views on work and training, and aspirations for the future. Little difficulty was encountered in completing the questionnaire.

In all 41 people completed the questionnaire all on the same day, 36 in the squat and five elsewhere, e.g. Waterloo Station. Informal interviews were carried out with a number of the younger squatters in a cafe opposite the squat and more details of their history and background were obtained. It was felt that taking notes at the time might act as a constraint so notes were made as soon as possible after the interview. It was during this stage of the research that the issue of young people who had experienced local authority care was highlighted.

A third pilot study was attempted in the London Borough of Ealing but this proved less successful. Anecdotal evidence suggested a large squatting population but research could not confirm this. The researcher spent fruitless hours visiting addresses where squatters were alleged to live but in only two cases were squatters found. The borough had no squatting organisation and it was difficult to make initial contact with all but a few squatters who, since the researcher was unknown to them, were suspicious and hostile. These difficulties proved insurmountable and the research was aborted. It was this failure that led to future data collection being carried out where the researcher was either known or could make contacts who would allay any fears.

PHASE TWO

Research into homelessness in such situations as on the street poses specific problems. The conditions are not conducive to long interviews, privacy is almost impossible, interviewees may be constrained by other people around them from co-operating and, as well, interviewers may feel uncomfortable and threatened by drunks. If hostel residents are being interviewed the additional factor of staff being nearby may also pose problems to those being interviewed. These problems are magnified when group discussions are required.

It was therefore decided that a total of five workshops would be held at the University of Surrey where it was hoped that members of each sub-group would attend. The workshops provided opportunities to;

1. further refine the questionnaire for the main data collection period and to determine the capability of respondents in completing it,
2. hold group discussion with participants,
3. enable them to take part in a participatory design exercise,
4. carry out a sorting task
5. carry out (on one occasion) the Thematic Apperception Test.

Proceedings were videoed eliminating the need to keep notes of the workshops. This raised the problem of whether at the outset people should be informed of the video at the risk the person refusing to attend. As a compromise the researcher said that proceedings would be recorded and if there were further questions the use of the video was admitted.

On arrival in the department participants were informed of the reason for the research. In addition the reasons for the sessions being videoed were explained. Participants were also introduced to the operators of the video in order to reassure them and were encouraged to watch themselves on television. The latter proved extremely popular even with members of the third group. On two occasions an objection was raised by someone who had not been informed, but once people were assured that it would not be used in public it was accepted. Either one or two researchers would be present at the workshop all times.

Sorting Task

After the initial introduction a sorting task was carried out. This consisted of 20 cards on which were printed various types of places, e.g. family home, hostel, hospital, which participants were asked to arrange into groups. This was in order to determine their conceptions of 'place' and 'home'.

Questionnaire

Next, participants were asked to complete the questionnaire and help was available from the researchers. In order not to embarrass participants who found difficulty in reading, help was offered if they found the print too small. They were also encouraged to mention any question they found difficult to understand. See Appendix 3 for details of the questionnaire.

It was found that many respondents needed assistance, finding the seven point scale complicated and difficult to understand. However most, with assistance, were able to complete the questionnaire.

Group Discussions

A varied cross selection of homeless people attended. Participants were selected either by the researcher meeting them at the hostel or on the street and directly inviting them, or indirectly when someone already attending asked another person along. On the day of the workshop the participants were met at Waterloo Station and taken by train to Guildford. Tickets were purchased beforehand, lunch, coffee and cigarettes were provided and each person was paid £5. Of the five workshops four were completed. The one which failed to take place would have consisted of people from the hospital squat whose population and leadership had undergone a complete change. The researcher approached the present 'leader' who appeared enthusiastic and promised to co-operate by asking a number of residents to attend, but on the morning of the workshop no one turned up at the station. The researcher visited the squat to find out why no one had arrived and was told that no one had wanted to attend. However, future conversation with squatters at the hospital suggested that she had failed to ask anyone.

Broadly speaking participants at workshops consisted of four diverse groups.

1. A group of younger men from the street and a hostel. Most were articulate, well adjusted and had high aspirations for the future of their own place. A total of seven people attended the first workshop.
2. A group of older men from a Salvation Army hostel. All but one found difficulty in communication and seemed to expect little from the future. A total of six people attended the second workshop.
3. A group of younger people from a number of hostels some of whom

had experienced sleeping rough on the street or had squatted. They were articulate, balanced and hopeful for the future. A total of six people attended the third workshop.

4. A group of younger people most of whom earned money by begging or occasionally by prostitution, who were aggressive, had a history of offending and/or mental illness, and were pessimistic about future opportunities. A total of seven people attended the last workshop.

Discussion focused on their perception of all aspects where they were staying at the present, aspirations for the future and understanding of how they had reached their present state in life. The quality of discussion varied. Most difficulty was experienced in the second and fourth workshops. With the older group there were problems in maintaining the level and momentum of discussion with two members being almost continually withdrawn. In the final workshop the aggression and unco-operative behaviour of the participants required a great deal of concentrated effort in supervision and motivation of the group.

Participatory Design Exercise

Participants were asked to record activities which they considered to be important in their ideal home onto pieces of paper. These could be connected with the interior of their home or aspects of the external environment which they considered important. Participants were then asked to think of the places they would need in their home to carry out all their activities. Typical of internal elements were bedroom kitchen, music centre, library while external elements included nearness to the shopping centre, countryside, or sports centre. Participants were then asked to attach the various elements onto a sheet of paper on which was superimposed a large circle divided into segments. They were thus enabled to conceptualise their ideal home and to relate each element to the others.

On one occasion the Thematic Apperception Test (TAT) was used. The TAT consisted of a number of pictures of ambiguous meaning and participants were required to make up a story about the picture. The rationale was that their accounts might reveal something of their background and the way they viewed the world. Results were mixed with a minority of people unable or refusing to make up accounts.

In parallel with the workshops data collection continued from other sources. Four hostels were visited:

at traditional women's hostel,

a small emergency shelter for young males with an evangelical Christian ethos

a hostel for young people with a secular ethos,

a large traditional hostel which was part of a group.

Firstly, contact with the management was made by telephone which was followed by a visit to talk with the manager and staff. Subsequently another visit was made and residents were asked to complete the questionnaire. Great importance was attached in stressing the voluntary nature of completion, the anonymity of the results and that the questionnaire would not be given to the staff.

As in the workshops some respondents had difficulty in understanding the seven point scale and a few statements proved difficult for people to understand. The questionnaire was, in fact, continually modified and any comments by respondents were noted.

Through discussion with both staff and residents information was gathered on the hostel's regime, what residents did throughout the day and relationships between staff and residents.

Another visit was made to the large squat. Whereas previously payment had been made to those who completed the questionnaire, on this occasion commodities were purchased for general use. Between the first collection of data and this visit a number of visits had been made to the squat and the researcher was able to see the population undergo a complete change. New 'management' was in existence and there was now an established hierarchy with 'leaders' having their own quarters which were comfortable and well heated apart from the main building, while the majority of residents occupied the main building which by now had been stripped of lead, wiring and other saleable items. Water came through various leaks in the roof. There was now also, a higher proportion of severely disturbed people, four people began the questionnaire but were unable to concentrate sufficiently to complete it. On two occasions the researcher had to listen to long and rambling accounts from people about their past and once a another person began shouting and screaming and acting in a hostile manner. Despite the difficulty 13 questionnaires were completed.

A number of people living on the street were approached and asked to complete the questionnaire. A total of six agreed to do so. In all, 56 questionnaires were completed in this phase of the research.

PHASE 3

This phases consisted solely of data collection through questionnaires and visits to facilities. The questionnaire is detailed in Appendix 2.

From experience in the previous phase the questionnaire was refined and ambiguous and difficult questions were eliminated and a five point scale was substituted for the seven point used previously. The questionnaire was also professionally printed instead of being photocopied and questionnaires were printed on two different coloured paper, blue for residents and yellow for staff. The two questionnaires were almost identical but staff were requested to complete the parts of the questionnaire which dealt with the residents' perception of the facility by responding to a statement as they thought their average resident would respond.

Two targets were set:

1) to visit and collect data from at least 30 different and varied facilities including all Salvation Army hostels, and settings of homelessness,
2) to complete 600 questionnaires.

It was necessary to ensure that apart from all the Salvation Army hostels, as far as possible a representative sample of hostels would be visited. A classification of hostels was drawn up based upon the following criteria.

1. Number of people in hostels.
2. Gender, age and ethnicity of residents.
3. Degree of support and staffing level.
4. Whether direct access or referral only.
5. Whether hostel met special or general needs.
6. Ethos and philosophy of hostel.
7. Degree of independence for residents.

Besides the Salvation Army hostels the managers of 34 hostels and projects were initially contacted by telephone over a period of six weeks. The object and nature of the research was explained to them and they were asked if they would allow a researcher to visit in order to show them the questionnaire and to explain more about the project. Of the 34, five refused to take part of all while the remainder agreed to a researcher visiting them. Reasons for refusing were,

privacy of residents (2)
disagreed with research,
did not have sufficient time,
not interested.

In six cases it was difficult to contact the person who was able to give permission and in two instances it was decided not to proceed with the attempt.

When agreeable, the initial contact was followed up as soon as possible by interviewing either the person in charge of the hostel or a delegated member of staff. This interview generally lasted for about an hour and, as well as elaborating on the research, questions were asked about the residents, staff and philosophy of the management, and observation was carried out on the physical aspects of the hostel. At the interviews a copy of the questionnaire was shown to the member of staff and any difficulty regarding the questions was discussed. The procedure for data collection was carefully explained and in every case the researcher asked that rooms were set aside for the field workers to interview the residents and times and dates were arranged when data collection could be carried out. As far as possible any limitation to access was respected, e.g. some hostels did not want the interviewers to go to individual rooms.

All but two of the Salvation Army hostels were co-operative. Neither of the two exceptions saw any need for research while in one case the statement was made that their residents were not homeless. In a similar manner to other hostels initial interviews were arranged with the Officer in charge of the hostel with the exception of the two mentioned. The interviews were particularly helpful in gaining from officers their underlying primary values and view of their role, and of their perception of the relationship existing between them, residents, other members of staff and the Salvation Army hierarchy.

Interviewers

Interviewers were selected from post and undergraduate students at the University of Surrey or in two cases from outside the university. They were paid expenses and a set sum per hour. This ensured that there was no pressure upon them to speed up the interviewing. An initial interview was held to determine their suitability, to explain to them in full the purpose of the research project and the procedure to be followed, including the sampling method. This was carried out by either one of the researchers employed on the project. All interviewers were issued with a list of instructions for interviewing and each point was carefully gone over to ensure that they understood what was expected of them. The list of instructions were;

Things to have, e.g. pencils, Identification.
Things to do; e.g. introducing themselves to manager or staff and the person to be interviewed.
Things not to do, e.g. not to go into bedrooms alone, not to get into debate or arguments.
Description of the questionnaire and how to apply it.
Describing the facility in physical, organisational and social aspects.

They were given directions as to how to find the hostel (all found their way and returned safely), and who to report to on arrival. In addition to following the instructions and assisting respondents they were encouraged to note any points about the facility they found interesting but which did not fall under any of the headings on the instruction sheet. Initiative in this respect was encouraged and points were noted that were either ignored or unnoticed on previous visits.

Sampling

In large hostels a random sample based upon bed numbers was developed and interviewers were given this sample list. So as to take account of residents who might be unavailable or incapable, even with assistance, of completing the questionnaire, more than the required sample were selected. Despite this, in general this proved, in practice, difficult to observe owing to the high number of people unavailable or incapable of completing the questionnaire. In order to overcome this two visits were made to the large hostels at different times of the day, e.g. one in the morning and one in the evening, in order to increase the chances of contacting different groups of people. Interviewers were also encouraged to go to as many parts of the hostels where residents gathered and ensure that as large as possible response was made from each group. Comparison of a full list of Salvation Army residents in all hostels with the sample group showed that in regard to age and length of stay the two groups were approximately equal in the hostels which had co-operated. Ethnicity was also similar except that for some reason Irish people were under represented in the responding sample.

In the small hostels, e.g. those of 40 or under, interviewers were requested to encourage as many residents as possible to complete the questionnaire. This proved successful in that of two hostels with nearly 40 beds, 50% of the residents of each completed the questionnaire while in some of the smaller hostels a higher response rate was achieved.

Some difficulty was encountered in facilities which had more than two small units with a small number of residents in each. In general the units were kept as separate entities. Sometimes one of the two researchers accompanied the interviewers or the former carried out the data collection on their own. Although this was necessitated by practical considerations it proved valuable in cross checking the interviewers' remarks and also gaining direct experience of the difficulties in sampling and interviewing. A number of points were noted:

Generally staff tended to question the wording on the questionnaire more than residents.

The two Salvation Army hostels were opposition to research had been experienced also proved the least co-operative and responses were less than other Army hostels.

Occasionally when it was explained to them that the Salvation Army was sponsoring the research some residents refused to co-operate.

There was a wide range of the ability or respondents to complete the questionnaire, in some cases respondents were extremely passive and had difficulty in understanding the questions, while in other instances the problem was not so much encouraging them to

voice their views but to get them to stop.
Occasionally abuse from respondents was encountered.
Residents were often willing to criticise both the facility and the staff.

No staff member of any hostel appeared to have difficulty in completing the part of the questionnaire which required them to assess the average resident's response although one manager of a hostel asked why it was necessary for residents to complete it if staff were able to state the residents' response. In two hostels which had proved hostile to the research only one staff member completed the questionnaire.

Hotels

A similar approach was made to hotels as was made to hostels, with the first contact being made through the telephone following with a visit being made to the hotel in order to explain the purpose of the research. The previous difficulty in gaining entry to hotels continued with similar problems being encountered. Increasingly the number given in telephone directories was unobtainable while the obstacles of lack of a persons able to give permission or, in some cases, to speak English continued. Others made it clear by their response that they were unwilling for us to gain access to residents. In total, 52 hotels were contacted at this stage. The response was as follows.

12 number unobtainable,
7 no one able to speak English,
7 no longer took homeless people,
7 refused permission,
5 referred to manager or owner who was unobtainable,
3 referred to manager who declined permission,
4 referred to manager who said they no longer took homeless people,
6 gave permission.

A Salvation Army officer carried out most of the data collection in the hotels. A total of 15 residents and six staff completed the questionnaire.

Once permission was given co-operation varied with one manager - who was leaving at the end of the week during which the research was carried out - being enthusiastic and extremely co-operative, and who gave a great deal of information about the hotel, residents and management, while at the other extreme two managers gave very little assistance to the researcher but left him to get on with the research as best as possible.

Such a low response rate, both in terms of actual numbers responding and hotels visited renders the final sample unrepresentative. It is difficult to know how a more representative sample could have been achieved given the time and scale of the research programme. Any sample is likely to be biased by the fact that it is almost certain to be limited to residents of hotels whose management permits the research to be carried out. Putting it at its most blunt, the managers with most to hide are least likely to give permission. However, the sample proves useful for comparison with people in other facilities.

One comment made by a respondent pointed out that in her opinion the questionnaire was made with homeless single people particularly in mind and did not specifically deal with her problems. This again raises the dilemma of how far one questionnaire can deal with different aspects of homelessness.

Street

Data from people living on the street was gathered from four centres in different parts of London. Two were traditional day centres, one was a Methodist Church providing Sunday lunch for homeless people, and the final venue was a centre which was attached to a housing project.

If there are difficulties regarding the representativeness of samples from hostels and hotels, in the case of homeless people living on the street, this difficulty is compounded many times over. To be certain of a truly representative sample one has to know where the great majority of street homeless people stay at any one moment in time, to know that a set period of time, and also able to carry out a sampling procedure which takes accounts of such variables as age, gender, ethnicity, education etc. Alternatively, one has to target such a large group so as to be reasonably certain that sufficient heterogeneity will be achieved in the final sample. Neither paths were practicable although a small number of questionnaires were completed by people encountered by the researcher during visits to London.

Hence the choice of four different and varied centres where homeless people congregated. But this approach, itself, poses difficulties as the visit to one centre particularly illustrated.

When the researcher visited this particular centre it was found that the majority of the people there were what can only be called, 'self defined homeless'. That is, although they had flats or bedsitters of their own, they visited this particular centre for homeless people for various reasons such as being able to be with friends or to gain the specific benefits of the centre. This difficulty was also thought to exist at other centres and therefore the interviewers were warned of this problem and asked to ensure that people who responded did, in fact, live on the street. Examination of the completed questionnaires from the other centres resulted in two being extracted and placed in the group for squatters. It was judged that nearly all of the remainder were from people who lived on the street.

Two or three visits were made to each of the centres, the first visit as with other facilities, to explain the purpose of the research and the following one or two visits for the completion of the questionnaire. Staff appeared enthusiastic and co-operative and no objections were raised regarding data collection. At one evening centre where well over a hundred people attended, the researchers appeared to be shocked by the degree of perceived disturbance in the people they encountered. On the whole people living on the street were willing to complete the questionnaire. At one centre the researchers attended a staff meeting where they were expected to give the staff an account of the visit and their impression of the centre and the clients, as well as any particular events they thought significant.

As with residents of hostels, the ability of people to complete the questionnaire varied considerably and about 10% of the questionnaires were rejected because they failed to give sufficient information.

Squats

Since three visits had been made to the hospital squat and despite the continual changing population, it was decided that it would not be included in the final phase of data collection. However some problems had risen in regard to contacting squatters, since some of the researcher's squatting informants had moved from their squats either to other parts of London or, in four cases, outside of London. This was partly the consequence of one borough initiating and maintaining a very forceful campaign of taking squatters to the courts for eviction orders. This was taking place in a borough where pilot work had been carried out in the first phase and some thought was given as to whether data should be gathered from this borough.

Since there was a well established housing advice group which had strong connections with squatters - previously it was a squatting group - which had continually proved helpful, and attracted many squatters under threat of eviction who might otherwise have not been contacted, it was decided that the advantages outweighed any methodological objection. Because of the lack of research and knowledge about squatting, access took precedence of strict methodological criteria.

Because of the researcher's strong connection with this agency it was decided to send two interviewers who were unknown to squatters working there to collect the data. There was little difficulty in persuading squatters to complete the questionnaires and in the report there was mention of the large number of people who were passing through.

Data was also gathered from three other sources. One was a squat in large building in the Strand which housed about 20 people at the time. Access to squatters was dependent upon the researcher navigating a rather hazardous entry to the squat but as a consequence seven questionnaires were completed. Three questionnaires were completed by squatters who attended a centre for homeless people in Highbury and another five were obtained from squatters in the area. A visit to another borough produced seven completed questionnaires. These were added to the total of 22 from the advice centre making a total of 44 completed squatting questionnaires.

Additional Information

A section was provided on the questionnaire for any additional information the respondent wished to provide. While other questions were broken down into values suitable for a data matrix such a method proved impossible for the additional information. Therefore it was decided that a content analysis would be made of the information provided.

The first step was to examine all questionnaires and those with additional information of any kind were put aside. Next those selected were examined and a brief note consisting of one to three words was made to describe the contents. If the additional information mentioned more than one subject then a number of notes were made. The final stage was to place all the notes into a respective category. Including 'others' a total of twenty four categories was obtained.

Some questionnaires were put aside since they provided useful information for determining steps and events that may have proceeded homelessness and other difficulties encountered as a consequence of homelessness.

TOPIC	NUMBER
Difficulty in obtaining accommodation[1]	9
Respondent in Childrens' home or in care	16
Criticism of research.	7
Humorous, cryptic or unexplainable.	8
Political, e.g. attacks against the government or praise of Margaret Thatcher.[2]	12

[1]. This category included the high cost of accommodation, the lack of accommodation and difficulty in obtaining access.

[2]. These included anti-government remarks, defence of squatting or general remarks about the political situation.

APPENDIX TWO

Mapping sentences of sub-sections of the questionnaire

The framework for each of the sections in this questionnaire are described below. Many sections are separate questionnaires which have been developed from mapping sentences and from previous research.

Section A: meaning of home
Q's 1-6/11-19

Derived from Sixmith's (1986) three aspects of the meaning of home, this questionnaire allows an exploration of the meaning of home to homeless people. It focuses on the benefits of the places where people are staying as well as of the places in which they would like to live in the future. In this way it provides information on their existing situation and further explores their goals and aspirations.

1. The extent to which (X) agrees that

A
1. (particular
2. (general

B
1. (social
2. (personal aspects
3. (physical
4. (financial
5. (environmental

of the place where he/she stays provides

C
1. (present
2. (future

benefits, by stating whether he/she very strongly agrees to very strongly disagrees, where (X) is a resident of squats, hostels and bed and breakfast hotels.

Self Esteem and Perception of Others Items
Q's 7,9/8,10

These self esteem items were taken from standard self esteem questions and interrcorreleted highly in the pilot study.

Section B:Moos Community Oriented Programmes Environment Scale Q's 20-39

These questions have been taken from Moos (1974) and aim to explore different aspects of facilities such as staff control, resident involvement etc. This questionnaire has been adapted for use by all respondents, that is from the street and squats as well as from hostels and hotels and by staff as well as residents.

The extent to which staff (X) and residents (Y) of this (hostel
(hotel
(project

agree that aspects of Involvement
Support
Spontaneity
Autonomy
Practical Orientation
Personal Problem Orientation
Anger and Aggression
Order and Organisation
Clarity
Staff Control

are present/absent by stating whether they strongly agree to strongly disagree, where X and Y are staff and residents of hotels, hostels and projects in London.

Section B2

This section contains similar items to section B1 but is aimed at facilities with staff(Qs 32-39). There are also a few items which explore the perceived role of staff in the place by both staff and residents (Qs 40-51). It is based on the mapping sentence:

The extent to which (residents agree
(staff

the role of staff (provides
(should provide

(medical support to residents.
(instrumental
(interpersonal
(spiritual
(societal
(physical/fabric

Section C General Health Questionnaire

The General Health Questionnaire is a basic self-administered screening test which focuses on psychiatric disorders. The short 12 item version is used here in order to compare levels of psychiatric illness within and between populations.

Section D:Personal Views/Locus of Control: See Questionnaire Q 1-7
It was thought important to explore how people perceive the control of their lives, and there are two questionnaires in this study which aim to do that.

The extent to which (X) agrees that

A
1. (personal factors which enable or prevent him/her
2. (external
3. (chance

B
from getting 1. (job
2. (housing

by stating whether he/she strongly agrees or strongly disagrees, where (X) is a resident of hostels, projects and bed and breakfast hotels.

Section E Model of Residents
Q.8-13 after Section D

These six items explore how residents and staff perceive the people in general that stay in the facilities. These have been used previously in hospital wards (Shattock 1988) and Salvation Army hostels (Moore and Canter 1990) and are loosely based on six models of therapeutic care (Canter and Canter 1979).

Personal Details Section

These 20 questions are largely on residential history, but include a wide range of questions on background and other details.

APPENDIX THREE

A Brief Outline of Facet Theory

The facet theory approach to research offers a set of principles to guide research design, has a companion set of multivariate statistical procedures to analyse data, and establishes a framework within which to construct theories.

The facet theory provides the means to define the context of the area under investigation. The definition is based on the literature, previous research and pilot investigations. Consequently, the potentially arbitrary nature of the questionnaire is reduced, so that, a reasonably complete definition of the domain of study is specified.

Facets are basic conceptual units into which an area of interest is broken down. In the example of the Meaning of Home sub-section, there is a facet which specifies the varieties of experience of home. Each facet consists of a number of elements. The elements are an exhaustive, mutually exclusive list of the possible components of a facet. In this example, social, personal and physical are elements of the facet 'home'.

Once the facets of an area are defined, and their elements are identified, they can be arranged in the form of a mapping sentence. The mapping sentence links all of the facets together using normal language. Examples of mapping sentences can be found in Annex B.

Using this technique it has been possible to test empirically the hypotheses underlying the construction of attitude measures. The approach allows the specification of a reasonably complete definition of the domain of study. This definition acts as a powerful set of hypotheses that are tested directly by multivariate analysis procedures.

APPENDIX FOUR

The two analyses used in this paper are multivariate analyses and are discussed in full in Lingoes 1973 and Shye 1978. For the purposes of this discussion a brief description of both analyses is provided.

Smallest Space Analysis

SSA is used to examine structural relationships between variables. The program calculates a matrix of associations between all of the items:every item is correlated with every other item. The program then plots each of the items or variables into 2 or 3 dimensional space. The points of the items are plotted in such a way that the rank order of the distances between the points is the inverse of the rank order of the correlations between the items, that is, the greater the distance between two points the lower the correlation. In other words the closer two items are on the plot the greater the relationship between them.

Partial Order Scalogram Analysis

POSA is an attempt to find order in a profile of responses to a set of variables. The analysis essentially consists of finding a partial order configuration that best accommodates the data whilst having a relatively simple structure. A partial order representation of a set of profiles (scores on variables) has two dimensions. It allows two dimensions in the order, that is to say there is not just one way of looking at the respondents, in this instance, hostels, but two. The first dimension runs from top right to bottom left of the plot and is simply the adding up of the scores in each profile: it represents the amount of a particular quality an individual or hostel possesses. This axis is termed the joint axis and the score on it is the joint score. The second dimension runs from top left to bottom right of the plot and is the lateral axis. The lateral axis represents the qualitative difference between the profiles.

Thus one considers the distribution of hostels throughout the POSA in relation to the two axes or dimensions. The profiles are located in space in the way that the more similar a profile (the more alike the hostel scores on the variables), the closer together they will be on the plot. A plot is provided for each item or variable which presents the same relationship, but indicates how each hostel responded to each item. In this way it is possible to work out through a series of partitions (ways of dividing up the space) how the hostels differ according to their responses to the questions.

UNIVERSITY OF SURREY

Guildford Surrey GU2 5XH
Department of Psychology

Telephone (0483) 571281
Direct Line (0483) 509175

Telex 859331
Fax 0483 32813

David Canter, Head of Department and Professor of Psychology
Harry McGurk, Professor of Developmental Psychology

University of Surrey

HOUSING RESEARCH UNIT

The University of Surrey is conducting a large survey of people in hostels and hotels in London to learn more about the experience of living and working in these facilities. This questionnaire will be filled in by staff and residents.

We are very interested in <u>your</u> experience of **the place you are working in at present.**

PLEASE READ THIS CAREFULLY

The following questionnaire consists of a number of statements for you to agree or disagree with on a scale of 1–5 from strongly agree to very strongly disagree. There are no right or wrong answers. It is your opinion that counts. <u>Where indicated</u> we would like you to answer in the way you think the residents in general would answer.

PLEASE ANSWER ALL QUESTIONS
Some sections may not seem relevant to you but it is important that you answer all the questions so that we can compare the results for residents and staff.

The questionnaire will not have your name on it and your answers will be treated in the strictest confidence. Only the research staff at the University of Surrey will have access to these questionnaires.

If you have any questions about filling the questionnaire in, or would like some help, please talk to the researchers who will be around the hostel for a day or two.
If you would like to know more about the project or have any questions, please contact:

Jeanne Moore or Des Stockley
Psychology Department
University of Surrey
Guildford GU2 5XH
Tel:(0483) 509175 ext. 2894

Facility: Male/Female
Sample No.: Resident/Staff
Case Number: Date:

SECTION A: ASPECTS OF HOME QUESTIONNAIRE

These are statements which could be made about where people stay or would like to stay. Please indicate how YOU THINK THE RESIDENTS WOULD ANSWER THESE STATEMENTS.
Please circle the number which describes your view.
1= Strongly Agree 2= **Agree** 3= **Neither Agree Nor Disagree**
4= **Disagree** 5= Strongly Disagree

HOW MUCH DO YOU THINK RESIDENTS AGREE WITH THE FOLLOWING ?

1. The social life is good here.	1	2	3	4	5
2. I can do what I want here.	1	2	3	4	5
3. I think this is a comfortable place to be in.	1	2	3	4	5
4. I can get a good night's sleep here.	1	2	3	4	5
5. Being here is the only way I can afford to live.	1	2	3	4	5
6. Overall I like staying here.	1	2	3	4	5
7. I feel I make a valuable contribution to society.	1	2	3	4	5
8. I feel part of a community living here.	1	2	3	4	5
9. I feel a failure.	1	2	3	4	5
10. The people here are just like me.	1	2	3	4	5
11. I feel safe here.	1	2	3	4	5

IN YOUR OPINION, HOW IMPORTANT ARE THE FOLLOWING TO THE RESIDENTS?
1= **Very Important** 2= Important
3= **Neither Important Nor Unimportant** 4=Unimportant
5= **Very Unimportant**

12. To be able to decorate where I live in a style that suits me.	1	2	3	4	5
13. To live somewhere that's quiet.	1	2	3	4	5
14. To have a place of my own.	1	2	3	4	5
15. To be in a place where my friends could stay overnight.	1	2	3	4	5
16. To find somewhere cheap to live.	1	2	3	4	5

IN YOUR OPINION HOW IMPORTANT ARE THE FOLLOWING TO RESIDENTS?
1= Very Important 2= Important
3= Neither Important Nor Unimportant 4=Unimportant
5= Very Unimportant

17. To have the use of a kitchen.	1	2	3	4	5
18. To have a room of my own.	1	2	3	4	5
19. To live in London.	1	2	3	4	5

SECTION B: PLACE DESCRIPTION QUESTION
1= Strongly Agree 2= Agree 3= Neither Agree Nor Disagree
4= Disagree 5= Strongly Disagree

HOW MUCH DO YOU AGREE WITH THE FOLLOWING?

20. Generally people here are very proud of this place.	1	2	3	4	5
21. There is very little group spirit here.	1	2	3	4	5
22. People here seldom help each other.	1	2	3	4	5
23. The people here tend to hide their feelings from one another.	1	2	3	4	5
24. The people here can leave anytime without saying where they are going.	1	2	3	4	5
25. Training for new kinds of jobs is highlighted here.	1	2	3	4	5
26. There is little discussion about what people will be doing after they leave.	1	2	3	4	5
27. People who break the rules are punished for it.	1	2	3	4	5
28. The people here rarely argue.	1	2	3	4	5
29. It's very well organized here	1	2	3	4	5
30. If someone breaks a rule he knows what will happen.	1	2	3	4	5
31. Personal problems are openly talked about.	1	2	3	4	5
32. Staff have little time to encourage residents.	1	2	3	4	5
33. Residents say anything they want to the staff.	1	2	3	4	5

HOW MUCH DO YOU AGREE WITH THE FOLLOWING?

1= Strongly Agree 2= Agree 3= Neither Agree Nor Disagree
4= Disagree 5= Strongly Disagree

34. Residents are expected to take part in things here.	1	2	3	4	5
35. Residents often criticize or joke about the staff.	1	2	3	4	5
36. Residents are rarely asked personal questions by staff.	1	2	3	4	5
37. The staff make sure this place is always neat.	1	2	3	4	5
38. Staff rarely give residents a detailed explanation about what this place is all about.	1	2	3	4	5
39. If someone fights with someone else here, he will get into real trouble with the staff.	1	2	3	4	5

40. Staff here provide care and support to residents.	1	2	3	4	5
41. Staff here supervise residents	1	2	3	4	5
42. Staff here offer a housing advice service.	1	2	3	4	5
43. Staff here caretake the building.	1	2	3	4	5
44. Staff here provide spiritual help to residents.	1	2	3	4	5
45. Staff here offer practical advice.	1	2	3	4	5

HOW MUCH DO YOU AGREE WITH THE FOLLOWING ABOUT STAFF'S ROLE IN GENERAL? IT IS YOUR OPINION THAT COUNTS.

46. Staff should provide care and support to residents.	1	2	3	4	5
47. Staff should supervise residents.	1	2	3	4	5
48. Staff should offer a housing advice service.	1	2	3	4	5
49. Staff should caretake the building.	1	2	3	4	5
50. Staff should provide spiritual help to residents.	1	2	3	4	5
51. Staff should offer practical advice.	1	2	3	4	5

SECTION C: HEALTH QUESTIONNAIRE

We should like to know if you have had any medical complaints and how your health has been in general over the past few weeks. Please answer ALL the questions on the page below by circling the answer which you think most nearly applies to you. Remember that we want to know about present and recent complaints, not those you that you had in the past.
CIRCLE THE ONE WHICH DESCRIBES YOUR FEELINGS.
It is important that you answer ALL the questions.

Have you recently

1. Been able to concentrate on whateve you're doing?	Better than usual	Same as usual	Less than usual	Much less than usual
2. Lost much sleep over worry?	Not at all	No more than usual	Rather more than usual	Much more than usual
3. felt that you are playing a useful part in things?	More so than usual	Same as usual	Less useful than usual	Much less useful
4. felt capable of making decisions about things	More so than usual	Same as usual	Less so than usual	Much less capable
5. felt constantly under strain?	Not at all	No more than usual	Rather more than usual	Much more than usual
6. felt you couldn't overcome your difficulties?	Not at all	No more than usual	Rather more than usual	Much more than usual
7. been able to enjoy your normal day-to-day activities?	More so than usual	Same as usual	Less so than usual	Much less than usual
8. been able to face up to your problems?	More so than usual	Same as usual	Less able than usual	Much less able
9. been feeling unhappy and depressed?	Not at all	No more than usual	Rather more than usual	Much more than usual
10. been losing confidence in yourself?	Not at all	No more than usual	Rather more than usual	Much more than usual
11. been thinking of yourself as a worthless person?	Not at all	No more than usual	Rather more than usual	Much more than usual
12. been feeling reasonably happy all things considered?	More so than usual	About same as usual	Less so than usual	Much less than usual

SECTION D: PERSONAL VIEWS: ABOUT THE RESIDENTS.
This part of the Questionnaire is designed to assess some of the ways in which you understand the world.

There are no right or wrong answers.

CIRCLE THE NUMBER WHICH DESCRIBES YOUR VIEWS ABOUT THE RESIDENTS IN GENERAL.

1= Strongly Agree 2= Agree 3= Neither Agree Nor Disagree
4= Disagree 5= Strongly Disagree

HOW MUCH DO YOU AGREE OR DISAGREE WITH THE FOLLOWING WITH REGARD TO THE RESIDENTS IN YOUR HOSTEL?

1. Just unlucky in finding somewhere else to live.	1	2	3	4	5
2. Too lazy to find somewhere else to live.	1	2	3	4	5
3. Stopped from finding somewhere else to live by the shortage of housing in London.	1	2	3	4	5
4. Would work if offered a job.	1	2	3	4	5
5. Just had no luck in getting a job.	1	2	3	4	5
6. Stopped from getting a job by a lack of skills.	1	2	3	4	5
7. If could settle down would get a job.	1	2	3	4	5

Most of the residents here

8. are normal people.	1	2	3	4	5
9. are physically or mentally ill.	1	2	3	4	5
10. Able to change for the better.	1	2	3	4	5
11. Threat to self and to society.	1	2	3	4	5
12. Require some kind of support.	1	2	3	4	5
13. Able to go back into society.	1	2	3	4	5

PERSONAL DETAILS:STAFF
Please tick the answer which applies to you.

1. GENDER

1 Male	2 Female

2. AGE:

under 18	19-29	30-39	40-49	50-59	60-69	70+

3. FAMILY STATUS:

Single	Widowed	Married	Cohabitating	Divorced	Separated

4. What level of education have you reached?

Degree or Higher	GCSE/O Level
Professional Qualifications	Other
A level	None of these

5. Do you have any trade qualifications? If yes, please state what they are.

Yes	No

6. What position do you hold in the hostel?

7. How long have you been working at the hostel?

8. In what country were you born?

9. What is your ethnicity? (race)

White European	Black Asian
White Other	Other
Black	

10. Which of the following best describes the place in which you **now** live?

House/flat	Hotel	Squat	Street
Room in shared house	Bedsit	Hostel	Other

11. And is it?

Owner occupied	Rented from a local authority or housing association
Rented from a private landlord	Co-operative
Other: (Specify)	Salvation Army

12. How long have you been staying there?

Less than 1 month	7 months to 1 year
1 to 3 months	more than 1 year
4 to 6 months	

13.At what age did you leave your childhood home?

Under 10	19-25
11-15	26-30
16-18	31+

14.Approximately how many different places have you lived in since you left your childhood home?

____

15. Was the last place you lived in, before this one a ?

House/flat	Hotel	Squat	Street
Room in Shared House	Bedsit	Hostel	Other
Prison	Hospital/Care Institution		
Friend's House	Tied Accommodation		

16.And was it?

Owner occupied	Rented from a local authority or housing association
Rented from a private landlord	Co-operative
Other: (Specify)	Salvation Army

17.How long did you stay in your last place?

Less than 1 month	7 months to 1 year
1 to 3 months	more than 1 year
4 to 6 months	

18.In what area do you live now?

____

19.In what area did you live prior to this?

____

20. Other Background Information if any:

UNIVERSITY OF SURREY

Guildford Surrey GU2 5XH   Telephone (0483) 571281   Telex 859331
Department of Psychology   Direct Line (0483) 509175   Fax 0483 32813

David Canter, Head of Department and Professor of Psychology
Harry McGurk, Professor of Developmental Psychology

University of Surrey

HOUSING RESEARCH UNIT

The University of Surrey is conducting a large survey of people in hostels and hotels in London. We are very interested in your experience of **the place you are staying in at present.**

PLEASE READ THIS CAREFULLY

The following questionnaire consists of a number of statements for you to agree or disagree with on a scale of 1–5 from strongly agree to very strongly disagree.

There are no right or wrong answers. It is your opinion that counts.

ANSWER ALL QUESTIONS

The questionnaire will not have your name on it and your answers will be treated in the strictest confidence. Only the research staff at the University of Surrey will have access to these questionnaires.

If you have any questions about filling the questionnaire in, or would like some help, please talk to the researchers who will be around the hostel for a day or two.

If you would like to know more about the project or have any questions, please contact:

Jeanne Moore or Des Stockley
Psychology Department
University of Surrey
Guildford GU2 5XH
Tel:(0483) 509175 ext. 2894

Facility: Male/Female
Sample No.:   Resident/Staff

Case Number: Date:

SECTION A: ASPECTS OF HOME QUESTIONNAIRE

These are statements which could be made about where people stay or would like to stay. Please indicate how much you agree or disagree with these statements with regard to the place you are staying in at the moment.

Please circle the number which describes your view.
1= Strongly Agree 2= Agree 3= Neither Agree Nor Disagree
4= Disagree 5= Strongly Disagree

HOW MUCH DO YOU AGREE WITH THE FOLLOWING?

1. The social life is good here.	1	2	3	4	5
2. I can do what I want here.	1	2	3	4	5
3. I think this is a comfortable place to be in.	1	2	3	4	5
4. I can get a good night's sleep here.	1	2	3	4	5
5. Being here is the only way I can afford to live.	1	2	3	4	5
6. Overall I like staying here.	1	2	3	4	5
7. I feel I make a valuable contribution to society.	1	2	3	4	5
8. I feel part of a community living here.	1	2	3	4	5
9. I feel a failure.	1	2	3	4	5
10. The people here are just like me.	1	2	3	4	5
11. I feel safe here.	1	2	3	4	5

HOW IMPORTANT ARE THE FOLLOWING TO YOU?

1= Very Important 2= Important
3= Neither Important Nor Unimportant 4=Unimportant
5= Very Unimportant

12. To be able to decorate where I live in a style that suits me.	1	2	3	4	5
13. To live somewhere that's quiet.	1	2	3	4	5
14. To have a place of my own.	1	2	3	4	5
15. To be in a place where my friends could stay overnight.	1	2	3	4	5
16. To find somewhere cheap to live.	1	2	3	4	5

HOW IMPORTANT ARE THE FOLLOWING TO YOU?
1= Very Important 2= Important
3= Neither Important Nor Unimportant
4= Unimportant 5= Very Unimportant

17. To have the use of a kitchen.	1	2	3	4	5
18. To have a room of my own.	1	2	3	4	5
19. To live in London.	1	2	3	4	5

SECTION B: PLACE DESCRIPTION QUESTION

1= Strongly Agree 2= Agree 3= Neither Agree Nor Disagree
4= Disagree 5= Strongly Disagree

HOW MUCH DO YOU AGREE WITH THE FOLLOWING?

20. Generally people here are very proud of this place.	1	2	3	4	5
21. There is very little group spirit here.	1	2	3	4	5
22. People here seldom help each other.	1	2	3	4	5
23. The people here tend to hide their feelings from one another.	1	2	3	4	5
24. The people here can leave anytime without saying where they are going.	1	2	3	4	5
25. Training for new kinds of jobs is highlighted here.	1	2	3	4	5
26. There is little discussion about what people will be doing after they leave.	1	2	3	4	5
27. People who break the rules are punished for it.	1	2	3	4	5
28. The people here rarely argue.	1	2	3	4	5
29. It's very well organized here	1	2	3	4	5
30. If someone breaks a rule he knows what will happen.	1	2	3	4	5
31. Personal problems are openly talked about.	1	2	3	4	5
32. Staff have little time to encourage residents.	1	2	3	4	5
33. Residents say anything they want to the staff.	1	2	3	4	5

HOW MUCH DO YOU AGREE WITH THE FOLLOWING?

1= Strongly Agree 2= Agree 3= Neither Agree Nor Disagree
4= Disagree 5= Strongly Disagree

34. Residents are expected to take part in things here.	1	2	3	4	5
35. Residents often criticize or joke about the staff.	1	2	3	4	5
36. Residents are rarely asked personal questions by staff.	1	2	3	4	5
37. The staff make sure this place is always neat.	1	2	3	4	5
38. Staff rarely give residents a detailed explanation about what this place is all about.	1	2	3	4	5
39. If someone fights with someone else here, he will get into real trouble with the staff.	1	2	3	4	5

HOW MUCH DO YOU AGREE WITH THE FOLLOWING ABOUT STAFF HERE?

40. Staff here provide care and support to residents.	1	2	3	4	5
41. Staff here supervise residents	1	2	3	4	5
42. Staff here offer a housing advice service.	1	2	3	4	5
43. Staff here caretake the building.	1	2	3	4	5
44. Staff here provide spiritual help to residents.	1	2	3	4	5
45. Staff here offer practical advice.	1	2	3	4	5

HOW MUCH DO YOU AGREE WITH THE FOLLOWING ABOUT STAFF IN GENERAL? IT IS YOUR OPINION THAT COUNTS.

46. Staff should provide care and support to residents.	1	2	3	4	5
47. Staff should supervise residents.	1	2	3	4	5
48. Staff should offer a housing advice service.	1	2	3	4	5
49. Staff should caretake the building.	1	2	3	4	5
50. Staff should provide spiritual help to residents.	1	2	3	4	5
51. Staff should offer practical advice.	1	2	3	4	5

SECTION C: HEALTH QUESTIONNAIRE

We should like to know if you have had any medical complaints and how your health has been in general over the past few weeks. Please answer ALL the questions on the page below by circling the answer which you think most nearly applies to you. Remember that we want to know about present and recent complaints, not those you that you had in the past.
CIRCLE THE ONE WHICH DESCRIBES YOUR FEELINGS.
It is important that you answer ALL the questions.

Have you recently

1. Been able to concentrate on whateve you're doing?	Better than usual	Same as usual	Less than usual	Much less than usual
2. Lost much sleep over worry?	Not at all	No more than usual	Rather more than usual	Much more than usual
3. felt that you are playing a useful part in things?	More so than usual	Same as usual	Less useful than usual	Much less useful
4. felt capable of making decisions about things	More so than usual	Same as usual	Less so than usual	Much less capable
5. felt constantly under strain?	Not at all	No more than usual	Rather more than usual	Much more than usual
6. felt you couldn't overcome your difficulties?	Not at all	No more than usual	Rather more than usual	Much more than usual
7. been able to enjoy your normal day-to-day activities?	More so than usual	Same as usual	Less so than usual	Much less than usual
8. been able to face up to your problems?	More so than usual	Same as usual	Less able than usual	Much less able
9. been feeling unhappy and depressed?	Not at all	No more than usual	Rather more than usual	Much more than usual
10.been losing confidence in yourself?	Not at all	No more than usual	Rather more than usual	Much more than usual
11.been thinking of yourself as a worthless person?	Not at all	No more than usual	Rather more than usual	Much more than usual
12.been feeling reasonably happy all things considered?	More so than usual	About same as usual	Less so than usual	Much less than usual

SECTION D: PERSONAL VIEWS

This part of the Questionnaire is designed to assess some of the ways in which you understand the world. There are no right or wrong answers.

CIRCLE THE NUMBER WHICH DESCRIBES YOUR VIEWS.

1= Strongly Agree 2= Agree 3= Neither Agree Nor Disagree
4= Disagree 5= Strongly Disagree

HOW MUCH DO YOU AGREE WITH THE FOLLOWING?

1. Just unlucky in finding somewhere else to live.	1	2	3	4	5
2. Too lazy to find somewhere else to live.	1	2	3	4	5
3. Stopped from finding somewhere else to live by the shortage of housing in London.	1	2	3	4	5
4. Would work if offered a job.	1	2	3	4	5
5. Just had no luck in getting a job.	1	2	3	4	5
6. Stopped from getting a job by a lack of skills.	1	2	3	4	5
7. If could settle down would get a job.	1	2	3	4	5

Most of the residents here

8. are normal people.	1	2	3	4	5
9. are physically or mentally ill.	1	2	3	4	5
10. Able to change for the better.	1	2	3	4	5
11. Threat to self and to society.	1	2	3	4	5
12. Require some kind of support.	1	2	3	4	5
13. Able to go back into society.	1	2	3	4	5

PERSONAL DETAILS
Please tick the answer which applies to you.

1. GENDER

1 Male	2 Female

2. AGE:

under 18	19-29	30-39	40-49	50-59	60-69	70+

3. FAMILY STATUS:

Single	Widowed	Married	Cohabitating	Divorced	Separated

4. EMPLOYMENT STATUS:

Employed Full-time	Employed Part-time	Retired	Casual Work	
Unemployed	Self Employed	Government Scheme	Invalid/Ill	Other

5. If you are staying in a hostel, are you a member of staff?

Yes	No

6. Do you carry out voluntary work?

Yes	No

7.How often do you visit day centres? Please tick the box which comes closest to your answer.

Once a day	Once a week	Once a month	Twice a year	Never

8.What level of education have you reached?

Degree or Higher	CSE/GCSE/O-Level	School Certificate
Professional Qualifications	Other	
A level	None of these	

9.Do you have any trade qualifications?
If yes, please state what they are.

Yes	No

10. In what country were you born?

11.What is your ethnicity? (RACE)

White European	Black Asian	Black	White Other	Other

12. How long have you been staying where you are now?

Less than 1 month	7 months to 1 year
1 to 3 months	more than 1 year
4 to 6 months	

13. Was the last place you lived in, before this one a ?

House/flat	Hotel	Squat	Street
Room in Shared House	Bedsit	Hostel	Other
Prison	Hospital/Care Institution		
Friend's House	Tied Accommodation		

14.And was it?

Owner occupied	Rented from a local authority or housing association
Rented from a private landlord	Co-operative
Other: (Specify)	Salvation Army
Don't Know	

15.How long did you stay in your last place?

Less than 1 month	7 months to 1 year
1 to 3 months	more than 1 year
4 to 6 months	

16.At what age did you leave your childhood home?

Under 10	19-25
11-15	26-30
16-18	31+

17.Approximately how many different places have you lived in (could include the street) since you left your childhood home?

____

18.What was the last place you felt was your home?

____

19.When you left the last place you felt was your home what sort of place did you go to? Was it a

House/flat	Hotel	Squat	Street
Room in Shared House	Bedsit	Hostel	Other
Prison	Hospital/Care Institution		
Friend's House	Tied Accommodation		

20.And was it?

Owner occupied	Rented from a local authority or housing association
Rented from a private landlord	Co-operative
Other: (Specify)	Salvation Army

21. Approximately how long ago was that?

____

22.In what area do you live now?

____

23.In what area did you live prior to this?

____

24. Are you on a housing waiting list?

Yes	No	Don't know

25. If yes, please specify.

Same Local Authority	
Other Local Authority	
Housing Association	
Other (please specify)	

26. Other Background Information if any:

Acknowledgements

The origin of the present volume was in 1979 when Major Ray Oakley, a senior architect with the Salvation Army, was seconded full-time to study for an MSc in Environmental Psychology at the University of Surrey. Following his experience on that course, he went on to design a number of hostels drawing on environmental psychology ideas. Some years later, when faced with the task of building new hostels in London, he returned to the University of Surrey. Together we developed a series of studies that went beyond the concerns solely of the Salvation Army to cover the issues dealt with in the present volume. Throughout all this time Ray has been a source of support and enthusiasm who has also had to act on many of the conclusions of research.

Early on in the work Tom Littler was appointed from the Salvation Army to act as coordinator and general advisor in which he was extremely helpful, particularly during the counts of people sleeping rough. A research advisory group and working committee was set in place to oversee the work and always acted in a constructive manner. It would be difficult to single out any individuals without implying that others did not give very strong support, sharing their vast expertise with members of the research team. We will therefore list the various people who contributed throughout the project.

At the University of Surrey three people in particular kept the project going at various stages, Jane Ball, Janice Pearce and Margaret Schofield. We are grateful to them all for their tolerance and professionalism.

Mercury communications provided free phone lines during the count and we are very grateful to them for that service.

We will list as many of the names as we have of the staff and volunteers who so kindly and willingly contributed to the various surveys. Without this army of volunteers, drawn from a very wide range of agencies, the project would not have been possible. Many of them were active workers in the homelessness field and readily gave advice and information throughout the project.

We are grateful to the ESRC for funding aspects of the studies, under their grant no: R000233029 "Varieties of Transitional Home Experience and Significance for Homeless People". We are also grateful to the anonymous donors who provided the Salvation Army with funds to support other aspects of the research.

Finally, our sincere thanks are due to the subjects of this research, we hope they never felt mere objects for study, the homeless people themselves. The frequent indications of wit and determination that characterise so many of them in the most difficult of circumstances was a constant source of inspiration.

Members of the research and working committees over the period

Beryl Steele
Thames Reach Housing Association

Mick Caroll
St. Mungo's

Tony Price
Central London Social Security Advice Forum
and Board and Lodging Information Programme

Remke Verzee
Simon Community

Peter Nagel
Central London Housing Advisory Service

Major Ray Oakley
Staff Architect

Major Doreen Crockford
Resettlement Officer

Edward Alsop
Chief Executive
The Salvation Army Housing Association

Lt. Col. Margaret White
Asst. to the Chief Secretary Salvation
Army Social Services

Lt. Col. David Barker
Provincial Officer

Major Trevor Smith
Research and Development Officer

Major Keith Lloyd
Director Salvation Army Whitechapel Complex

Captain Charles King
Press Officer

Col. F. Fullerton
The Leader, Salvation Army Social Services

Lt. Col. P. Hofman
Chief Secretary, Salvation Army Social Services

We also gratefully acknowledge the assistance of the following:

Rupert Chandler
Resource Information Service

Mike Satchell
St. Mungo Housing

Commander W.E.E. Boreham
Head of Community Involvement Branch

Brian Snellgrove
Squatters Network of Walworth

Southwark Housing Information Project

Brixton Squatters Aid

Metropolitan Police

City Police

Superintendent B.F. King
British Transport Police

Ken Wise
Chief Operations Officer
Heathrow Airport

Hal Porsen
London Research Centre

John Hall
Bayswater Homelessness Project

Mercury Telecommunications PLC

We would like to thank the following volunteers for their part in the counts. There are many more for whom we have no names.

Tower Hamlets

Paul & Dawn Scott
Mrs Agnes Rice
John Turner
Martin Busby
John Stott
Bob Gluck
Stephen Jobson
Tony Nickson
Wilma Malcolm
Adrian Scott
Sean Wright
John Holloway
Alison McIntosh
Jackie Birch
Cornel Neil
Lesley Gunn
Capt. Paul Kingscott
A/Capt. Eric Dowling

Hackney

Capt. David Bailey
Major Eerde Pawels
Capt. James Williams
Mr Ken Guest
Capt. Fred Thompson
Major K Pell
Lieut. A Molloy

Mrs M Bailey
Capt. E Palfrey
Steve Crook
John Crosby
Helen Wightman
Joe Murphy
Phil Graystone
Capt. M Caddy
Ian Cooper

Chelsea/Kensington

Fr. Paddy Smyth
Capt. Alan Read
Michael Dorgan (Chaplain)
Capt. Philip Haigh
Simon Parsons
Mike Alliston
Peter Hammond
Sue Hammond
Nigel Hill
Bob Pilcock
David Johns
Asif Khels
A Stringer (Envoy)
Lt. Ian McBride
Lt. Sally McBride
David Wise
Capt. Ivan Olivar
Nigel Boyd
Annabel Hackney
Louis Panton

Ealing

Mr & Mrs Payne
Cherie Linton
Peter Dysney
John Liary
Margaret Roberts
Bill Burridge

Lambeth

Grant MacDonald
David Vidler
Jeremy Swain
Oliver Mason
Cathy Symes

Heathrow

Major T Davis
Mrs Major M Davis
A Kerslake
Mrs M Kerslake
D Cooper
Mrs J Cooper
J Denyer
Mrs J Denyer
R Kerslake
Mrs E Betts
Mrs E Newnes
Mrs Y Atwill

Camden

Ben Lanchester
Hazel Dumford
Stuart Marriott
David Powell
Chris Roberts
Tony Smith
Adrian Tate
Caroline Earland
Paul Avison
Sean O'Shea

Croydon

Graham H Kinsley
Margaret Jackson
Graham Dolby
Keith Francis
Audrey Francis
Pauline Hill
Mark Bartlett
Peter Carpenter

Laurence Dolby
Mark Scott
George Scott
Hazel V Scott
Maureen Chapman
Karin Allen
Steve Findlater
Mark Bruce
Alistair Dawson
Trevor Dawson
Paul Dawson
Philip Howe
Alex Bienfait
Sarah Cooper
Joy Cooper
Alan Howe
Valarie Howe

Islington

Val Henley
Mick Cornall
Robert Nightingale
Charles Brennan
Frank Cruise
Jim Doyle
Robert Watt
Rod Henley
Brian Boylan
Sally Yarwood

City of London area

Lt. Col. Len Grinstead
Miss Miriam Blackwell
Capt. Roland Sewell
Mrs Captain Dawn Sewell
Mrs Lieut-Colonel Du Plessis
Major John Amoah
Major Geoff Ashdown
Miss Eileen Marron
Mr Geoff Nunn
Capt. Ruth Richards
Lt. Col. D Blackwell
Mr George Wilson
Mrs Jean Wilson
Capt. Graham Jones
Mrs Brenda Oakley
Capt. David Lewis
Mrs Major Maureen Sands
Mr Roy Bullock
Mrs Captain Hart
Mr Andrew Phillips
Major N Armistead
Major Ray Oakley
Miss Diana Dupigny

Names which appear on slips

Mrs Gildersleve
R Sylvester
Heather Ray
Tom Gillespie
Sean Smith
Shyama Perera
Mary Teh
Major Katherine Foreman
Luke Anthony McQuade
Denis Plum
Elizabeth Caird
Peggy Baumber
Gerald Clifford
Lee Simpson
Rowena Lowe
Nuala O'Duffy
Joan Martin
Derrik Tribble
E Kavanash
Major Gordon Kent
Jason Clifford
Nigel Hill
Jason Scannell
Bert Inward
Robert A Halliday
Kathleen Francis
H Waterman

Index